AFGHAN WAR 2001

By

Emil Tzolov

The Author Emil Tzolov was born in Sofia in the Family of journalists. His Father Peter Tzolov was commentator at the Bulgarian Radio. His Mother Petya Tzolova was TV moderator at the Bulgarian Television. His grandparents kept hiding allied prisoners of War and rescued a great many of them.

1979 graduated the German College in Sofia
1983 graduated the English College in Sofia in the class of the British historian Mercia McDermot who has been living in Bulgaria since 1949
1988 graduated Economy at the Humboldt University in Berlin in Germany
1993 came to live in exile in Western Europe
1999 was awarded with EU-citizenship for his contributions to journalism
Since 1992 he is citizen of the World (World Service Authority Washington)
His books are widely accepted and welcomed by the broad public

     Other books:
     May 1975 - on economic integration
     May 1984 - on Bulgarian Agriculture (HfO Berlin)
     Nov 1986 - on East-West relations (HfO Berlin)
     Feb 1988 - on state economic monopoly (HfO Berlin)
     May 2004 - on Afghan war-a book in the form of diary

Order this book online at www.trafford.com
or email orders@trafford.com

Most Trafford titles are also available at major online book retailers.

Print information available on the last page.

ISBN: 978-1-4120-2444-0 (sc)

Trafford rev. 07/07/2015

North America & international
toll-free: 1 888 232 4444 (USA & Canada)
fax: 812 355 4082

I DEDICATE MY

BOOK TO MY MOTHER −THE TV COMMENTATOR PETYA TZOLOVA-

AND TO HER FRIEND − THE TV JOURNALIST NINA PANITZIDOU −

FROM WHOM I LEARNT JOURNALISM.

THE AUTHOR

TABLE OF CONTENTS

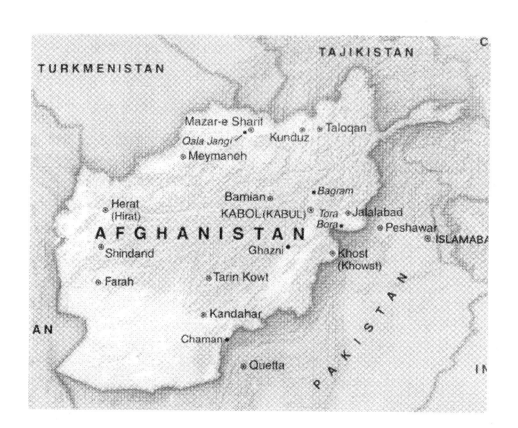

Chapter 1

USA (PART1)

09 Sept 2001

The supreme Commander of the Northern Allience General Ahmed Shah Masood was assassinated in a suicide bomb attack: 2 AL Qaida members posing as journalists detonated their explosives hidden in their video equipment. Ahmed Shah Masood died of his wounds on 11 Sept 2001

At 04 :45 GMT the plane attack took place on the twin towers of the World Trade Center in New York in which estimated some 7,000 people died. Another plane was deliberately crashed Into the Pentagon-building in Washington where some 150 people died. The 4th plane was shot Down near Pittsburgh in Pensylvannia. On this plane almost nothing has been reported up to date.

At 20:42 GMT-rather late-the NATO Secretary General Lord Robertson extended the condolences of the NATO to the American President and to the American people - after the President of Pakistan General Pervez Musharraf who was obviously sleeping at that time; similar did also the president of Iran .The US Secretary of State Colin Powell was already called back from his visit in Peru, when George Robertson extended his condolences in English. The statement of the Israeli Prime Minister Ariel Sharon came on time but it took too long to be translated from Hebrew into English.

At 21:06 GMT A huge flotilla incl.2 war plane carriers left its base and headed to New York

At 02:06 GMT Multiple rocket explosions shook Kabul - the capital of Afghanistan; the rockets hit ammunition depot which caught fire; before it a few missiles were seen in the night sky - it was 3 o'clock in the night in Kabul. In the press conference US official said it is not the proper time to discuss if America was behind this rocket assaults.

The US Defence Secretary Donald Rumsfeld said also America is not behind the rocket assaults but now is not the time to be specific and to discuss on intelligence matters.

Another official said America is not behind the assaults, which may be work of the anti-Taleban coalition in the North of the country – the Northern Alliance.

12 Sept 2001

00:00:00 Pakistani time 20:00 GMT A written statement (poem) in Arabic was delivered to a Pakistani Urdu newspaper editor Hamid Mir in Urdu from Osama ben Laden in which he, according to the translation of the chief editor, says:

"Osama ben Laden is not responsible for the assault but he is very cheerful with it: now Americans can understand how do feel innocent Palestinians under bombardment. Osama ben Laden continues to fight for the liberation of

1

Palestine and Kashmir. He knows that he is wanted by the USA but his death will change nothing because it will spring off 1000 new Osama Bens."

The jurnalist Hamid Mir - editor in Urdu-says the poem was brought after a phone call by the same bodyguard who attended a previous interview with Osama ben Laden.

12:00 GMT UN staff was evacuated from Afghanistan in fear from US-reprisal against it

14:00 GMT President Bush said no difference will be made between those who carried out the assaults and those who harbour them (unconsciously he used of the word "Harbour" hinting the assault on Pearl Harbour in December 1941.

15:00 GMT A statement of Osama ben Laden was revived made back in 1998 where he says "Black times are coming for America". Osama ben Laden denied any involvement but stressed his pleasure from the attack.

At 15:00 GMT The President of the EU Central Bank in Frankfurt Wim Duisenberg offered to the US any financial help necessary. It is not clear whether and when the US accepted his proposal.

18:30 GMT Michael Connelly from Centre of terrorists studies in London said,low tech equipment of the doers will soon lead to their ends: Osama bin Laden has his phone and fax bugged: the attack must be planned inside of N. America the same way Irish terrorist action were planned and fulfilled from the British mainland not from Ireland itself,he said in a TV-interview.

17:59 GMT The US-Aviation Authority says US airport will remain closed until further notice: earlier reports suggested they would reopen on Wednesday.

18:30 GMT NATO joint statement remembered that attack on one member would invoke retaliation by all member states. But: it is up to the state concerned to evaluate, take decision and ask for the help" - George Robertson blunt and clumsy statement at 22:39 GMT after he failed for hours to express his condolence on Tuesday. His condolences were announced by the BBC even after the condolences of the Pakistani President where was meanwhile after midnight.

18:56 GMT Yasser Arafat volunteered to donated blood for US-Victims; Palestinian children held up candles in a silent march in memory of the victims.

20:15 GMT In a radio interview the former US Secretary of State in the Clinton administration Madeleine Albright said : "The bombing of a pharmaceutical plant in Sudan in August 1998 was not a mistake!"

At 20:16 GMT Mr. Ashcroft, US Attorney General,said "A number of the hijackers were trained as pilots inside the USA".

20:38 GMT : the slogan was coined:"Bomb them, kill them, stop them!", implying the Al Qaida terrorists.

22:30 GMT President Bush visited the Pentagon wreckage:he looked very pale and nervous.

13 Sept 2001

Police in Germany arrested one suspected terrorist in Hamburg while FBI believes to know who the hell the other terrorists are. Excesses in the USA against the Arab and Islamic community. Osama ben Laden open his website www.jihad.com

NATO offered full military help;while Russia called for closer co-operation to NATO

China called for coordinated measures but asked to be consulted in advance.

14 Sept 2001

Several persons were arrested in New York while trying to board a plane with false papers and faked pilot licence. The German police release one of the arrested men without charges and arrested new few students in Hamburg belonging to Islamic terrorist organization. Iranian man waiting a deportation to Iran had tried in vain to phone the White House from Germany on the whole day of 10th of September 2001-the day before the attacks-and to warn for the planned assaults on Tuesday-11th of September but nobody paid attention to his warnings. This man is now in German custody waiting further decision for deportation or detention.

Chapter 2

USA (PART2)

14 Sept 2001

20:00 GMT Newshour: President Bush slightly tearful in New York where he emerged after 3.5 days of hiding from the calamity. After such a grandiose mistake he should resign after all. Many suspected terrorists and hijacker said to be taken in (=arrested) but later released.

22:06 the BBC staff said that Osama bin Laden is hiding in Pakistan not Afghanistan.

15 Sept 2001

09:00 GMT Congress voted full support to President Bush for eventual military action although he is entitled already Richard Pearl, Chairman of the defence board of the Pentagon said, by the end of the day we will set up the mission and than form the coalition and not set up the coalition without mission thus looking for the smallest common denominator.

President Putin called for restrain and caution speaking during a visit in Armenia.

Colin Powell warned the Taleban, they would pay the price if they harbour Osama bin Laden.

The Taleban vowed retaliation if they were attacked.

Ahmed Shah Massoud, commander of the Northern Alliance died meanwhile of his wounds.

The Taleban stated that every country, which helps American attack on Afghanistan, would be punished; Afghanistan's neighbours must understand that good neighbour relations with Afghanistan are more important than a country far away.

Americans are going to kill innocent Afghans to pay the price for the death of innocent Americans.

Not only Osama bin Laden must be held responsible. Saddam Hussein also harbours terrorists and wrote checks to Palestinian suicide attackers. Military reservist started to report and appeared to their duties

Only Chicago airport was working in the USA-all other airports were closed for security reasons.

Washington asked Pakistan to use its airspace to launch air strikes to the Taleban. Igor Ivanov asked for caution and restrain. Russia has no objection to use force against the terrorist, but not the use Russian bases against them. Russian team of advisors is prepared to travel to Washington.

Russians tried to subdue American intervention efforts the black boxes of the Pennsylvania crashed plane were found. A material witness was arrested.

4

Colin Powell declared state of emergency. Pakistan negotiated which steps to take to satisfy the American demand for cooperation.

14:00 GMT Pakistani foreign minister said Pakistan would act in accordance with UN resolutions combating terrorism. The Iraqi president Saddam Hussein issued an open letter to the West warning not to attack any country. He was toppled in April 2004 and arrested by US forces on

13ᵗʰ December 2004 near his home town in Northern Iraq.

The Russian President Wladimir Putin warned the West not to act as bandits.

President Bush said the struggle will be long and persistent and the American people will pay high price but they will prevail. Pakistan stated it will support Washington but it will take part in no military action. Pakistani delegation is due tomorrow to leave to Afghanistan to pursue the Taleban to hand over Osama ben Laden.

There was a bomb treat in the Empire State Building in New York this night. FBI was alarmed three weeks earlier following a tip-off from the CIA on the September attacks but this became clear only now.

The head of the Northern anti-Taleban Alliance offered to help the USA to trace down and arrest Osama ben Laden.

Pakistani delegation is expected in Afghanistan to try to persuade the Taleban to hand over Osama ben Laden but senior Taleban – the Taleban supreme leader Mullah Mohamed Omar stated that US would wage a war against Afghanistan even if they hand over Osama ben Laden to the USA.

Pakistani President, General Pervez Musharraf is expected in Beijing for consultations with the Chinese leadership. Later on these talks were cancelled-Beijing said it does not consider them for useful. So Pakistan had to accept the US proposal for giving its ground and air space to the US forces for military use to unleash a war against Afghanistan where Osama ben Laden is supposed to be hiding. Later on Kirgizstan, Turkmenia and Kazakhstan also agreed with the Americans to give their air spaces and territories for US military to use and so Afghanistan was encircled even before the beginning of the war.

17 Sept 2001

The Pakistani delegation landed in Afghanistan in the city of Kandahar; the visit to China was cancelled because Beijing did not feel it was necessary.

17:00 GMT President Bush stated that Osama ben Laden was wanted-dead or alive. His slogan remembered the old cowboy times of Texas where George W. Bush was governor and as such signed over 150 dead penalties.But the Taleban fear that Washington will still target them even if they would have delivered Osama bin Laden to the US.

The Egyptian President Muhammad Hosni Mubarak and the Iranian Supreme religious leader Ayatollah Ali Khameini warned for premature actions: they will only increase the Washington's unease if the US would establish military presence in Pakistan. But finally Washington prevailed.

In the Washington's Islamic Centre President Bush called to stop violence against Muslims after Muslims were lynched and killed in Dallas and Texas. It became clear they had had nothing to do with the 11ᵗʰ September attacks.

18 Sept 2001

The Taleban delayed taking the decision since many clerics failed to arrive in Kabul.

Unconfirmed reports said the Taleban's are set to deliver Osama ben Laden if he is put to trial in a neutral Islamic country.

Graham Richard - President of EU Commission of Human rights, Civil liberties and Home affairs spoke against premature US actions.

19 Sept 2001

The Taleban refused to extradite Osama ben Laden to the US unless there is a solid proof of his involvement of the terrorist attacks on 11th of September. The Taleban Supreme leader

Mullah Omar accused Washington of using the allegations as pretext of attacking Afghanistan and asked for patience for punishing the culprits.

The written statement rei-terated that Osama bin Laden is innocent and did not have the communication links to organize the attacks of 11th September

The Taleban said they would abide by any decision made by the clerics. Observers say such meetings usually support existing Taleban policy.

A senior UN official urged the USA to bring Afghanistan in its coalition against Osama bin Laden. Francesc Vendrell who later became special UN envoy to Afghanistan said the crisis offered a historic opportunity to end the civil war in Afghanistan, establish a government acceptable to all Afghans and deal with the presence of Islamic militants. He said many Taleban are increasingly unhappy with the radical government and want change.

Iraqi foreign minister Naji Sabri denied US government reports that Iraq is behind the bombing although Iraqi intelligence officer met the terrorist

Mohammed Ataf in Prague in July 2001. He said that USA, Britain and the entire world knew that Iraq had no links with the attacks of 11th of September

President Bush met President Megawati Sukarnoputri of Indonesia and President Jacque Chirac of France.

German, Russian and Saudi foreign ministers are due in Washington, but Germany refused to take part in any military action against Afghanistan unless there is a proof that Afghanistan is involved. Germany approved the US military strikes weeks later.

The German Chief Prosecutor NIEM announced that there were signals before the bombing but they were ignored in Germany.

US Vice President Dick Cheney and US Secretary of State Colin Powell said they don't suspect Iraq of any involvement on this stage. On 18-09 Baghdad sent condolences to the relatives of the victims of the suicide hijack-attacks on New York and Washington.

Chris Davis became the new Labour Director of the BBC while Greg Dyke retained his post as BBC Chairman. The former BBC-Director Mr. Blunt became chairman of British Telecom.

EU passed a new law under which arrest warrant is valid in all EU member countries.

General Pervez Musharraf stated Pakistan would maintain friendly relations with Afghanistan.

USA stationed 100 combat aircraft in Bahrain and Kuwait preparing carefully for a strike at Afghanistan.

20 Sept 2001

The Taleban clerics forum asked Osama bin Laden to leave Afghanistan but they do not reckon he will soon leave the country.

Washington insisted he must be handed over to responsible authorities; FBI overwhelmed with help offers from Arab speaking translators for a payment of $ 25-38 an hour.

The US Secretary of State Colin Powell met the Chinese foreign minister Tang Jia Xuan in Washington. On his plane also to Washington, the British Prime Minister Tony Blair spoke to the Iranian President Mohammad Khatami. Later on Tony Blair met G. W.Bush in Washington.

21 Sept 2001

Washington set an ultimatum to Afghanistan to deliver Osama ben Laden or to share his faith; also to close all training camps. Taleban rejected again this US request.

Protesters came in the streets of Karachi to protest against the Pakistani policy of cooperation with Washington. The British Foreign Secretary Jack Straw visited Iran which share a large border with Afghanistan. Practically he asked Iran to pass British troops through its territory to encircle Afghanistan from the West. Iran rejected the "secrete" British proposal but never denounced it publicly. Iran condemned the attacks of 11th September but warned from premature actions, which would trigger unpredictable avalanche of anti-Western activities.

German chief prosecutor N I E M issued arrest warrant for two more Arabic students: Mohammed Attaf and Ramzes Said. Three further arrests were made in London.

Colin Powell said in BBC interview that he does not know for sure where is Osama bin Laden but he assumes he is in Afghanistan. This statement of the US Secretary of State triggered off a wave of speculations: the Israel intelligence named Ibrahim Moodnier, head of the Hezbollah, as prime suspect of the latest attacks on the W.T.C. and the Pentagon.

Suspicion was cast also on throwing poisons in reservoirs of water. Gui Verhofstadt - Belgian prime minister and EU President at that time stated that the strikes against Afghanistan must be authorized by the UN-something what the US refused.

22 Sept 2001

America started a military build-up: warplane carrier USS. Kitty hawk left Japan while carrier USS. Roosevelt heads towards Pakistan. The United Arab Emirates U.A.E. broke its diplomatic relations with Taleban. To please America.

General Mohammad Fahim - Commander of the Northern Alliance - met the Russian Commander General Kvazhnin to secure Russian military support for the war in which the oppositional Northern Alliance played the crucial role.

Pope John Paul II visited Kazakhstan though it has no Catholic population

US warplanes and German special troops stationed in Uzbekistan starting thus practically to encircle the Taleban from the North-West amid peaceful anti-war demonstrations in the German cities of Berlin and Cologne against retaliation strikes of the Americans.

7

23 Sept 2001

The Security Advisor Condoleezza Rice & President George Bush stated they will be not deterred to strike Afghanistan by the Taleban statement they have lost the trace of Osama ben Laden.

Arab countries' foreign ministers meet in Jeddah to discuss how much to cooperate with USA Saudi Arabia came under pressure to break diplomatic relations with Afghanistan which it did on 25th of September when the war already well under its way. The Northern Alliance under General Abdul Rashid Dostum took strategic regions in the North of Afghanistan.

The Taleban shot down US recognisance plane over Afghanistan. 10,000 British troops arrived in Oman for training.

FBI & CNN published the names and the photographs of the hijackers many of them however falsified. Two of the real persons intend to sue CNN for libel and falsification. Similar falsification occurred also on 31st December 2002-the FBI placed the photo of an alleged wanted terrorist in several newspapers. He came forward with the stament that he is a juwelry

Trader and had never left his shop. He was obviously frightened because he could face dead penalty.

The exiled king of Afghanistan Mohammed Zahir Shah (86) spoke for unification of the nation.

President Putin of Russia spoke by phone with the presidents of Central Asia republics on how to combat terrorism. His practical advice certainly excluded Chechnya.

Osama ben Laden accused of training militant Islamists in Kosovo and Macedonia which actually supported the US and NATO war on Serbia in 1999.

Chapter 3

USA (PART3)

24 Sept 2001

President Bush froze all-financial assets of Osama Ben Laden. Mullah Omar urged Washington to withdraw all troops from the Middle East and stop its support for Israel in the combat against terrorism or to face all-out vain bloody war.

The Northern Alliance took another region in the north - Zara - on the route to Mazar-e Sharif. Heavy fighting was reported in region of Shamali. The Taleban are reported to have mobilized some 300,000 fighters nationwide.

The price of Afghani opium dropped from $700 to $200 per kilogram. US delegation discussed military cooperation with Pakistan.

The Taleban closed the UN-Office in Kandahar and seized 1500 tons of food.

President Putin opened Russian air space for humanitarian help and promised intelligence help for the Americans. He will supply additionally the Northern Alliance with weapons.

Iranian President Khatami denounced sharply US-police and demanded the closure of the oppositional Mudjahedeen-office in Washington.

25 Sept 2001

Saudi Arabia broke diplomatic relations with the Taleban.

But the Pakistani President General Pervez Musharraf refused to break diplomatic relations to

Afghanistan and warned all parties not to support the anti-Taleban opposition on a conference with a high-leveled EU delegation which arrived in Islamabad for talks. In 2003 Pervez Musharraf-who converted Pakistan into nuclear power -survived unharmed 2 assassination attempts. Pakistan receives solid US military aid.

Russian President Putin and President Hosni Mubarak of Egypt arrived in Berlin for talks .

The British Foreign Secretary Jack Straw visited Iran and spoke with the Iranian foreign minister Kamal Kharrazi. Pope John Paul visited in Armenia till the evening of 26th September.

British war ships passed the Suez Canal heading to the South coast of Pakistan.

FBI-investigators arrived in Germany to investigate connections of Mohammed Attaf to Al Qaida and probably directly to Osama ben Laden. The British Prime Minister Tony Blair warned the Taleban to hand over Osama Ben Laden or face war.

FBI issued international arrest warrant for the Egyptian Imon Eazawari.

26 Sept 2001

The US Embassy in Kabul set afire by angry mobs. The Taleban Supreme leader Mullah Omar appealed to the Afghani not to leave the country as the danger from US-strike has receded., he assured them. The Iranian spiritual leader Ayatollah Khomeini criticized bitterly Washington for its anti-Islamic policy and asked for closure of the oppositional Mudjahedeen-office in Washington.

In Brussels lord George Robertson –Secretary General of NATO-gave evidence against Osama Ben Laden. His evidence was never made public-even after the fall of the Taleban.

Italian Prime Minister Silvio Berlusconi spoke of the superiority of Western nations. His remark caused a storm of outrage among Muslim countries.

27 Sept 2001

President Bush is to reassure air flight security in Chicago or to face another blow among the public scrutiny.

The Taleban Supreme leader Mullah Mohamed Omar warned Afghans not to cooperate either with Russia or with America. Russia promised Soviet era weapons to the Northern Alliance in Afghanistan to combat the Taleban.

President Bush ordered to shoot down all hijacked planes in order to avoid disasters similar to those in New York and Washington on the 11th of September.

The Arab League denounced the remark of Silvio Berlusconi about the superiority of the Western nations and asked him either to deny it or to apologize for it.

The Taleban asked Osama Ben Laden to leave Afghanistan.

28 Sept 2001

Pakistani Delegation arrived in Afghanistan to try to persuade the Taleban to hand over Osama Ben Laden. Both sides decided to keep in touch with each other. At this stage Pakistan-being key American ally in the region-did not fear America too much and was not convinced yet the US would launch war on Afghanistan before all diplomatic means were exhausted. But George W. Bush showed very soon that he is a tough president with a heavy hand. Or he simply bowed to the pressure of the military.; who knows?

King Abdullah of Jordan visited President Bush in Washington to please America. Jordan is one of the poorest Arab countries.

US-special Delta-force troops entered Afghanistan on intelligence gathering mission. They are believed to have been joined by British troops.

01 Oct 2001

Talks in Rome between the Northern Alliance, special US-Senate delegation and the former King of Afghanistan Zahir Shah. The talks established Emergency Council under the King and 120 local representatives - called later with their true name-war lords. The Northern Alliance advised the USA not to take any military action against the Taleban ,said the Voice of Russia.

Terrorist attacks took place in Sri Nagar in Kashmir and in Jerusalem.

President Putin of Russia arrived in Brussels for talks with Gui van Verhoven and George Robertson ,said the Voice of Russia. The other media kept silent on his visit till the next day.

02 Oct 2001

The US DefenceSecretary Donald Rumsfeld said the strike against Afghanistan would be within days. Senior American official said toppling the Taleban is not their explicit aim and they are looking also for a peaceful solution but British Foreign Secretary, Mr. Jack Straw, ruled out every negotiation with the Taleban who he compared with the fascists.

President Bush is at the moment more low key than Tony Blair: this is a different kind of war and Americans won't see on TV-screens what had taken place but the US started a huge police investigation on all they can put their hands on.

Telephone call of Osama Ben Laden to his Mother Al Khalifa Ben Laden from 09 Sept 2001 published in which he told her that something **B I G** is about to occur and that he will off for some time. His mother was in Syria for holiday on 09 Sept 2001 when the phone call occurred. Upon her return to Saudi Arabia she was arrested. To the Saudi police she confirmed the details of this conversation and altogether cooperated with the Saudi police. If correct this intercepted phone call will be the most serious evidence against Osama Ben Laden. Reports of this conversation came as Tony Blair stated he had seen incontrovertible connection between Osama Ben Laden and the attacks on New York and Washington. So far the US-Government has not confirmed this conversation and up to date has refused to reveal his case against Osama Ben Laden. The FBI however has been slowly building the prosecution file following the money trail-money transfers had been treated as fingerprints at the scene of the crime.

Terrorists dispatched unused cash back to their pay masters in the Middle East in the days before the attacks: Mohamed Attaf sent $4,000 to Mustafa Ahmed, who disappeared after the 11th September and 2 other hijackers transferred money to a man in The Middle East, who reportedly fled afterwards to Pakistan.

President Bush attempted to show the American people that progress is been made by saying 50 bank accounts with $6,000,000 had been frozen - 30 accounts in the US and 20 overseas.

Only today US Government announced they were planning opening speech of the US Secretary of State Colin Powell to the UN General Assembly referring to the neglected Israeli-Palestinian peace negotiations but his speech was delayed by the attacks of 11th September against New York, Washington and Pittsburgh. India asked Washington to extend its struggle against terrorism also to Pakistan and the Islamic separatists in Kashmir. India accused Pakistan of taking only cosmetic measures against terrorism while Pakistan stated this is reprehensible.

Franco-Algerian terrorist Jamal Bigal revealed the role of Osama Ben Laden - he received attacks orders against US-interests in France from a close associate of Osama Ben Laden but not direct from Osama Ben Laden himself. Jamal Bigal was arrested at the beginning of July in the United Arab Emirates UAE and extradited to France on 01 Oct 2001 in the evening.

The BBC correspondent Jackie Rowland reported from the northern Afghani town of Hodga Bahaldin where she was speaking with the Northern Alliance Foreign Mr. Abdullah Abdullah.

11

The Northern Alliance reported defection from the ranks of the Taleban. The attacks of the Northern Alliance will be focused on small towns, which will be identified as vulnerable. Successes were reported from the western province of Bahres, where several hundreds Taleban defected. Defections were reported also from the Pashtun dominated province of Lahaman in the east. Dr. Abdullah said the Council will convene in 2 weeks time and the Taleban will be defeated with or without US help but international support will hasten the process and US military action will begin in the matter of days.

George Robertson gave a news conference in Brussels prior to his meeting with President Putin in which he said the attack on the USA was from outside and the alliance will support the USA. Now what will be happening: negotiations between Putin and George Robertson will divide Afghanistan in 2 Sectors by joint NATO-Russian offensive?? George Robertson said all NATO Ambassadors were briefed on evidence linking Osama Ben Laden to the attacks; this was classified information and cannot be revealed. US terrorism specialist Robert Taylor briefed George Robertson.

Labour MP Tony Benn said in Parliament UN must authorize any strike.

The Taleban Ambassador to Pakistan Abdul Salem Zaeef said Afghanistan needs help not war and asked Washington for peace, negotiations and evidence on Osama Ben Laden's involvement but Washington refused, as it maintains no direct contacts with the Taleban. After the war Abdul Salam Zaif asked political asylum in Pakistan but was refused and delivered to the US for inter rogation.

03 Oct 2001

USA asked formally NATO for support - logistical and military.

The Russian President Vladimir Putin arrived in Rome for talks with Sylvio Berlusconi.

General Pervez Musharraf indicated in a speech that he might abandon Afghanistan. Only 8 days earlier-on 25th of September he declared exactly the opposite-that Pakistan would never abandon its ally and neighbour Afghanistan. It is not clear up to date what caused this turn in Pervez Musharraf behaviour. Maybe it will become clear after his planned resignation in 2005.

He spoke of multiethnic society in tribal Afghanistan where the war-lords are local commanders

President Putin hold talks with NATO Secretary General George Robertson in which he supported NATO. Actually Russia opposed the extension of NATO eastwards close to its borders. A new milestone was set in NATO development.

After a bus-jacking in the USA the whole bus fleet-90,000 strong was grounded among huge panic and public transportation disruption.

04 Oct 2001

Taleban arrested a Sunday Telegraph journalist in Jalalabad for entering illegally Afghanistan.

Tony Blair met President Putin in Moscow - a reliable partner as he put it.

The US Defence Secretary Donald Rumsfeld held for talks in Amman and Cairo.

Pakistani Government spokesman Aziz Ahmad Khan said Pakistan had received reliable evidence for the participation of Osama Ben Laden in the attacks on America but refused to convey them to the Taleban. Than to whom ?

Mujahideen war lord Abdullah Haq said he would organize a national uprising against the Taleban.

A Russian passenger plane exploded over the Black Sea on its way from Tel Aviv to Novosibirsk.

Kamal Ahib - Islamic terrorist was arrested in Britain and than extradited to France.

05 Oct 2001

Anti-war demonstrations in Japan against US-military strikes. The British Prime Minister Tony Blair continued in Moscow his talks with the Russian President Putin and later on flew up the Pakistani and Indian capitals Islamabad and Delhi. He managed remarkable achievement compressing the 3 capitals in record time.

The US Defence Secretary Donald Rumsfeld arrived in Uzbekistan; 1,000 US troops also on its way to Uzbekistan to encircle the Taleban from the North.

06 Oct 2001

Tony Blair arrived in India-Pakistan's arch-rival-but not much reported. Taleban failed to shoot down a plane over the capital Kabul. The arrested female Sunday Telegraph journalist Yvonne Rigley will be released under the direct order of supreme leader Mullah Mohamed Omar who showed humanity and morality to the world.

On 06 Oct 1981 The Egyptian President Anwar Sadat assassinated by Egyptian Islamic Jihad.

The 20th anniversary was commemorated under gloomy subdued mood. No photos or film documentaries on the assassination were shown. Nothing new!

In a BBC-interview Robert Fox from the Evening Star newspaper and his colleague Philip Nickly said,it takes decades for the truth to come-take the murder of Aldo Moro and President Kennedy. "We try to combat the asymmetric war by symmetric measures", they added.

07 Oct 2001

Taleban said they might arrest Osama Ben Laden and put him on trial if they receive formal request from the USA but they did not receive any evidence so far. But the USA rejected their proposal saying it is time for deeds not for words.

Taleban placed 8,000 additional troops on the boundary with Uzbekistan.

The W A R began at 18:30 GMT = 12:30 ET with air strikes on targets in Kabul, Kandahar, Quetta, Mazar-e-Sherif: 15 strike-aircrafts, 25 bombers and 50 Cruise missiles were shot on different targets from navy vessels in the Arabian Sea. The Airport of Kabul was destroyed together with 15 Taleban MIG-21 planes. A terrorists training camp near Jalalabad was also hit.

Osama Ben Laden issued televised interview in which he says a war on the entire Islamic world has been declared. At 19:29 GMT the BBC program broke down for 4 minutes. It is not clear whether it was for technical reasons or it was a black-out.

The ex-king of Afghanistan Mohamed Shah expressed his shock and regret of the strikes while Iran protested. Iraq called it aggression. Indonesia called for restrain but EU and NATO reaffirmed their full support for the US air strikes. Russia took no official position.

08 Oct 2001

It 's public holiday in USA. Anti-war demonstrations took place in Pakistan, Cairo etc. Police shot tear gas to disperse them. The Palestinian leader Yassir Arafat arrived in Cairo for talks with the Egyptian President Hosni Moubarag. Sense of shock and panic in the Arab world.

Russia and China supported the strikes where some 30 targets were hit and 30 civilians died.

The Northern Alliance said it will capitalize from the strikes.

Several Austrian newspapers said this mission would be more successful than the Vietnam War. The BBC broadcasted interview with the NATO Secretary General, Lord George Robertson, and British Defence Secretary, Jeff Hoon. They called the air strikes "a legitimate act of self-defence "and said "the strikes had just begun". Special ground troops are later to deploy.

Taleban condemned the attacks and called it act of terrorism.

Taleban Ambassador in Islamabad Salam Zaif gave press conference in which he said a war on the Islamic world has been declared. In Quetta the UNICEF-office was set alight by protesters. Donations were only possible to the "War Child",P.O.Box 20231, London NW5 3WP tel. 0870 4427 565. The NATO Secretary General George Robertson says that upon US request NATO will deploy AWACS reconnaissance planes over Afghanistan which actually never happened.

The British Foreign Secretary Jack Straw arrived in Luxemburg for EU-Foreign Ministers conference. The Taleban ex-communicated the former Afghan king Mohamed Zahir Shah.

At 16:00 GMT the 2nd night of bombardments began over Afghanistan.

In his weapon information websites www.globalsecurity.com & www.tradingweapon.com the weapon expert John Pyke said the US will launch attacks beyond Afghanistan.

09 Oct 2001

Daylight bombardment over Afghanistan. 4 UN workers were killed after a UN building took a direct hit although it was clearly marked. Alone in Kabul the civilian casualties were well over 1,000 , BBC said. Anti-American demonstrations took place in Jakarta and London.

10 Oct 2001

The military Academy in Kabul was bombarded together with a living-block section in Kabul.

The Taleban issued a defiant message that the Americans have not destroyed the air defence system of the country. The US refuted this statement. Taleban called for global jihad on their website www.jihad.com. In pre-recorded BBC interview Mullah Omar addressed the nation and said the Americans are strong but not invincible. Turkey offered its bases and airspace for American use.

President Bush issued a list of 22 most wanted terrorists including Osama Ben Laden, Ali Muzahaferi and Mohamed Attaf and thanked NATO for its support to America.

The World Islamic Congress condemned the terrorist actions but warned strongly Washington not to attack any other country under pretext of combating terrorism.

Pakistani Government threatened to deport any Afghan refugee participating in pro-Taleban demonstrations in Pakistan.US-Embassies round the world started to pile up antibiotics in case of anthrax-attacks .

11 Oct 2001

The Northern Alliance took the northern Afghan town of Chah Charahn while Americans bombarded civilian objects and hit a mosque in Jalalabad. US used bunker-buster bombs, which penetrate deep underground and destroy bunkers and underground facilities.

200 civilians were killed in the town of Kadam where previously was a training camp.

The British Prime Minister Tony Blair arrived in Cairo after having been refused audience by the Saudi King. The Jordanian King Abdullah visited Berlin, where the Bundestag adopted new anti-terrorist law. Anthrax letters were reported in Germany. The Palestinian leader Yassir Arafat visited Greece for talks with the Greek leadership.BBC defended its right to broadcast Taleban messages including the message of Osama Ben Laden as they did on 10 Oct 2001 and interviewed the Pakistani Interior Minister Moinuddin Haider. Anti-war demonstrations took place in Cape Town in South Africa around the US Embassy.

FBI warned against new terrorist strikes.

The nephew of the Saudi King said USA must reconsider its Middle East policy and take more moderate stand and donated $10,000,000 to the municipal of New York. The Mayor of New York Rudolph Giuliani dismissed his remark as irresponsible and refused to accept the $10,000,000.

12 Oct 2001

US will stop the bombardment if the Taleban deliver Osama ben Laden and used forbidden cluster bombs at concentrations of Arab and Pakistani Taleban soldiers. Destroyed are up to date:

The Kabul airport, the Ministry of defence, the Presidential Palace, Radio and TV stations, residential areas,the home of Mullah Omar and the airport in Kandahar. Altogether the civilian

Casualties are some 174 people, said the Iranian radio. The Northern Alliance is ready to rush up towards Kabul and finish the war.

In Gaza, Jakarta, Teheran, Dakar and Karachi anti-war demonstrators clashed with police.

The UN declared it is unable to cope with the huge refugee influx from Afghanistan.

UNHCR condemned the attacks and asked them to stop. Al Jazzera, which has correspondence office in Kabul, has shown the destroyed mosque in Jalalabad and the killed civilians.

The insurance company AXA which had insured the international football games in Japan and South Korea pulled out of the contract in fear of new attacks. Equinox-British astrology company predicted a successful war for the USA. The British prime minister Tony Blair cancelled again his visit to Saudi Arabia. No reasons were given but he was once rejected audience at the Saudi King on 11th October 2001.Palestinian leaders warned US President Bush to match his words.

13 Oct 2001

Colin Powell is due in Islamabad

International Muslim Organization - British Organization with extended international links. Against the strike because other means also may be pursued, so Chairman Imam Tahir Ishak. Dr. Sahad al Fahid - movement for Islamic reforms. Afghanistan claimed 300 dead civilians.

14 Oct 2001

A 2,000 pound air bomb was dropped in the residential area of Kabul;many civilians died.

The Egyptian president Hosni Mubarag sent 80 terrorist members under the leadership of Al Zuihri to a military court where they have no right to appeal. The Palestinian leader

Yasser Arafat arrived in London for talks with the British prime minister Tony Blair.

Taleban organized journalist journey to an eastern town of Kouram where a bomb went astray and killed 200 civilians. In a defiant manifesto Al-Qaida said it would hit back for the strikes on Afghanistan. For Tony Blair this amounted to a confession for the strikes on Washington and New York on 11th September. Many new anthrax cases were reported world wide

Protest anti-war demonstration took place at the Pakistani base of Jakobabad, which is used by US forces. The new BBC-news director Richard Sambrook-who broadcasted earlier the Al Qaida message defended his decision.In Afghanistan the whole village of Holumn was almost fully obliterated by US-bombing. The Northern Alliance decided not to attack Kabul until political agreement is reached on post-Taleban settlement, said its spokesman Dr. Abdullah Abdullah in the town of Shamali only 40km north of Kabul.

Taleban Maulvi Abdul Kabir offered to surrender Osama ben Laden to a neutral country but US President Bush refused any negotiations with Kabul.

15 Oct 2001

Taleban opened massive anti-aircraft fire.

The Palestinian leader Yasser Arafat arrived in London for talks with the British Prime minister Tony Blair; Arafat rejected accusations his movement has fallen down to terrorists.

Kuwaiti Ambassador to Washington Sheikh Saud called for more support to the Americans in a newspaper article. Afghani cricket team played in Peshawar against Pakistan to show they are not terrorists.The Taleban Foreign Minister Wakil Ahmad Mutawakel arrived in the United Arab Emirates UAE and there are speculations he may defect there. 12 civilians were killed in an air raid at the northern Afghan city of Bagdaz. Taleban Foreign Minister Wakil Ahmad Mutawakel may have arrived in Islamabad and the speculations continued that he may defect there as Pakistan supports the US in its war on Afghanistan. The US Secretary of State Colin Powell also arrived in Islamabad for talks with the Pakistani leadership and this enhanced speculations that there might be a meeting between the two foreign ministers. Pervez Musharraf advised Colin Powell first to remove the Taleban and than to hunt down Osama Bin Laden. Democrat Senator Tom Daschle received an anthrax letter in his office which cause great panic in Washington.

16 Oct 2001

In talks with Colin Powell Pervez Musharraf reassured him of Pakistani support but stressed there must be post-war help for Afghanistan. The US Army used low flying slowly moving 4 engine ground attack air planes AC-130 with 100mm cannons to underline its air superiority;many civilians died in the raid. Later on the US planes hit the Red Cross compound in Kabul. Many civilians died, although the building was clearly marked with the Red Cross emblem 3 by 3 meters on its roof well visible from the air;the fire destroyed many food supplies. The Red Cross lodged formal complaint with the US.

Pro-Taleban Pakistani cleric Abdul Rahman was charged with treason after he called fellow Taleban to destroy Government institutions. Abdul Rahman could face dead penalty if found guilty.

The Northern Alliance was closing its troops round the Northern Afghan city of Mazar-e Sharif I by that time.

17 Oct 2001

The PFPL-the Popular front Liberation of Palestine-shot dead the hard line Israeli minister Rahme Zaevi to revenge the death of Ali Abdul Mustafa in August 2001.

The US Secretary of State Colin Powell in India for talks with Indian Foreign Minister Jaswan Singh. Singh disagreed that Osama Bin Laden was a terrorist and that Kashmir was a central issue. Colin Powell reassured India of good relation despite the strong ties with Pakistan in the war against Afghanistan. India called against the state sponsored terrorism of Pakistan in Kashmir.

In Kandahar clashes took place between Taleban authorities and Al-Qaida fighters.

US-planes stroke a refugee camp near Kandahar killing a number of people. The Taleban Supreme leader Mullah Omar said holy war is on and the Taleban fighters will not fear death.

CNN tried to establish contacts with Al-Qaida to take interview. CNN was approached by Al-Qaida representative with an offer of Osama Bin Laden to respond questions on videotape. Contact was made through the Arabic TV station Al Jazzera that has presence in Afghanistan and will send back the videotape answers. CNN put 6 questions incl. whether Osama Bin Laden was behind the attacks in New York and Washington and whether Al-Qaida has nuclear weapons. After a review CNN will emit the interview if it is newsworthy. In fact this never occurred. 6 world aid agencies called for the air strikes to stop temporarily to allow food aid to get through.In Washington both Houses of Senate were closed because of anthrax. Anthrax found also in the house of the Governor of New York George Pataki which increased the panic even furter. The USA and Britain closed their embassies in Sarajevo, Banja Luka and Mostar because of fear of terrorist and anthrax attacks. The US Secretary of State Colin Powell arrived in China to secure Chinese support for the US strikes on Afghanistan in a war which is still not declared. China shares a common border with Afghanistan-some 200 km in the mountains. The Taleban Supreme leader Mullah Omar told his soldiers they are fighting holy war jihad and their victory is certain. Taleban seized 7,000 metric tons of UN food and dispenced it not to the civil population but among themselves.

17

On 17 Oct 1961 French police killed 200 peaceful Algerian demonstrators in Paris. The day was commemorated in France by many people - Muslims and non-Muslims.

Russia closed the radar base in Cuba to save $200,000,000 - enough to buy 100 new sophisticated radar stations. The closure of the naval base in Vietnam will bring up money for one more Russian nuclear submarine.

18 Oct 2001

US planes hit fuel depot in Kabul, which burst into flames.

Russian-Indian talks took place for post-war settlement in Afghanistan.

The Russian General Kvazhnin arrived in in Dushanbe for 6-hour visit with the Tadzhiks.

The Saudi Interior Minister Prince Nayaf called on Saudi-Arabians not to support Taleban.

On 23th October 2001 the Saudi Defence Minister Prince Sultan took exactly the opposite position -called for peace in the Afghan conflict.

The US President Bush and the Russian President Putin arrived in Shanghai for talks.

The British prime minister Tony Blair arrived in Turkey for talks. Concretely he wants Turkish troops to occupy Afghanistan.Turkey rejected the British proposal. Anthrax panic broke out in Kenya from a letter posted in the USA on 08 Sept 2001. Scott Ritter, former weapon inspector on Iraq, said in a BBC-interview the anthrax may come from some Timothy McVeigh cell. Indirectly he excluded the Taleban and Al Qaida from the anthrax-front. Meanwhile psychological warfare experts warned Taleban to surrender or be defeated.

19 Oct 2001

US-ground troops entered South Afghanistan. Taleban denied this report.

Senior Taleban official Abdul Nasir Mastri killed in an accident.

Taleban brought cease-fire plan to Pakistan although they refused to hand over Osama Bin Laden.

Anthrax fears cause panic in India. Taleban denied any link to the anthrax and called the people not to eat US food drops because it was poisoned. While CIA agitated local tribes to break away from Taleban, Taleban advised that every food with Afghan blood on it is unclean.

CIA broadcasted the propaganda from a special aircraft flying slowly over Afghanistan.

EU-top took place in Gent, Belgium;before the top France, Germany and Britain met separately which triggered off Italian protests. After the meeting Tony Blair said that a l l agreed that Taleban harbour Al-Qaida and it is OK to destroy it.

25,000 anti-war demonstration took place in Gent in Belgium against the war in Afghanistan.

The Polish governments warned that Israel were going to put Yasser Arafat under pressure with the Clear aim to topple or to isolate him. In 2004 Poland contributed some 2,000 Polish troops in Iraq to the US-led coalition. The Russian-Indian 2-day talks ended with the resolution that any new post-Taleban Government must be broad-based and independent. Germany issued international arrest warrant on the Moroccan Zakharia Essemar for his part of the New York bombing. General Abdul Rashid Dostum received US food, munitions and money to capture Mazar-e Sharif.

18

20 Oct 2001

100 new US rangers entered Afghanistan overnight said Taleban Education Minister Amir Khan Mutaki. After a battle with Taleban militia in the Baba Sahib mountains west from Kandahar they pulled out. The rangers tried to destroy airfield, which had sustained the air strike.

A US helicopter was shot down by Taleban fire. 2 US soldiers died in the crash

A bomb explosion was reported at Islamabad international airport but no further details came in.

The Russian General Wladimir Popov said in Shamali-40km from Kabul- that Russia had helped sufficiently the Northern Alliance and the NE needed no additional (i.e. American) help.

Geologist recognized the rocks on Osama Bin Laden videotape-they were from an area 150 km southeast from Kabul.

Canadian Government decided to by-pass Bayer pharmaceutical antibiotic "Sipro" meant to combat anthrax. Only few mounts ago USA and Canada were against such by-pass by cheap generic copies. But the harsher the war the harsher we do it .The BBC-Today-program investigated that UN-foundation donated $2,000,000 to Sudan but finally that money came to the pockets of Osama ben Laden. 5,000 Afghan refugees crossed the border to Pakistan. 10,000 more still wait to cross. The Palestinian leader Yasser Arafat held talks with the Russian representative Andre' Volovan.

21 Oct 2001

The 10-years old son of Mullah Omar was killed in a US air raid. Doctor Abdul Barry told BBC when he crossed the border with Pakistan with a wave of refugees the boy was already badly injured in the first days of the war and Mullah Omar brought him personally to the hospital in a desperate vain to save his life. The uncle of Mullah Omar was also killed.

Taleban shoot dead any Westerner who tries to approach the border at the crossing point Chaman while Americans raided the Kabul airport Bagram. Angry protesters in India attacked the Coca Cola plant in Delhi to protest against the strikes in Afghanistan.

22 Oct 2001

US planes hit a hospital in Herat killing over 100 civilians - nurses, doctors and patients.

Taleban accused US of using also chemical and bacteriological weapon - judging from the injuries of their patients. There is no comment from the Pentagon but the Americans bombarded mistakenly also positions of the Northern Alliance.

Taleban produced the wreckage of the helicopter they had shot down yesterday to the TV-station Al Jazzera. According to the German Radio Deutschland Funk there were 2 helicopters.

The Northern Alliance called upon the Pentagon to step up its bombardment of Taleban front position. The fortress Mazar-e-Sharif was hit but not destroyed. With recent Taleban victories over the Northern Alliance, God had shown clearly He sides with the Taleban, not with the Northern Alliance, the supreme Taleban leader Mullah

Omar said. The Russian President Vladimir Putin stated his full backing of the anti-Taleban Alliance in military, technical,logistical and humanitarian terms.

President Putin held all night talks with the Tadzhik President Rahmaninov and the deposed Afghani President Rabbani in the Tadzhik Capital Dushanbe. Putin said that the Taleban had discredited themselves by supporting terrorism. The British Foreign Minister Jack Straw called in London also for similar all-party Government after the war.Iran, India and Russia are against Taleban participation in the post-war Government but again the Iranian President protested against the US air strikes.

Pakistani President General Pervez Musharraf called the strikes to end before beginning of the holy month of Ramadan mid November. Actually this did not occur.On the border crossing Chaman to Pakistan many Afghani refugees managed to cut the border wire and to get through into Pakistan but many others were beaten back by Pakistani border guards and stranded into no-man's-land without food, water and shelter. Later on high-energy biscuits and blankets were given to the Pakistanis who passed them on to the Taleban for further distribution among the population.

In London Tony Blair was bitterly criticized by Labour MPs Bob Marshal, Hilary Armstrong, Paul Martens and Alan Simpson for his opposition to end the high level strikes, especially the high level bombardment - 30,000 ft.- which inflicts many civilian casualties and will not achieve the aim of arrest of Osama Bin

Laden. British Defence Minister Jeff Hoon called for ground troops to enter sooner Afghanistan to achieve the main aim - the arrest of Osama Bin Laden. Till today-10-02-2004- this has not happened.

New anthrax cases were reported in USA: a postal worker in Washington-Brentwood contracted the disease after 2 further postal workers had already expired from anthrax. For more information on how to prevent anthrax a special website was established: www.uspost.gov.

The US Defence Secretary Donald Rumsfeld denied earlier reports that US-planes hit Afghani hospital in Herat in which 100 civilians died. He said the allegations would be investigated.

UN called on Pakistan to open its border and to accept more new refugees from Afghanistan.

23 Oct 2001

The Northern Alliance resumed attacks on Mazar-e Sharif while US-planes bombed Taleban front line and Kabul itself. As the Taleban had entrenched themselves no success was achieved. USA and the Northern Alliance are not explicit allies but they share a common enemy. The US planes started this time from a military base in Uzbekistan to underline US disagreement with the Northern Alliance. Senior Taleban Mohamed Haib Aga used the disagreement to boost moral saying said Taleban will not be defeated and they will celebrate victory over USA and the Northern Alliance. US planes bombed and destroyed a mosque West of Herat killing all the people praying inside. Pentagon did not comment. UNHCR called Pakistan to open its border to Afghanistan for more new refugees. The Pakistani decision to establish a refugee camp inside Afghanistan set a dangerous precedent as it puts lives at risk. UNHCR reckons the conditions for sheltering refugees inside Afghanistan are not suitable because expose the refugees to additional risk and called on Pakistan to open its border.

Anti-anthrax measures were taken in Washington including irradiation of the postal envelopes with low-level radiation machines. The purchase of the machines, which will bombard the mail with radiation, will cost

$1,000,000,000. Jonathan Fariti from the American Vaccination Association said it is not necessary to vaccinate people.

High-level international delegation arrived in Israel, to negotiate peace with the Israelis. The same delegation was yesterday in Gaza to negotiate with the Palestinians but BBC did not inform on it.

UN confirmed that a hospital was hit near Herat yesterday but Pentagon still refused to comment, a UN spokeswoman said at a press conference in Islamabad. But military observers in Afghanistan said USA used cluster bombs, which are vicious anti-personnel device. ritish Defence Secretary Jeff Hoon said Britain would decide soon on whether Britain will send in ground troops. He said 9 Al-Qaida train camps and 9 airfields were destroyed and 24 troops garrisons essentially hit.

In Pakistan angry anti-war protesters clashed with riot police. 9 people were injured while over 1,000 protesters were arrested. Russia stepped up its campaign in Chechnya. Many rebel strongholds were targeted; civilians tortured and summarily executed while the rebels too strengthened their attacks on Russian targets, placed landmines and shot pro Russian officials.

Pakistani President General Pervez Musharraf called again for the air strikes to end before begin of the holy month of Ramadan. Actually this did not happened.

Finally Pentagon broke its silence and came forward with description of what had happened on Sunday in Herat: a 1,000 pound bomb missed its target by approx. 300 feet and hit a senior citizens house. No one survived, Pentagon spokeswoman Victoria Clark said. However an UN spokesperson in Islamabad spoke of a hospital, not seniors' house. Pakistani Hirakulat (Hirakat) Mujahideen said in Islamabad their house in Kabul was hit and 22 civilians died. The civilian casualties amount so far to over 1,000. New anthrax letters were found in the postal office of the White House which increased the panic. The Saudi Defence Minister Prince Sultan called for peace in the Afghan conflict.

24 Oct 2001

US-planes bombed Taleban positions North of the Capital Kabul. Taleban moved their front lines closer to the Northern Alliance making difficult for the Americans to distinguish foe from friend. They took also positions in civilian areas in Kabul.

In Herat citizens were trapped in their houses, as the area is full with unexploded cluster bombs.

Afghani opposition forces met in Peshawar to discuss the future of the country after the defeat of Taleban. However the former king was not present and did not send any representative. The meeting will continue tomorrow and may come up with a resolution.

The Buddhist supreme leader Dalai Lama congratulated the recent US-strikes against Afghanistan and said the war has become much more humane and mature as food drops and precautions for civilians were made which is actually not exactly true. But some 2 years earliers Taleban had destroyed the 2 huge Buddha statues in Bamian. The Northern Alliance called for more strikes on Taleban esp. on their front line which was closing dangerously to the Northern Alliance positions UNHCR said up to 70% of the population of the big Afghan cities Jalalabad and Kandahar had fled either into refugee camps or to the rural areas where they feel safer. Up to 25% of the population of Kabul has also left. The situation in this refugee camps is desperate - people are crammed together like sardines,they've received no food for the last night, no clean drinking water let alone washing water;diseases were spreading, especially diarrhoea etc.

President Bush speaking in Maryland said, the USA will not back down until they defeat the Taleban. This war is with the Taleban, not with the Afghani people, he put it. The head of US postal office said that the post of US-citizens is not safe and they should handle it with care washing their hands each time after they had handled their post. Rear admiral John Stufflebeem said Taleban are tough warriors but USA will find way to destroy them even if they fall back to an urban war. He was surprised how strong Taleban cling to power.

Chapter 4

USA (PART4)

25 Oct 2001

Although the US-strikes on Taleban positions continue, the Northern Alliance complained they were insufficient and inadequate. Also the practical help it received is insufficient. Residential area of Kabul was hit, leaving 17 civilians dead. The village of Tarrin Kowt was entirely destroyed by US strikes in a 5-hour air raid. A bus with passengers was also hit by American shell near Kandahar. There was no independent confirmation.

14,000 Pakistani Taleban volunteered to join Taleban fighters in Afghanistan; most of them are from the radical Islamic organization Tanzia Niphat Isheriat Mohamedi. Local leader Mullah Soupy Mohamed gave the call to volunteers for the fight in Afghanistan. Many of them brought their own guns and weapons. However the Pakistani Government is not likely to allow them to cross the border. Pakistan had given all its support to USA so it will not allow massive numbers of Pakistani guerrillas to cross the border with Afghanistan.

The village Tarrin Kowt-80km north from Kandahar-was destroyed by US strikes in a 5-hour air raid. The villagers said they have no idea why the village was targeted by US-planes. The Taleban Education Minister Amir Khan Mutaki called for the Organization of Islamic Congress to inspect the damage. Dr. Badawi from the Organization of Islamic Conference in London said in BBC-interview that the US strikes would alienate not only Muslims but also the entire world from the USA. Rear Admiral John Stufflebeem said it is strange that the Taleban does not realize the inevitability of their defeat.Israeli Foreign minister Simon Perez returned from his visit to Washington. Israel is the biggest recipient of US-foreign aid: it gets $3,000,000,000 of development funds and armory each year.

A series of explosions shattered an army weapon depot in Thailand. People from the surrounding villages were evacuated. No further reports came in on whether it was a terrorist attack but 3 years later on-in 2004-the Thai Prime Minister Thaksim Shinawatra introduced military law in 3 provinces in South Thailand – in Yala, in Pathani and in Narathiwat because of frequent Islamist attacks there.

On 29th of March 2004 a night curfew was imposed in Thailand from 10:00 pm till 04:00 am.

Prince Hasan Bin Tellal of Jordan called for the creation of World Congress that would to solve international issues such as terrorism. UN said even more and more Afghan civilians were killed in recent US raids.

The US Defence Secretary Donald Rumsfeld said in an interview with USA-Today that the USA may never succeed in catching or killing Osama ben Laden. Even if they succeed the activities of al-Qaida will continue,he said.. Osama has plenty of friends and money in many countries and even if he was captured the problem of international terrorism will remain, Donald Rumsfeld continued. The Taleban were described as tough warriors operating on a harsh terrain. This is the same like looking for a needle in a haystack. In his answer to the repeated question, if they can capture Osama ben Laden or maybe not , Donald Rumsfeld answered:"Well, you're trying to get me again".

23,000 British troops were staged in Oman for exercise planed long before the current crisis. 500 of them will be re-located to Afghanistan after the end of the exercises as special ground commandos, said the British armed forces minister Jeff Hoon, whose visit to Oman coincides with Donald Rumsfeld's statement. Tony Blair paid surprising visit to an Islamic conference in London.

USA distributed to the EU a 47-points list on how to combat terrorism. The list includes fast track extradition of terrorists to the USA, where they face dead penalty, and fast freezing of their assets.

The list was distributed to the Chief of the European Commission Romano Prodi and to the Belgium Prime Minister Gui de Hoofstad; Belgium holds currently the EU-presidency. The US list was not submitted to Russia on how to combat the Chechen terrorists who increased their recent attack on Russian soft civilian targets.

Georgia was recruiting Chechen fighters to fight in its break away republic of Ossetia. Since the 11th September the fighting in Chechnya has intensified.

Referring to the shot US helicopter few days ago many observers consider that Taleban had moved many of their troops and positions to Pakistan just crossing the border. Many of them had brought their families to Pakistan in safety or attend medical treatment in Quetta, reckons the author of the book "Taleban".

3 new cases of anthrax were registered in the USA:between the contracted was a NBC journalist.

26 Oct 2001

Mujahedeen Commander Abdul Hak arrested by the Taleban during his intelligence gathering Mission for the Americans.Mohamed Zaif -the grandson of the former Afghan king Zahir Shah-spoke out his condolences to the Hak's family.Daud Ossala-Abdul Hak's brother said he was on a peace mission, but in fact he was spying for the Americans and for the Pakistani intelligence. The success of this arrest was due to the wide popular support which Taleban enjoy among the ordinary people, said Pakistani defense analyst Kamran Khan in a BBC interview. A view clearly rejected by a British armed forces minister Adam Ingram. The campaign for the capture of the Mujahedeen Commander Abdul Hak lasted several days. The Taleban surrounded the village in which he was hiding and the American helicopters could not help him. Abdul Hak was executed together with his 2 adjutants already the very same day. One American who was with them is on the run. The execution came despite the calls of his brother and from the King's grandson Mohamed Zaif . A friend of Abdul Hak said he was betrayed in the dead of the night. His capture revealed his taste for secret Night missions. Abdul Hak fought against the Taleban although he has had already blown away one of his legs by a landmine. He was ethnic Pashtun;-ironically from the same large ethnic group from which Taleban draw most of their supporters. He was against the US air strikes and supported the idea of bringing back the Afghan King Zahir Shah-aged 86-to the Afghan throne.His death will deter many commanders and warlords from their intentions of traveling through Afghanistan in order to gain supporters for the Northern Alliance. Hak spoke fluently English and was invited by the British Prime Minister Margaret Thatcher to London for talks during the Soviet occupation of Aghanistan in the 1980s. Later on he indulged into business activities in the United Arab Emirates UAE, which brought him a big fortune. He was definitely opposed to the US strikes on Afghanistan, as I said already. When the Taleban came in to capture him he tried to escape on a horseback calling in American helicopters on his satellite phone but all was in vain. An unknown assailant in the Pakistani town of Peshawar killed his wife and 2 of his sons in 1999. This is not a major surprise knowing that even the former Pakistani President Zulfikar Ali Bhutto was hanged several years earlier-this a part of the political culture of that region.

The death of Abdul Hak is a major blow to the formation of a new broad-based democratic government after the defeat of the Taleban, which laid still in the future by that time.

The Taleban were very proud when they captured and killed the prominent opposition Commander Abdul Hak and 2 of his supporters. The Taleban told the BBC that at least one American was traveling with Abdul Hak and now is on the run. American helicopters are reported to have made unsuccessful effort to rescue the party when the Taleban found their hiding place South of the Capital Kabul.

The Taleban said Abdul Hak was executed under a decree that anyone helping US or British forces is liable to the dead penalty. The Commander's Family has confirmed that he was captured. Abdul Hak who was not member of the opposition Northern Alliance and he is thought to have entered Afghanistan to try to win over fellow Pashtun and moderate elements within the Taleban to turn against the Taleban. Abdul Hak was one of the best-known guerrilla commanders who fought against the Soviet occupation of Afghanistan country in the 1980s. After the Russians were driven out he stayed above the factional conflicts, which destabilized Afghanistan. He remained a leading figure of opposition in exile although he was not a member of the Northern Alliance. His main importance to the American led campaign against the Taleban was that he was Pashtun-the largest ethnic group in Afghanistan from which the Taleban draw most of its members.

American warplanes have continued to bomb the Capital Kabul today Friday-the Muslim day of religious prayer. Residents reported to have heard at least 2 loud explosions around midday and saw thick cloud of smoke rising from one area. Red Cross workers said storage facilities were hit destroying vital stocks of food. Doctors in Kabul have appealed to an end of the US attacks saying they have to operate the civilian casualties in worsening and primitive conditions. Film has been broadcast of a wrecked bus that was carrying civilian passengers when American bombs allegedly hit it on Thursday. Red Cross facilities in Kabul were also hit and destroyed. A spokesman of the International Red Cross said the US air raids were deplorable and the buildings were clearly marked with the Red Cross mark 3 by 3 meters big. BBC correspondent in Afghanistan William Reed said that each bomb that goes astray hits the US w a r efforts.

Britain has decided to deploy 200 commandos trained to operate in harsh winter conditions. A further 400 marines will be on a stand-by. This is the first time British ground forces were engaged in the theatre of military action. The British deployed also one carrier, one destroyer and 2 submarines armed with Cruise missiles. The British Prime Minister Tony Blair said the decision to deploy ground troops was not taken lightly. "We do not combat a state; we combat an idea", the British defense minister, Jeff Hoon said.

Activists from the Dutch Organization "Lawyers for peace" protested against the military strikes and said that article 51 of the UN-Charter, the right of self-defense, is not applicable since the aggressor is not a state but a terrorist organization.

US-plane manufacturers compete who will get the order for the production of a new strike plane, 3,000 of which are due to be produced.

An Algerian pilot trainer Lotsi Raisi was detained in London charged with training the suicide pilots of Osama ben Laden.

Providing security after the 11th September in London cost the Metropolitan police extra £100,000 weekly, said the BBC correspondent in London Terry Stiastny. Police officers slept in vans and in police stations to provide extra security in the Capital.

15,000 angry protesters gathered in Karachi and 20,000 in Quetta to protest against the strikes in Afghanistan. Pakistani police said the protest were organized by militant Islamic groups and were largely peaceful.

A mighty anti-American protest demonstration took place in Nairobi reported the BBC correspondent in Kenya Tom McKinley.

After the Friday prayer the mass of demonstrators took from the central Al Aksa mosque to the city center where was dispersed by tear gas of the riot police. Many of the protesters threw themselves to the ground to express their peaceful feelings but the riot police ignored this,beat them and arrested them massively.

Czech authorities said the Al Qaida terrorist Mohamed Attaf met allegedly with Iraqi intelligence officer in Prague in June 2001. The Iraqi official was expelled subsequently.

New anthrax cases were reported in the USA, the man who had contracted anthrax was identified as Alfred Blanco, reported BBC correspondent in Washing Tim Frank. Anthrax was also found in the mailroom of the US Supreme Court in Washington, the CIA-head quarters and a special military medical research center in Maryland, just outside of Washington. The Supreme Court was closed down. An official said that a Ph.D. having an equipment of a whole laboratory could only produce such big amounts of anthrax.

President Bush passed new laws to combat terrorism, which tightens immigration and banking procedures and lightens police surveillance.

27 Oct 2001

The Taleban authorities in Afghanistan said they have put to death 20 members of the opposition Northern Alliance. They said the men included 5 commanders and were captured when Taleban repulsed an attack north from Mazar-e-Sharif. The day before the Taleban captured and killed the prominent opposition leader Abdul Hak who apparently entered the country to rally support among the Pashtun ethnic majority for the expelled Afghan King Mohamed Zahir Shah.His body is expected to be handed over to his relatives in the Capital Kabul. The death of Abdul Hak was followed by a night of the heaviest air raids on Kabul so far. American planes bombed air base near Bagram. The air raids lasted 11 hours.

The President of neighboring Pakistan, General Pervez Musharraf, has expressed concern about the growing number of civilian casualties in Afghanistan following the persistent US air raid on civilian targets in Afghanistan He spoke against any continuation of air strikes during the forthcoming Muslim holy month of Ramadan that begins on 17th November. General Musharraf warned that the power vacuum in Afghanistan would lead to atrocities and chaos there. He said any political settlement following US military action should contain all segments of Afghan society.

The Pakistani authorities have halted a convoy of trucks and busses carrying thousands of armed Pakistani tribesmen near the Afghan border. The tribesmen say they were going to join the Taleban in fighting a holy war against the USA in response to a call to arms by a militant Islamic organization.

Muslim clerics traveling with the convoy have been holding talks with the authorities that were refusing to let them cross the frontier. Pakistani police said there was up to 9,000-armed men in the convoy but the organizers put the figure double so high. Witnesses said much of the tribesmen were carrying automatic weapons while others had axes and swords.

The head of the UN refugee agency is in Pakistan at the start of weeklong visit to the region aiming to ease the plight of thousands of Afghan refugees trying to flee their country. The refugee agency believes that up to 1,500,000 people may try to flee from American military strikes and starvation. Mr. Lubbers will visit new sites for the refugees in southwestern Pakistan where preparations have been made for a possible big influx of people. He also had talks with Government officials in Islamabad before traveling to Iran. The UN refugee agency called on both countries to lift their border restrictions and allow in more Afghans. 7 people were killed in Western India when police opened fire on Friday night after a protest of Muslims against the US strikes on Afghanistan. Police said at least 14 people were injured in the incident in the town of Maragon. The violence erupted after police tried to prevent a group of Muslims from distributing pamphlets calling for boycotting American goods. A curfew was imposed on the town following the shootings and extra police and army units were deployed. Thousands of Pakistani protesters blocked the main road Korol Koram from northern Pakistan to China to protest against the American war. The opposition Northern Alliance criticized bitterly the USA saying they could have inflicted much more harm to the Taleban if they have used tactics different from their air raids.

28 Oct 2001

5 Pakistani gunmen opened fire onto a Catholic Church congregation during Morning Prayer in the town of Bahawalpoor in the North-East Pakistan leaving 18 people dead and many more wounded. Before opening the fire the gunmen killed the policeman on the entry and closed the church doors. After the shooting they escaped on motorbikes. Voice of Russia said the worshippers bagged for mercy but the gunmen wouldn't listen. Pakistani President Pervez Musharraf said he was deeply saddened and promised the attackers will be tracked down and brought to justice. Pope John Paul II spoke out his regret for the attack and called it a tragic act of intolerance; as it did the Archbishop of Canterbury George Carery: every one should recognize it was conflict not between Christians and Muslims, he said. A bomb exploded in a bus traveling to Quetta. The bomb was apparently hidden under the bus seat and went off when the bus was passing through a military area. 3 people were killed and other 25 injured when the bomb went off. The city of Quetta in northwestern Pakistan was the scene of several huge anti-American demonstrations.

A bomb went off in a shopping area in Zambwanga in the Philippines-the former US colony; 11 people were killed and 50 others injured, said a hospital official.

American air raids continued also this night destroying 3 houses in Kabul and leaving 10 civilians dead. Witnesses saw also the bodies of 4 children who were found in the rubble.

27

On Saturday bombs were reported to have hit 3 villages 2 of them on the territory controlled by the opposition Northern Alliance. 8 civilians are reported to have died in those incidents.

As the bombing campaign is moving into the 4 weeks BBC correspondent said there is growing pressure on the USA over the growing number of civilian deaths. For the first time American planes attacked northern Taleban positions near the Tajik border at Katakala.

Heavy fighting was also reported round the Northern town of Talukan near the Tajik border.

British Foreign Minister Jack Straw said in a BBC-interview that the war with Afghanistan will be long and protracted and will last also after the holy month of Ramadan which begins on 17th November 2001, reported radio Voice of Russia.

The Afghan opposition leader Abdul Hak, who was captured and killed on Saturday, was buried inside Afghanistan. His relatives have taken his body to his native village near Jalalabad. Prayers were also been set in the Pakistani city of Peshawar where Abdul Hak's Family has been living in exile for a long time.Abdul Hak had gone clandestinely into Afghanistan to try to run support among his fellow Pashtun to rise up against the Taleban authorities. Speaking on TV US Defence Secretary Donald Rumsfeld described his last hours how he was been calling for American air assistance and that this American air assistance was provided all too late; it came not from the army but from o t h e r armed elements, Donald Rumsfeld said to the camera.

The 9,000 Pakistani armed volunteers still had been waiting on the border to cross into Afghanistan where they are eager to join the Taleban forces for a holly war against the USA.

A delegation of Muslim clerics among this huge group has gone into Afghanistan to meet Taleban officials. Local Pakistani officials were quoted to be saying they would not stop them from crossing the frontier with Afghanistan.

The UN High Commissioner for refugees Ruud Lubbers who's a native Dutch came to the border crossing in Chamani where many thousands Afghan refugee are stranded waiting to cross into Pakistan. Ruud Lubbers urged Pakistan to accept more Afghan refugees fleeing from American bombardment. Speaking at the Shaman border crossing between Afghanistan and Pakistan Ruud Lubbers said he hopes Pakistani officials would become bit more flexible. Pakistan already shelters 2,500,000 Afghan refugees and allows in only the wounded, women and children. Mr. Lubbers said the UN has 15 new sites ready to receive more than 100,000 Afghans if they are given permission to cross the border into Pakistan.

BBC-Talkingpoint on 28 Oct 2001 said the Taleban consists of 3 layers-top commanders, local commanders and Arab volunteers. The problem with the Northern Alliance is that they have not sufficient Pashtun representation and Pashtun are the largest ethnic group in Afghanistan. Other problems are that Russia will not allow moderate Taleban in the future Afghan government and the Taleban will not allow too big Russian influence in the region. 75% of the population in Afghanistan are women as the men are killed in the wars. Women play very important role in Afghan life: the most beautiful mosque in Herat-the Gor Heshad mosque-was built by a woman. Women should not be treated as other ethnic group . In many countries there is a kind of federalism, e.g. in Malaysia which is also an Islamic country. So why not to apply the same also for Afghanistan? A new Marshal-plan if necessary will be launched for Afghanistan to rebuild the country after the war. Probably it will be called Powell-plan after the name of the US Secretary of State Colin Powell

29 Oct 2001

A memorial service took place in the Pakistani town of Bahawlpoor for the 16 Christians shot dead on Sunday by gunmen who burst into their church. The Pakistani government said a major hunt is under way for the attackers. A huge crowd of Christians and Muslims gathered in the church compound for a service for those killed on Sunday morning. The local bishop, who called to the government to arrest those who were responsible and appealed to the community to remain calm, addressed them. There was heavy police security in the town as 13 of the bodies were taken in a procession of vehicles to the Christian graveyard for a burial. The shops in the town remained closed as a mark of respect. The gunmen burst into the church during the Sunday morning prayer and opened fire indiscriminately on the worshippers. No one had claimed responsibility for the attack but the local community blamed the local pro-Taleban hardliners who had recently held anti-American demonstrations.

USA broadcast from a plane, explanations to the "noble people of Afghanistan" in Persian and Pashtun languages how to distinguish food aid packages from unexploded cluster bombs as both are of the same y e l l o w color. The USA did not wish the people to mistake the cluster bombs for food packages. Both are colored yellow and it is easy to imagine how easily children might confuse the two. Twice the broadcast said that cluster bombs and food would not be dropped in the same area. The clear implication is that American planes have dropped food packages and cluster bombs near enough to each other to worry. Critics say the weapons often leave hundreds of unexploded bombs littering the ground.

British Muslims from the organization Al Mahajirune joined the Taleban and some of them died in the air raids. In Afghanistan the Northern Alliance was increasingly critical to the Americans saying the bombing campaign must be stepped up especially in the area of Dashta-Kule. The Americans are unwilling to allow the Northern Alliance to take the Capital Kabul before a post-Taleban agreement is made.

British Defence Minister, Jeff Hoon, said in a press conference that the recent strikes on Afghanistan had undermined dramatically the ability of Al Qaida to carry out further strikes. On question of civilian casualties Jeff Hoon said it was a central issue to keep civilian casualties as low as possible. He warned British Muslims not to join the war in Afghanistan as they face certain death there or legal actions for treason if they manage to return to Britain.

American planes stepped up their assistance for the Northern Alliance raiding an underground command center used by Osama ben Laden and his Al Qaida organization in eastern Afghanistan. A spokesman said that the caves and labyrinths in this area provided a safe heaven for Al Qaida in this area. Air strikes were completed also against Taleban positions in northern Afghanistan.

A suicide bomber exploded bombs wrapped to his body in the capital Colombo just before the arrival of the president Rahmasivi Inkriminayka.

The Japanese Parliament accepted controversial law allowing Japanese troops to serve abroad. De facto Japanese troops were deployed for the first time since the WW2 in 2004 in Iraq.

US army general Tommy Franks met with Pakistani President Pervez Musharraf in Islamabad and later went to Uzbekistan for talks with the Uzbek President Islam Karimov.

President Bush is to meet Pakistani President Pervez Musharraf on 10th November in New York.

German Chancellor Gerhard Schroeder visited India after a short visit to neighboring Pakistan.
The Dutch Prime Minister Wim Kok also visited Pakistan for talks.

30 Oct 2001

American planes continued to bombard Kabul and Kandahar. One bomb fell in the outskirts of Kabul. Taleban positions were also bombed near the Tajik border. A bomb hit a hospital in Kandahar. The pictures of a huge crater were shown on the al-Jazzera TV station.

A group of 25 journalists, including Simon Ingram, were convoyed by the Taleban when they showed them around the city of Kandahar to witness the massive destruction and civilian casualties.

They were allowed to take pictures but their passports were taken away from them. People in Kandahar tap about and grope in the dark as electric power supply had been virtually cut off days and weeks ago. There has been no food for so the people had to scavenge around.

The head of the UN refugee agency Ruud Lubbers called on Britain and on the USA not to allow Afghan civilians to become the victims of the ongoing military actions against Afghanistan. Ruud Lubbers, who is meeting the Pakistani President General Pervez Musharraf, asked Pakistan to open its border to Afghan refugees with genuine humanitarian needs. USA must fulfill its pledge that ordinary Afghani would not suffer because of the war and it must put refugees closer at the top of its agenda. The efforts to eradicate international terrorism should not mean endless unspecified strikes on Afghanistan "they are killing ordinary people," Ruud Lubbers said. He was not calling for a pause in the bombing, he said but any action should take civilians into account. He is interested in practical results, Ruud Lubbers said, and asked the Pakistani government to open the border to those in need.

Earlier Pervez Musharraf met the UN special envoy to Afghanistan Lakhdar Brahimi to discuss the formation of broad based government to replace the Taleban.

US-Government issued a new terrorism warning to the American public and law-enforcement agencies. The Attorney-General John Ashcroft said he has credible information on possible attacks on the USA or American interests abroad in the coming week (31st Oct-6th Nov 2001). It is the second time FBI is warning Americans that further terrorist attacks could be imminent, although there is no specific information on how or where they might come. John Ashcroft placed law enforcement agencies on the highest stage of alert; warnings were also sent to the government departments, which oversee US power stations, airports, bridges and dams. The new alert came as new cases of anthrax were reported in New Jersey and New York. The latest came in Manhattan, where a 61 years old hospital worker tested positively for inhalation anthrax. It is the most serious form of the disease and the first anthrax case in New York.

Egyptian dissident Yasser Assiri was charged in Britain with conspiracy to kill the leader of the Northern Alliance Ahmed Shah Masood. Yassar Assiri was granted political asylum in 1993.

Speech of Tony Blair to the Welsh Assembly in Cardiff on 30th October 2001: Tony Blair has confirmed some public concern on the progress of the campaign in Afghanistan. The British Prime Minister said that now is the testing time of the military campaign against Afghanistan. He did recognize that people want results as fast as possible but they are worried of civilian casualties and the refugee crisis. In a speech to the Welsh Assembly Tony Blair said the objectives of the military action are clear: to bring Osama ben Laden to justice, to destroy his Al Qaida network and remove the Taleban from power and the anti-terror coalition will not falter in these aims. Tony Blair said there is a flood of new evidence that confirms Osama ben Laden's guilt in the September the 11th attacks.

After his speech at the Welsh Assembly Tony Blair arrived in Syria for talks with the Syrian President Basher el Asad.Discussions took place to enable Afghan people to take control of their own future. In a BBC interview on 30th October 2001 General Wesley Clark denied any US intention of sending ground troops to Afghanistan. In fact this was not kept strictly:American ground troops invaded Afghanistan and captured the southern strongholds Kandahar and Tora Bora -something which the Russians failed to achieve in their war on Afghanistan in the 1980ies.In 2004 General Wesley Clark became candidate for the position of US president but failed to be elected despite his boasting of US success under his command in the 1999 war on Serbia (6 mln population). A Muslim suicide bomb attack occurred on an oil tanker in Sri Lanka. The tanker exploded and caught fire.

Some of the attackers in Bahawalpoor were arrested but not charged.

General Tommy Franks, Chief Commander in the Afghan war,spoke in the Uzbek Capital Dushanbe. He refuted the statement that the bombing campaign has reached a stalemate, said the BBC correspondent in Uzbekistan Catrine Davis.

31 Oct 2001

Tony Blair held talks with the Syrian President Basher el Asad after he'd arrived in Damascus the day before.Basher el Asad told Tony Blair that he supports international actions against terrorism, but international terrorism must be seen in the context of what is happening in the Middle East; in a news conference after their talks in Damascus he made plain his view that the campaign should not target Syrian based Palestinian groups which tried legitimately to free their land from Israeli occupation; terrorism should not be viewed with only one eye and Arab world saw no difference between Israel's terrorism against the Palestinians and the terrorism of the wider world. The word terrorist should not be used to describe Palestinians fighting for their freedom, Basher el Asad said.

Basher el Asad also criticized as unacceptable the many civilian casualties from the bombing in Afghanistan and denounced the Western aggression in Afghanistan but he praised Tony Blair for his respect for Islam. After his talks with Basher el Asad Tony Blair flew to Saudi Arabia where he held talks with King Fahad and Crown prince Sacram Prince Abdullah. But there he received only verbal and no practical support. This day was one of an embarrassing diplomacy for Tony Blair. At least he was granted an audience to the Saudi King Fahad after he's been rejected so many times. The Saudi rejection from 11th October 2001 was especially embarrassing to him,the media said.

The US Defence Secretary Donald Rumsfeld was due to Russia at the weekend to discuss progress of the US campaign in Afghanistan

Taleban foreign minister Mutomakil denied reports he had tried to meet secretly US officials, recently he was identified as a possible defector.

American planes carried heavy bombing raids to the Taleban positions north of the Capital Kabul. Witnesses reported about 100 explosions round the Bagram air base which is held by the opposition Northern Alliance but is to close to Taleban lines for operational use. Further north more air raids were reported against the Taleban-held town of Mazar-e Sharif. Small groups of American soldiers are in the area helping to identify targets. The southern city of Kandahar has also been hit again but BBC correspondent Simon Ingram, who has been allowed in the stronghold, said that normal life is still carrying on to a surprising extent. 1500 people were killed since the beginning of the war against Afghanistan said the Taleban Ambassador in Pakistan Abdul Salam Zaif. The UN special envoy to Afghanistan Lakhdar Brahimi warned that setting up a new government in Afghanistan would be a long process. Pakistani officials told the Taleban ambassador in Pakistan not to meet Mr. Brahimi. The Taleban Ambassador Abdul Salam Zaif accused him of cooperating with the USA. Lakhdar Brahimi who was visiting Pakistan said he was trying to find a consensus among Afghans and their neighbors but old problems could not be solved in a week. He said there should be a structure to enable dialog between the opposition Northern Alliance and the Pashtuns-the largest ethnic group and Taleban's main source of support. Lakhdar Brahimi said he did not feel it necessary to talk to Taleban at this stage.

The USA tightened security around nuclear facilities following the latest warnings of possible terrorist air craft attacks on them attacks. The measures include a w e e k l o n g ban on aircraft movements close to 18 US nuclear plants. Aircraft will be allowed over the sites only if they fly at high altitude or are escorted by US fighter planes. Rigid flight restrictions were also imposed over New York during this week's World Series Baseball matches. The authorities say airport security will be more rigidly enforced after reports of continuing lapses despite the 11th of September attacks. They said airport buildings would be closed if necessary. Dagestan political activist Arcen Kamaev was shot dead in the city of Mahachkala while returning home. The car of the killers was later found together with Kalashnikov AK-47 rifles. The city prosecutor said the assassination would be treated as an act of terrorism. The Swiss Chief Prosecutor has frozen the bank accounts of 24 persons and organizations suspected of terrorism.

The UN high Commissioner for refugees Ruud Lubbers arrived in Tehran for talks with Iranian President Khatami. He failed to convince him to open Iranian borders to Afghan refugees. Both sides agreed to disagree.

BBC correspondent in Kandahar reported on the surprising confidence Taleban still have.

US Attorney General John Ashcroft announced tougher emigration restrictions and had given new approach to set up special task forces.

01 Nov 2001

Tony Blair in Jordan for talks with Jordanian King Abdullah. King Abdullah warned that any escalation of the aggression against any further Arab countries will be catastrophic. Later on Tony Blair arrived in Israel for talks with Ariel Sharon and Yasser Arafat. Tony Blair acts for and reports back to Washington after a British newspaper wrote: "Asad humiliates Blair". In a news conference BBC correspondent Andrew Marr asked him if he approves of "the targeted killings" of suspected Palestinians. Tony Blair ended his visit to the Middle East with an impassionate plead to Palestinians and Israelis to end their bloodshed.

Pakistani finance minister asked Japan for financial help to stabilize the region.

American bombs hit the power plant of Kandahar-the biggest in Afghanistan-cutting electric supply for Kandahar and Lashkagor. There also been strikes on the dam that feeds the power station. The Taleban spokesman expressed concern for the consequences for nearby villages and farmland if the dam would collapse.The Americans intensified their attacks on front line Taleban troops Using B-52 bombers called flying fortresses; their other name is B U F F which Means Big, Ugly, Fat & F ..... BBC correspondent Simon Ingram in the southern Afghan city of Kandahar said that Taleban has taken journalists to a village, which was flattened by American strikes a week earlier. Of the village Chokokarez only mud bricks ruins remained; 90 civilians were killed in the air attack. There was no comment from the Pentagon but the journalists were shown fresh graves where some of the victims were buried. Their relatives have been treated in a hospital in the Pakistani city of Quetta. There was no evidence of Taleban presence and no evidence of Al Qaida -activities. There is no comment from the Pentagon, but Human Rights Watch asked the Pentagon for explanation. The Pentagon declined to make any comment.

A statement reported to come from Osama ben Laden broadcasted by the Arabic TV station al-Jazzera urged Muslims in Pakistan to defend Islam against Christian crusade. Al-Jazzera, the only TV station allowed a correspondent in the Capital Kabul, said the letter was signed by Osama ben Laden.

The letter said one half of the world is under the flag of Christian cross while the other half is under the flag of Islam. The letter said that the Pakistani Government has chosen to side with the Christians and it accused the Pakistani Government of being hypocritical and they will face a painful punishment. The letter was also faxed to other media organizations including the BBC. An Arab journalist inside of London conveyed the letter to the BBC. The BBC was unable to track him down for an interview. The letter appears to capitalize on the anger of many Muslims on the US-led war on Afghanistan.

A prominent Afghan opposition leader said his supporters fought off an attempt by Taleban forces to capture him as he rallied support in southern Afghanistan for the former Afghan King. Hamed Karzai, who comes from the same Pashtun Clan as the former King and is an important leader in his own right, slipped over the border into Afghanistan a few weeks ago. Speaking to the BBC from the mountains north of the Taleban stronghold of Kandahar Mr. Kharezy said other tribal leaders had joined him and that during skirmishes with the Taleban they have captured 12 Taleban soldiers.

Another opposition leader-Abdul Hak-was killed by the Taleban a week earlier while he was on a similar mission.

The American Defence Secretary. Donald Rumsfeld said the USA is planning to send more Special Forces to Afghanistan to assist the anti-Taleban opposition and help direct air strikes. Donald Rumsfeld said there had been delay putting in extra troops for several reasons including the bad weather, but he said a number of teams were now ready to go.

In another development the American National Security Advisor Condoleezza Rice said the USA could not afford to stop its war on terrorism for the Muslim holy month of Ramadan.

Turkey announced it is sending a contingent of 90 troops of its Special Forces to assist the US-led military operation in Afghanistan. The announcement that marks the first Muslim country contribution to the campaign and follows media reports that the USA had asked Turkey to provide military instructors for the Northern Alliance. The Turkish Parliament approved the deployment of troops abroad d shortly after the September attacks on New York and Washington.

The Prime ministers of Malaysia and Indonesia met to discuss the crisis in Afghanistan. The Prime minister of Malaysia, Mohamed Mohateer said the prolonged campaign undermines the forces of the international coalition against terrorism. The problem will remain even if Osama ben Laden was captured tomorrow, he said. Mohamed Mohateer stepped down voluntarily as President of Malays on 31 OCTOBER 2003. Before doing this he said on an ASEAN-conference:" We know that we are exploited but let the West exploits US fairly!"

USA became increasingly concerned about the successes of Osama ben Laden in the media war.

Russian foreign Minister Igor Ivanov arrived in Washington for talks for reducing strategic weapons. Practically the whole American scheme worked so: the Americans promised to reduceits strategic atomic weaponry if they receive in return Russian agreement to station American troops in the former southern Soviet republics of Kazakhstan, Uzbekistan and Turkmenistan to encircleAfghanistan from the North together with opposition Russian-backed Northern Alliance. The Russians gave their permission but finally were betrayed by the Americans and received nothing at the end -certainly no American strategic nuclear weapons reduction. Even worse-the US President George W. Bush started a strategic shield defense program to humiliate the Russians even further. This despite the Russian space help to the Americans-after the disastrous crash of the US space Shuttle in February 2003 Russian remained the only space nation to deliver supplies to the space Station Mir, which in translation means P E A C E .

02 Nov 2001 Wednesday

The International Agency on Atomic Energy, the body that sets standards for atomic safety, is meeting in Vienna. It had called a special session on the threat of terrorism. Opening the session the Director of the Agency Mohamed el Baraday said the idea of terrorists acquiring nuclear weapons is a doom scenario. But the IAEA is aware that such attack could take place. The Agency had singled the former Soviet Union as a region where nuclear material was not adequately regulated.

American B – 5 2 bombers called flying fortresses or B U F F - Big, Ugly, Fat and F... had been pounding Taleban front lines north of the Afghan Capital Kabul and around the northern city of Mazar-e Sharif. Opposition forces of the Afghan Northern Alliance estimated that as many as 60 bombs had fallen on Taleban positions including on a village said to be used as Taleban command center. The opposition Northern Alliance had received a harsh blow last week when a key Afghan Commander in the East of the country Abdul Hak was captured and executed. He was on a mission inside the country to try to recruit local leaders to the cause of the Loya Jirga-a gathering of all the tribes-to try to build an alternative government for Afghanistan. Another influential Pashtun leader from the Pakistani city of Quetta-Hamed Karzai-is on a similar and equally perilous mission. His Brother Ahmed Karzai-explained his reasons for going to Afghanistan:" He is trying to bring people together to end the misery of the Afghan people and form a broad-based government in Afghanistan; he is there to bring peace and stability to Afghanistan". There were reports on Thursday night that Taleban had captured more than 20 of Hamed Karzai's men and possibly himself when he was involved in fight with Taleban forces in Uruz-ghan province. Ahmed Karzai told the BBC that none of his brothers' supporters has been killed or captured in the incident. Ahmed Karzai said: "There was an incident yesterday around evening time and there is no one killed or captured from our side and they say they are ok" Although Hamed Karzai is supporter of the former King Zahir Shah he had given no detail as yet about the extent of his mission or how many fighters might support him.

The Taleban are certainly keen to capture Hamed Karzai. He is an influential tribal leader who comes from the Taleban heartland of Kandahar. He belongs to the same clan as the King and potentially commands the loyalty of large numbers of Afghans. He currently looks like the currently Afghan opposition best hope for alternative Pashtun power base to the Taleban. A former deputy foreign minister of Afghanistan he supported the Taleban when they first emerged. But he quickly became disillusioned with the Islamic movement, saying it has been infiltrated and controlled by foreigners, including Pakistani and Arabs. Recently he said it is time for the Afghans to get rid of such people: "3 years ago these Arabs together with their supporters and with the Taleban they went and destroyed miles and miles of homes, orchards, vineyards and life: they have killed Afghans; they have trained their guns on Afghan lives; these Arabs are in Afghanistan to learn how to shoot and they learned it on live-targets and these live-targets are Afghan people-our children and our women-who want them out". Mr.Karzai and his supporters are currently hiding in the mountainous area of Uruz-Ghan province North of Kandahar-not far from the birthplace of the Taleban leader Mullah Omar.

But the full extent of his mission is not known. It had been reported that Abdul Hak-another royalist supporter who was killed by the Taleban last week-had gone into Afghanistan to raise a Pashtun rebellion.

However Abdul Hak was well known military commander while Mr. Karzai is more a leader and diplomat. It was more likely that he was concentrated simply on raising support for a Loya Jirga.

Nevertheless now the Taleban know he is there, he may be forced to fight. There are continuing difficulties in establishing a grand post-Taleban government-the stated aim of antiterrorist powers gathered around the USA.

As the USA intensifies its bombardment of Taleban targets in Afghanistan the lack of any viable political alternative to the extremist Islamic militia will be a growing worry for Washington. Western strategists had hoped military pressure would encourage Taleban commander to defect but the continuing absence of any credible opposition to defect to makes a large-scale shift relations less likely.

Among the worldwide Afghan Diaspora of intellectuals, tribal leaders and former politicians several groups are putting now their own solutions to the Afghan problem. The most widely supported internationally had been an attempt to weld together followers of the former Afghan King Zahir Shah and the anti-Taleban Northern Alliance. But so far they have failed to agree on a list of representatives for a council to discuss the shape of a future government. The Northern Alliance has even failed to manage to agree on their own list of their own representatives to this council. Beyond this some political groups have been promoted by former Mujahedeen leaders-such as Piel Ahmed Gulani or Gourmetin Hekmet Shah.

But a large gathering of Pashtun leaders organized by Piel Gulani in the Pakistani city of Peshawar last week (BBC did not report on it!) there were no representatives from the King's party or from the Northern Alliance. UN-Afghan envoy Lakhdar Brahimi is now due in Iran for talks on the problem. He has called for a government, which represents all of Afghanistan's range of ethnic groups. But Lakhdar Brahimi has in the past shown his frustration with the slow and painful negotiations necessary with Afghanistan's fractious political groups. He said it would take long time to create any alternative government for the country. The danger is that the military campaign will change the situation on the ground making a political solution even harder.

Sierra-Leonean spokesman said Sierra Leone had been selling illegal diamonds for the Al Qaida network. The rebels initially denied the facts exposed by the Washington Post but later agreed with them. Sierra Leone had mined

diamonds worth hundreds of millions of dollars and selling them to Osama ben Laden Al Qaida network. The claims were made in the Washington Post newspaper. A senior rebel leader Omri Goli told the BBC West Africa correspondent Mark Doyle that the allegations in the Washington Post were extremely serious and that his movement will find out the truth about them. The newspaper said the IUF had sold millions of dollars worth of illegally mined diamonds by men now named by FBI as Al Qaida members. The gems were than re-sold by Al Qaida for huge profits the paper said or used as secrete convenient depository of wealth in case that
Al Qaida bank accounts were frozen. The Sierra-Leone rebels and others in the region associated with them had been shown in the past including in the UN-reports as deeply involved in criminal activities.

Fire fighters in New York had angrily protested at plans to scale down the search for bodies in the ruins of the World Trade Center. Some 1600 of them marched on the site known as "Ground Zero" demanding the right to continue searching for the bodies of their colleagues who died in the attack. About 250 fire fighters are still missing.

The irritation in Washington at the warning issued by the than Governor of California Gray Davis: he announced on Thursday that there is credible evidence that terrorist are planning a rush hour attack within the next week on one or more of California bridges including the Golden Gate Bridge in San Francisco. Senior officials in Washington moved quickly to say that they advised the Governor not to release the intelligence to the public, as it was uncorroborated. The Director of Homeland Security Tom Rich explained more details. The FBI director Robert Muller acknowledged that there was a difficult balance to strike; he accepted that the general alert on Monday about an imminent terrorist attack had annoyed many law-enforcement agencies because of it was imprecise. Robert Muller also implicitly considered that the current investigation into anthrax is not going as well as it could be. The FBI director said he had expected that the $1,000,000 reward put up for information would have elicited more leads; it had not and he had appealed to the public to do more. The prevention and the investigation of terrorism have continuing to prove difficult tasks.

In heavy clashes in Indian administered Kashmir Pakistani troops used heavy gunfire to help Islamic fighters to escape back in Pakistan. An Indian official said the separatists are believed to belong to Harakatul-Mujahedeen and Terakul Jihad groups. 20 of them were killed on line of control that divides India and Kashmir.

President Bush reiterated there would be no bombing pause for the Islamic holy month of Ramadan, as the Islamists too will not pause.

03 Nov 2001

The opposition Northern Alliance in Afghanistan said they had captured a district south of Mazar-e Sharif following of defection of 800 Taleban soldiers to their side. They said they took Ak Hopruk during the night after 3 hours of battle capturing further 200 Taleban troops. An Alliance spokesman said a number of Taleban fighters had been killed and operations were continuing in the nearby area. The Taleban said they had been fighting in the region but gave no details. Elsewhere to the north of Kabul American planes have been again attacking Taleban positions.

The Taleban said they have shot down an American helicopter going to the aid of a crashed aircraft inside Afghanistan. They say 50 US troops were killed and the bodies were visible. The Taleban statement follows an announcement by the Americans that they had lost a helicopter on a Special Forces mission after a crash-landing probably caused by bad weather. The Americans said 4 people received injuries but they were not life threatening and the entire crew was safely recovered and brought out of Afghanistan. They said they later deliberately destroyed the crashed helicopter not to allow to be used by the Taleban. American officials would not say where it came down but the Taleban said the incident occurred to the south of Kabul in Naour-district. The information came from the Taleban information ministry-they insisted they have shot down the second helicopter by rocket fire. The Pentagon insisted on its version, no helicopter was shot down and troops were lost the Pentagon said. The Pentagon has flatly contradicted the Taleban version to what had happened to a helicopter Americans accepted has crashed inside Afghanistan. A Defence Department spokesman said it was not true that the Taleban shot down the helicopter and killed 40-50 US troops. The Taleban's claim came from the information ministry in Kabul. They said one US helicopter had crashed and another hit by rocket-fire as it tried to carry out a rescue operation. The Pentagon insisted that what it said happened really:all US troops involved in the incident were flown out, no helicopter had been shot down and not troops had been lost.

There are reports that Taleban decided to free the French journalist Michel Perar who was detained inside of Afghanistan just after the start of the American bombing campaign. Diplomatic sources say the French Ambassador to Pakistan was traveling to the Afghan border where Michel Perar is expected to be handed over. Michel Perar was disguised in the traditional clothing of an Afghan woman when he was discovered. The Taleban suspected him of spying for the Americans.

The US defense secretary Donald Rumsfeld has been held talks in Moscow with Russian President Vladimir Putin and Russian Defence Minister Sergey Ivanov. He was at the start of a tour to Central and Southern Asia in an effort to boost support for the military offensive in Afghanistan. The progress of the campaign is expected to dominate his meeting with President Putin and his defense minister Sergey Ivanov. Donald Rumsfeld was also paving the way for a meeting between President Putin and President Bush later in November 2001. The main issue is expected to be the American wish to press ahead with the controversial missile defense system. From Moscow Donald Rumsfeld was expected to go to Uzbekistan, where American soldiers are based and than to Tajikistan, Pakistan and India.

Osama ben Laden criticized sharply the UN, saying it stood by, as crimes are committed against the Afghan people and the Islamic world. Osama ben Laden denounced Arab leaders who cooperated with the UN saying no Muslim should resort to the UN, because they have suffered for years at the hands of the UN and its policies. Osama ben Laden was speaking on a recorded video address on the Arabic language satellite television channel Al Jazzera.

Charles Kennedy MP appealed for a stop to the use of cluster bombs in Afghanistan.

The Taleban claimed they have captured some areas lost earlier to the Northern Alliance.

04 Nov 2001

4th week since the beginning of the war in Afghanistan. American Defence Secretary, Donald Rumsfeld, visited Pakistan. The media did not cover his visits to Uzbekistan and Tajikistan. On his talks yesterday with the Russian President Vladimir Putin in Moscow was also reported very little. In his talks with Pakistani President Pervez

Musharraf, a meeting described as crucial for Pakistani support for American attacks, Donald Rumsfeld said there would be no pause in the bombing during the Muslim holy month of Ramadan. Donald Rumsfeld has gone to Pakistan after talks with the leaders of Russia, Tajikistan and Uzbekistan on which was reported very little. At the Press conference in Islamabad Donald Rumsfeld's message was clear: the bombing would go on despite the start in 17th November of the Muslim holy month of Ramadan. The US, he said, had to pursue aggressively the Al Qaida network and the Taleban.

Pervez Musharraf had said before his meeting with Donald Rumsfeld that he would press for a pause in the bombing. Donald Rumsfeld said he was aware of President Musharraf´s views and that this was a sensitive issue. But despite of this obvious disagreement the emphasis of the press conference in Pakistan was on the continuing cooperation between the two countries. Pakistan's foreign minister said Pakistan accepted that the USA are focusing on military targets and are doing its utmost to avoid civilian casualties.

At 20:00 GMT Donald Rumsfeld arrived in India for talks.

Nothing was reported also on a 2 days Islamic symposium in Mecca in which Islamic leaders criticized the Western way of reporting on the war in Afghanistan. The Islamic leaders rejected any connection between Islam and terrorism.

As the American offensive at the Taleban in Afghanistan enters its 2nd month heavy B-52 bombers called flying fortresses BUFF – Big, Ugly, Fat & F…have been pounding again Taleban positions in the northeast of Afghanistan.

For several hours B-52 bombers dropped thousands of tons of bombs sending huge plumes of smoke into the air. A BBC correspondent who saw the attack said they were the heaviest since the bombing campaign began.

The US top military officer General Richard Myers said the more teams of special ground forces were deployed in the past 2 nights to support the offensive of the Northern Alliance. He was speaking after another series of air attack of American heavy bombers on the northeast of Afghanistan. "The more teams we get on the ground the more effectively we'll bring air power to bear on the Taleban lines and we're continuing to do that." General Myers denied a magazine report that Taleban forces have injured American soldiers during a raid into Afghanistan last month. He said US forces had the initiative against the Taleban and were prepared to fight throughout the winter.

The Leader of Jemaah Islamiya in Pakistan Hussein Emez was put under house arrest to prevent him from organizing anti-war demonstrations.

The British Prime Minister Tony Blair is to have talks in London shortly with several EU-leaders to discuss the international campaign against terrorism. A spokesman for Tony Blair said the dinner provided a good opportunity to exchange information on the latest developments following Tony Blair's recent trip to the Middle East and the German Chancellor Gerhard Schroeder's visit to Russia (not to China??). The meeting comes in advance of a flurry of diplomatic activity as members of the US-led coalition against terrorism consider how to proceed with their campaign.

Now, when the US bombing campaign enters its 5th week, what exactly has been achieved? The Pentagon's military planners envisaged that it would begin, as it did, with the big bang as the Taleban air defenses would be destroyed; phase 2, to begun soon after with establishing bridgeheads and from this bases the US could embark on lightening strikes against the Taleban and the Al Qaida network, but it had clearly not worked out like that. The Taleban had proved to be more resilient than they had been thought, the opposition Northern Alliance has failed to take advantage of the American bombing, the anti-Taleban coalition has failed to materialize while civilian casualties have mounted.

US defense secretary Donald Rumsfeld said today that the military campaign was showing measurable progress but, by odd and odd stick. Thomas Willington-from the Institute of Defence Studies at the Kings College in London said it is very difficult to point any success of the military campaign against Afghanistan. In a BBC-interview he said, "moreover stage-2 of the campaign, the establishing of bridgeheads had failed to materialize so far; we have seen the Special Forces raids which are quite interesting but in terms of degrading and destroying the Taleban is very difficult to say that the elite units of the Taleban have retreated up into the mountains, they've got out of the firing lines leaving there the conscript armies there so they are safeguarding their crack troops, only few of the Al Qaida sites have been destroyed successfully." Where have the Pentagon's planners got it wrong? "The country is a natural fortress, the Taleban are battle-hardened troops, they know better than anyone else how to fight in this terrain, the Americans have to fight a very bitter campaign, this is 21st century warfare technology against the traditional warfare methods on the Afghan side and the Afghans at the moment appear to have the upper hand. Absolutely, if the ground forces are not employed, the American forces are no match for the Taleban. The only way to destroy the Taleban and the Al Qaida is by putting significant ground troops but that means preparing the US public and the British public for very significant military casualties and it will be a long, a very bitter and very dirty campaign. And if you want to go for a ground invasion you also have to move ground forces into Pakistan too, get airborne troops ready to be dropped into the country; you need to be planning this now. Maybe it's been planned but we do not know. Washington has also provided ammunition in the form of civilian casualties, which the Taleban had made much of, and the war was characterized as a war against Islam". (Thomas Willington from the Institute of Defence Studies at the Kings College in London in a BBC-interview with Julian Marshal on 04 Nov 2001)

The Secretary General of the Arab League Amr Moussa said that Arabs wouldn't be fooled into accepting of Middle East peace accord, which does not aim the establishing of Palestinian state. Speaking at the start of Arab foreign ministers in Damascus he said Arab would not be "victims of a political fraud". Amr Moussa also dismissed the latest broadcast message by Osama ben Laden calling the Muslims to join for a holy war against the West. He said Osama ben Laden spoke only for himself and not for the Arab world or for all Muslims. Amr Moussa was referring to Osama ben Laden latest broadcast message in which he calls for Muslims to wage a holy war against Christianity.

But Amr Moussa strongly attacked Israel's policy on the West Bank and Gaza describing the Israeli forces as an Army of occupation in the Palestinian territories.

The Egyptian Foreign Minister Ahmed Maher said Osama ben Laden is at war with the world.

Airbus announced that the Dubai based Emirate Airlines will buy 25 new jet airliners from the European Airbus group at the cost of $5,000,000,000. 25 will be the world's biggest passenger planes the giant A-380 double-decker jets. The Dubai based Emirate Airline announced it intends to buy 40 more airplanes both from Airbus and from its American rival Boeing. This huge purchase order showed how much our Western world is depending on the Arabs.

05 Nov 2001

The Taleban authorities are appealing for a large-scale humanitarian aid for thousands Afghan people displaced by the American bombing campaign. They said their country is facing a humanitarian crisis of catastrophic proportions. They called for a major humanitarian operation to help the thousands of people displaced by the American bombing campaign. The Taleban representative in the Pakistani Capital Islamabad Mullah Abdul Salam Zaif said the UN and aid agencies should conduct the operation. But he accused the UN of putting political concerns before the humanitarian needs of Afghanistan an allegation denied by the UN spokeswoman.

A BBC correspondent in the region said the risk is that this dispute would obscure the huge and pressing humanitarian needs of millions of Afghans as winter approaches fast. American aircrafts have again attacked the Afghan Capital Kabul and hit a hotel in the city, which has been used as a base by Taleban fighters.

Reuters news agency reporting from the city quotes eyewitnesses to be saying that a number of Taleban fighters have been killed in a hotel attack, which they say appeared to be made by helicopter gun ships firing missiles. This cannot be confirmed. A Taleban information ministry spokesman said that some Taleban fighters have been wounded in the attack but he did not confirm any deaths. However some hours later the Taleban education minister Amir Khan Mutaki said a house near the hotel had been hit not the hotel itself. He did not elaborate.

Forces of the opposition Northern Alliance in Afghanistan have staged a big military parade in the area of the country they control. Some 7,000 troops took part. They paraded 20 Russian tanks along with personnel carriers and other vehicles. They were told by their leader-the ousted President Buhanuddin Rabbani-that they would begin a major assault soon to recapture Kabul and the rest of the country. However the BBC defense correspondent said questions are been raised about the effectiveness of the Northern Alliance and whether it is ready to launch such an offensive. Some analysts in Washington argue that there is no alternative to American troops on the ground.

The Saudi Crown prince Abdullah criticized the USA because of their coverage of the Afghan war.

The Pentagon said it believes substantial numbers of Taleban soldiers have been killed by air fire, as their positions do not return the fire.

06 Nov 2001

As American air raids continue the opposition Northern Alliance in Afghanistan said it has achieved some success in fighting round the strategic Northern city of Mazar-e Sharif. There was fierce fighting round the strategic city of Mazar-e Sharif. The Northern Alliance said it captured the Zare district and has taken more of the neighboring district Ak Kuprakh. But a Taleban spokesman said Taleban forces had fought off an attack on Ak Kuprakh by opposition forces supported by American air strikes. American planes have again bombed Taleban positions defending Mazar-e Sharif but the BBC correspondent in the region said there is no sign yet of a major offensive by the Alliance on the city, which controls major supply route.

40

International aid agencies said conditions inside Mazar-e Sharif are deteriorating and a number of people have died after fleeing to camps around the city. The UN had warned that a 100,000 more children will die in the Afghan winter unless aid reaches them soon. A spokesman for the UN children fund said that worsening weather will compound the misery of those in need and many will freeze to death unless they get clothes, tents and blankets. Heavy snows are expected soon blocking roads used by aid supplying trucks. UN officials say they will use bulldozers to keeps the roads open for a few more weeks. The Taleban authorities have called for a major humanitarian operation inside Afghanistan to help those displaced by the air strikes. The Taleban representative in Pakistan said the UN and other agencies should conduct the operation.

The US Transport Minister Mineta called for more security screening for people boarding planes after a man with weapons was detained while boarding United Airlines flight. The weapons-bombs, knives and pepper spray-were only found in a last minute check and the man was arrested and charged. The man said the weapons were for his own protection and there was no indication that he was planning any illicit activity. Mr. Mineta has recommended the United Airlines should be punished and fined. 4 workers who were involved in the breech have been fired and 5 others suspended.

Germany announced it would send 3,000 soldiers in Afghanistan. Full details are not clear but it is known it will involve personnel and not just equipment. Some reports suggested that Germany would contribute Special Forces units as well as flying hospitals, transport aircraft and personnel carriers designed for use in areas contaminated by chemical or biological weapons. The plan needs the approval of the German Parliament. The BBC Berlin correspondent said the main opposition parties had indicated they would support the government but that Chancellor Schroeder coalition partners, the Greens, may have more difficulty in doing so.

President Bush has said that the Al Qaida network of Osama ben Laden is trying to acquire weapons of mass destruction. In a speech replayed by a video link to a meeting of 17 Central and East European countries in Warsaw Mr. Bush said that "if successful Al Qaida could become a threat to civilization itself." Al Qaida operates in more than 60 nations, including some in central and Eastern Europe. This terrorist group seeks to destabilize entire nations and regions. They are seeking chemical, biological and nuclear weapons. Given the means our enemies will be a threat to every nation and eventually-to civilization itself".

The Taleban said at least 2 villages near the city of Herat in northwest Afghanistan have been hit during US bombing raids. The Taleban made the statement to an Iranian journalist who was among a group of reporters invited to see the city by the Taleban. The journalist told the BBC that he had seen about 20 badly injured civilians at the local hospital who were hurt in the bombing attacks. The Taleban told him that the raids had mostly targeted their military facilities in the northern outskirts of the city. The reporter said he had seen wide spread poverty but that life was more or less normal during daytime. He added that there were also an increasing number of refugees coming from other parts of Afghanistan.

President Jacque Chirac has arrived in Washington where he will meet President Bush for talks intended to strengthen the American campaign against terrorism. It is Mr. Chirac's 2nd visit to the US since the September's attacks on Washington and New York. While the French government continues to give strong support to the campaign the French public is showing evidence of serious doubt about the American war in Afghanistan.

There has been an explosion on the grounds of the Australian international school in the Indonesian Capital Jakarta. No group claimed the responsibility for it.

07 Nov 2001

The President of Pakistan General Pervez Musharraf has made a brief visit to Iran at the beginning of weeklong diplomatic tour. He met the Iranian vice-president and the deputy foreign minister during his stop over at Tehran airport. Pakistani Embassy officials said the discussions had not been very substantive. However General Musharraf is due to meet the Iranian President Mohamed Khatami at the UN General Assembly in New York next week. Iran and Pakistan discussed US air strikes in Afghanistan and its political future. During a stop in Turkey on his route to France General Musharraf repeated his call for a broad-based multi-ethnic government in Afghanistan.

The opposition Northern Alliance in Afghanistan said American bombing raids on Taleban frontlines had helped to make significant advances near the key northern city of Mazar-e Sharif. It said the bombing had knocked out Taleban heavy artillery easing the way to its forces to move to within 7km off the city and captured several districts to the south. The Alliance told the BBC it would not launch now planned push on the Capital Kabul until after Mazar-e Sharif has fallen. A BBC Afghanistan correspondent said the Alliance had to withdraw 2 weeks ago after similar advances near Mazar-e Sharif because it ran out of ammunition and commanders say they have not still received promised American military supplies.

Police in Turkey released details on the seizure of over a kilogram of uranium enriched for use in nuclear weapons. A police official said 2 men have been detained when they offered the uranium wrapped in newspaper to an undercover police agent in exchange of $750,000. He said the men did not appreciate the significance of the uranium, which is believed to have come from a former Soviet republic.

On Tuesday President Bush warned that members of Al Qaida network are trying to require chemical, biological and nuclear arms. Correspondents say the trafficking in illegal substances has increased since the collapse of the Soviet Union and Istanbul has become the center of so called suitcase trade.

There was an unenthusiastic response from some aid workers in Afghanistan to the call by President Chirac of France on an urgent UN conference to establish a new relief program for the country. Mr. Chirac said that without it there could be a humanitarian catastrophe but some aid workers said they are fearing that preparing for another big international conference would divert them from their main concern-the operations inside Afghanistan to get sufficient relief stocks in place before winter. The main supplier-the World Food Program is now moving significant quantities of food into the country after virtually stopping shipments for several weeks after the September attacks in the USA.

A gunman opened fire at the American airbase in Qatar injuring a lot of servicemen. The Pentagon denied this reports.

The Pakistani government decided to open a refugee's camp inside of Pakistan near Jalalabad.

In Afghanistan Americans used for a first time powerful daisy-cutter bombs incinerating everything in 600m radius.

UN food convoys reached Taleban controlled northeast Afghanistan carrying wheat and flour for distribution among the starving population.

08 Nov 2001

Pakistani President General Pervez Musharraf held talks in London-his latest stop in round of intense diplomacy before the UN General Assembly in New York at the weekend. He pressed again the British Prime Minister Tony Blair for a short and more targeted war in Afghanistan. Speaking in Paris before leaving for London, General Musharraf underlined his desire to see an end to the bombing as soon as possible. Speaking after talks with the French Prime minister Lionel Jospin, President Musharraf called on America to halt its attacks on Afghanistan as soon as possible. He said the whole world saw them as a war on poor miserable and innocent civilians and that continuing to bomb them throughout the Muslim holy month of Ramadan would cause trouble through the Muslim world. President Musharraf's words were listened carefully to in Washington where he is considered a vital ally in America's war against terrorism. Later in the day he brought this message to Tony Blair in London before flying to the US for a meeting with President George W. Bush. Tony Blair has just returned from Washington where he also held talks with President Bush.

American warplanes have resumed their attacks on Taleban forces striking at their front line positions in northeast Afghanistan for the 8th time in 12 days. The area is important because it is one of the places where opposition forces of the Northern Alliance could make a breakthrough in their efforts to capture the city of Mazar-e Sharif.

The Alliance said it is edging closer to the city but the Americans who have Special Forces in the vicinity say there is still air blunder flaw to the fighting.

The Afghan tribal chief Hamed Karzai who entered southern Afghanistan last month to rally opposition to the Taleban authorities told the BBC he is safe and still in the country after fighting off attempt to capture him by Arab and other foreign fighters supporting the Kabul regime. He denied reports made public by the American defense Secretary Donald Rumsfeld that he have been taken out of the country by a helicopter. He said his supporters helped by local villagers had fought off attacks of pro-Taleban forces. He criticized bitterly the US bombing of Afghanistan.

The Americans had said they would not stop their campaign of air strikes during the holy month of Ramadan despite the request of General Musharraf. If the bombing does continue the pressure on the Pakistani President and other Muslim governments to end their support for the coalition will increase. The Secretary General of the Pakistani opposition party, the Muslim League, Goyhan Ayutkhan who was the country's foreign minister said it becomes increasingly difficult for General Musharraf to reign in the protest against his policies: "In Pakistan they Usually are holding some demonstrations of religious parties after the Friday's prayers. What General Musharraf is just saying and I am also of this conviction the Ramadan on 17th November 2001 every evening will be a prayer at every mosque in the Muslim world. This fall out will be reiterated and the prayer for the Afghan people, for the bombing to stop, support for them will increase."

The coalition has been also called on to stop the bombing by those in the humanitarian community. Their concern is that millions of Afghans who stay in the country face starvation during the long winter. They want a pause in the bombing to allow them to distribute food stocks to those suffering from 3 years of famine and drought. The Human Rights group Amnesty International warned that the number of refugees fleeing from Afghanistan is

43

growing. It said many are leaving because of the bombing. Amnesty called on the international coalition to take grater responsibility for them.

But the British Foreign Office Minister Ben Bradshaw said the root cause of both the refugee and the humanitarian problems lay within Afghanistan. As the American air strikes continues the opposition Northern Alliance said it is edging closer to the strategic Northern city of Mazar-e Sharif.

The Alliance spokesman said they are preparing to attack Taleban forces once more in the valley of Cheshma Asafa- about 17km south of Mazar-e. The spokesman said they are hopeful the city itself would fall in the next day or two.

But the Taleban denied Alliance claims to have captured 4 key districts South to the city in the last 48 hours saying just one district has fallen. Obviously both sides are willing the impression that they are the winning side. In Mazar-e Sharif is the grave of Prophet Mohamed's son-in-law. Northern Alliance spokesman said they believe the population is ready to rise up and large numbers of Taleban soldiers were also about to defect The Taleban are equally adamant that they can and will hold Mazar and revenge every woman and man there to be ready to sacrifice their lives for the holy war jihad.

The UN Commissioner for Human Rights, Mary Robinson, warned China not to use the current situation in Afghanistan for diminishing the rights of ethnic minorities. Speaking on the first day of her visit to China she expressed concern for the situation in Tibet.

The UAE had frozen the bank accounts of 66 persons and organizations believed to be terrorists.

The Pakistani authorities asked the Taleban to close down their consulate in Karachi because it served no purposes but the main office in Islamabad remains open. It is another attempt of Pakistan to distance itself from the Taleban. On the EU-summit in Brussels the Green Parties of France, Belgium and Finland condemned the use of American cluster bombs.

09 Nov 2001

American planes pounded Taleban positions through the night. The Pentagon confirmed a fierce battle is under way around the key city of Mazar-e Sharif.

The Taleban claimed to have repulsed major offence there by the opposition Northern Alliance.

The American General in charge of the military campaign made it clear that the USA is leaving open the option of deploying more ground forces if the Northern Alliance is unable to advance on its own. There was also heavy American bombing on other Taleban frontline positions clearly audible 40km away in the Capital Kabul.

The Taleban said Americans were firing rockets at vehicles behind the front lines and killed 10 civilians.

BBC correspondent in the Afghan Capital Kabul said there was no sign at all that the Taleban authority was about to collapse and they remain even more defiant than when the bombing started.

As for ordinary Afghans in Kabul he said people were quite calm though they are fewer around. This contrasts with the mood a month ago when many people were very frightened by the US attacks on Afghanistan. Most people are pre-occupied with the business of simply existing. The BBC correspondent is part of BBC-team, which entered Kabul by road under Taleban escort.

Opposition forces made significant advance to seize the key northern city Mazar-e Sharif. The Northern Alliance advanced to the airport of Mazar-e Sharif from the north to while another opposition force is advancing from the South and the population is fleeing the city. The Taleban rushed reinforcement to Mazar-e Sharif and will hold the city the fall of which will open a land route from Uzbekistan. Opposition Commander General Rushed Dostum claimed his forces were only 6km from the center of Mazar-e Sharif and they have taken already the outskirts of the city.

BBC correspondent in the area advised caution because Alliance forces edged closer to the city few weeks ago but than eventually withdrew.

Police in Central Pakistan shot dead 4 people in the most serious incident of violence yet in demonstrations there against American raids on Afghanistan. The police opened fire after several thousands demonstrators blocked a railway line near the city of Moultan halting an express train by placing bolts on the track and took 4 policemen hostage. The clash took place during a nation-wide strike called by hard-line religious parties, which called the President of Pakistan General Pervez Musharraf to withdraw support from the military action. Tight security is enforced and less serious clashes were reported from Peshawar and Karachi where police fired tear gas at protesters. A BBC correspondent in Islamabad said it is difficult to gage how many people took part in the strike, as it is a public holiday.

Saudi Arabia expressed anger and frustration at the failure of the Bush administration to come forward with an expected initiative to resolve the Israeli-Palestinian dispute. The Saudi foreign minister Prince Saud al Feysal told the New York Times that President Bush's reluctance to get more involved in the Middle East "was enough to make a sane man go mad". His comment follows news from the White House that George W. Bush will not meet the Palestinian leader Yasser Arafat at the UN General Assembly this weekend. The BBC Middle East analyst said the Prince's remarks represent an unusually vigorous abandonment of the Usual Saudi reticence.

King Abdullah of Jordan said Jordan would send troops to Afghanistan if necessary.

Al Qaida issued a video message stating the organization remains intact despite the US bombing.

10 Nov 2001

The opposition Northern Alliance forces patrol the streets of Mazar-e Sharif after capturing it from the Taleban. The loss of the strategically important city is significant victory for the Northern Alliance and major setback for the Taleban. Reports from Mazar-e Sharif said the atmosphere is calm; people are out in the streets and many shops and part of the bazaar are open for business. The BBC correspondent in the area said the Taleban had withdrawn in several directions abandoning positions they would undoubtedly fought hard to defend had it not been the pulverizing American air strikes.

The Northern Alliance said it took 2 provinces in the region. General Dostum boasted: "It took only 90 minutes to take the city". 90 Taleban died in the fighting and many hundreds were captured. 20 Taleban tanks were also captured.

The Northern Alliance's drive northwards from Mazar-e Sharif towards to the Uzbek border would enable the opening of a bridgehead into the country-potentially not only for additional US troops and weapon supplies but also for much needed humanitarian aid. The BBC defense correspondent said the Taleban might try to recapture

45

Mazar-e Sharif but to do so they would have to regroup their troops, making them especially vulnerable to the decisive factor in the battle so far-the US air power. The fall of Mazar-e Sharif is vital propaganda victory for the Americans who want to persuade various tribal groups to abandon the Taleban but had no hope to do so as far as there was no fundamental change in the circumstances on the ground.

The Northern Alliance said it is ready to capitalize on their major victory and to launch an offensive on Kabul. After the fall of Mazar-e Sharif the value of the Afghan currency rose up 10% to the value of the Dollar, which will stimulate the economic life.

The "Don"-newspaper in Pakistan published an interview with Osama ben Laden in which he said he had access to nuclear and chemical weapons. Osama ben Laden described such weapons as a "deterrent" but said he might use them if the USA deployed similar weaponry against him. However an Urdu-language version of Osama ben Laden's interview published in another newspaper made no mention of Osama ben Laden's acquiring of nuclear or chemical weapons. A Pakistani journalist who conducted the interview said the full interview would be published in his Urdu-newspaper shortly.

Hamed Mir-biographer of Osama ben Laden spent last week inside Afghanistan and confirmed the Taleban were loosing the war together with Osama ben Laden's forces. Hamed Mir said in BBC-interview: "Osama ben Laden is no more a rich person: he depends entirely on Afghanistan. If he were a rich person he would go to Saudi Arabia or to Palestine; he had chosen Afghanistan;

Afghanistan is his country-this means that he is depending on Afghanistan. He is not that powerful, he is not as powerful as the US thinks he is. You see the US asking help from Britain, from Australia, from the EU, from Pakistan-the US is fighting against a single man. There was a time when the US was fighting against the Soviet Union and against China. Now the level of the US is Osama ben Laden, a single person. Once the level of the US was the Soviet Union-a superpower versus superpower; now the superpower is fighting against a single person. This is the level of the superpower; to justify the war we must see the evidence that Osama ben Laden is behind the September attacks and we have seen nothing"-Hamed Mir, biographer of Osama ben Laden in a BBC interview with Judy Swallow on 09 Nov 2001 at 21:00 GMT.

President Bush made his speech at the opening of the UN General Assembly in New York in which he called for a "global war on terrorism".

President Musharraf of Pakistan warned him, that his approach was superficial. He still waits for talks with President Bush.

The President of Iran warned that the roots of terrorism must be approached and the reasons for terrorism quitted. He said violence could incite even more intolerance; even more injustice will be generated. Major conflicts must be solved with justice he said.He himself faced uncertain elections in February 2004.

2 mighty demonstrations took place in Rome, both pro and anti the war. Italy is due to send shortly 2,700 troops to Tolikum-a northern Afghani town.

11 Nov 2001

Forces opposing the Taleban authorities in Afghanistan captured an important town on the road to the Capital Kabul. The Northern Alliance said it took the town Pulihumri after a fierce fighting with the Taleban troops. The

46

Alliance said it is advancing down the main road linking the newly recaptured Northern city of Mazar-e Sharif to Kabul.

The BBC Afghanistan correspondent Kate Clark in Shamali-just north of the front line near the Capital Kabul-said the Taleban are seriously on the run in north and central Afghanistan as commander after commander is reportedly defecting to the Northern Alliance which claimed to have captured Pulihumri, a mining town half a day drive South from Mazar-e Sharif. That would mean that Taleban forces in the northeast would be cut off. The Alliance claimed also that commanders south of Pulihumri have defected leaving the Taleban garrison in Bamian vulnerable.

The Northern Alliance took also the town of Taloqan while in Kabul Taleban were setting road blocks in the center of the Capital. 5 US bombs hit a marble factory in Kabul. There was no indica tion it was serving any military purpose. The bridge over Pulicharki River in Kabul was also destroyed.

Chapter 5

USA (PART5)

Reports from Mazar-e Sharif said that the situation there is still tense. Armed groups were robbing the streets and the Northern Alliance forces are seldom seen to assure law and order. A French journalist was killed in the skirmishes; Johannes Sutton worked for Radio France International. Two further journalists were also killed, a French and a German.

President Bush and President Musharraf of Pakistan called the Northern Alliance not to capture the Capital Kabul to avoid atrocities and ethnic violence and because the virtual capital of the Taleban was Kandahar; but Dr. Abdullah from the Northern Alliance said it would go for the Capital Kabul.

The British Government stated publicly it put some British ground troops into Afghanistan but did not specify the number of the troops. Britain said the pace of the Alliance troops was directly dictated by the US.

In Fox-TV interview Donald Rumsfeld said that Kabul was destroyed by the Soviet Union.

The UN refugee agency said it began to move Afghan refugees to the first of 11 new camps set up inside Pakistan. A UN spokesman said more than 50 families were expected to be transferred to the Rogani camp near the Pakistan town of Quetta. They come from the border transit camp of Kilifayso, which now holds 3,500 people. The UN has been pressing for permission to set up the camps where tens of thousands of refugees can be settled in safety, said the BBC correspondent in Islamabad Jill McGivering. Although the Pakistani authorities had initially allocated sites for camps, they were reluctant to give their final permission.

12 Nov 2001

A plane has crashed over New York's Queens district shortly after taking off from JFK airport. The plane was airbus A-300 flight Nr.587 with 246 passengers and 9 crew on board; the plane was bound to the Dominican Republic, belonging to American Airlines. All bridges, airports and tunnels in New York were closed. The UN headquarters also was sealed off as a precaution. The Mayor of New York Rudolph Giuliani said there was an initial explosion under the left wing of the plane, the left engine separated and fell down on a separate location than the plane itself-in Rockaway Beach in Queens; it is a dense populated residential area. 12 buildings are on fire. 60 people died on the ground when the plane hit a Catholic Church and gas station. The FBI said it believes there was initial explosion in the air before the plane crashed; the incident took place only 1 minute after take-off at 14:00 GMT 09:00 local time. The witnesses clearly contradict each other-half of them have seen no initial explosion, the other half say the initial explosion was under the right wing not under the left. At the time of explosion a military helicopter was in the air. After the crash a military jet fighter was seen patrolling the site. An expert said the security on New York airports is not tighter than on 11th September.

At 16:00 GMT Tony Blair gave already his reaction. At 17:11 GMT the White House spokesman Arie Fleischer gave a press conference. Arie Fleischer said the National Aviation Safety Board would lead the investigation not the FBI.

At 20:00 GMT the flight recorder was discovered

At 16:00 GMT President Putin of Russia said he is not discouraged to fly to New York for talks with President Bush. He was expected to land at 23:00 GMT in Washington not in New York; the next day the Russian newspaper Nezavisimaya Gazetta reported exclusively on the meeting between George W. Bush and Vladimir Putin.

At 21:15 GMT President Bush was speaking live from the White House not from New York.

The situation in Mazar-e Sharif in Afghanistan remained volatile. Warehouses of the World Food Program were looted along with UN-offices. A children relief convoy was seized unknown by whom.

American shrapnel hit another 10-truck convoy and the food was spilled around. There are many rumors that the Northern Alliance is not united. The Northern Alliance said its forces are fighting the Taleban at the western city of Herat near the Iranian border. Many defeated Taleban fighters fled subsequently to Iran and the US government accused Iran of giving them asylum .

An Iranian radio correspondent in Herat said the city had already fallen with many Taleban fighters killed or captured; the Taleban denied the claim. They also denied reports that the city of Kunduz in the north has been taken by opposition troops. The Northern Alliance captured large areas of northern Afghanistan in the past few days including the key city of Mazar-e Sharif. American aircraft bombed the Taleban frontline north from the Afghan Capital Kabul as Alliance commanders announced their advance towards the city. Taleban defenders responded with heavy fire and denied reports that Taleban were leaving Kabul. Taleban said they reinforce the Capital; reinforcement positions were said to have been built south of Kabul where a natural front line is very convenient for defense.

The UN High Commissioner for refugees expressed her concern of the situation in Mazar-e Sharif where looting, robbing and executions still continue; both sides were said to be responsible for it.

The UN children agency sent a convoy of trucks laden with humanitarian supplies from the Uzbek Capital Tashkent to the Afghan border. The Agency is hoping to get permission to take the supplies across the border by river barge from the Uzbek town of Termez. UNICEF wants to distribute the material among children living in refugee camps mainly in the province Balkh around the northern city of Mazar-e Sharif which was captured by the Northern Alliance on 10th November 2001. The Uzbek Deputy foreign minister said the first-aid shipments would cross the border on Wednesday.

The UN Security Council is expected to consider a resolution on the political future of Afghanistan. The UN special envoy to Afghanistan Lakhdar Brahimi will brief the Council on his latest talks with Afghanistan's neighbors and Russian and US representatives.

Officials from the 8 nations met Lakhdar Brahimi in New York on 11th November; they expressed support for the Afghan people to form a broadly based and freely chosen government to succeed the Taleban. A declaration on an interim administration was to endorse by their foreign ministers but it does not specify who is to take over if the Taleban were ousted.

More than 40 top Hollywood executives met President's Bush key adviser Karl Rove to discuss how they can contribute to America's war on terrorism. Karl Rove stressed that the President was not seeking to censor or influence the contents of films and TV-shows. It was remarkable that the powerful people from the fiercely competitive Hollywood film studios actually congregated together in a single room let alone agreed on anything.

13 Nov 2001

Hundreds of fighters from the opposition Northern Alliance moved into the Afghan Capital Kabul after Taleban defenders abandoned the city overnight. The Alliance columns included both regular troops and police. It is not clear how south from Kabul Taleban forces had gone but said they are very angry of the loss Kabul and regroup to recapture the Capital. However the same day they lost also the town of Bamian after a 2-hour battle. Taleban destroyed the town entirely before they left.

American bombing raids over night destroyed the building of the Qatari Al Jazzera TV station in Kabul to prevent it to fall to the Northern Alliance.

A convoy of Northern Alliance troops has been seen passing the main road not far from the BBC office in Central Kabul from where the BBC correspondent William Reef reported; the whole situation in the Afghan Capital has changed completely and very quickly. The Taleban forces simply left the city overnight without resistance.

It is not clear how far south of Kabul they have now gone. Mullah Mohamed Omar urged the Taleban to regroup and to fight not to desert. BBC correspondent Mike McWilliams said there is a real danger of civil war and partition of the country into 2 zones: Pashtun held south Afghanistan and Northern Alliance held north Afghanistan.

There was robbing and looting in the streets of Kabul; single armed men were roaming the streets and the Northern Alliance was unable to establish order in the city where chaos and political vacuum prevailed. All day long executions took place in Kabul and large crowds of people gathered in jubilation and to throw stones at the bodies of the executed Taleban.

There was no political authority in the Capital and the Northern Alliance just had started to establish itself into governmental buildings and set up checkpoints. Preachers were agitating the people not to take revenge. It was not clear if representatives of other political parties will be allowed in Kabul or it would stay only in the hands of one party only. Neither the Northern Alliance nor Hamed Karzai were able in a BBC interview at 13:15 GMT to give any assurance that violence, rape and bloody revenge will not happen again as the situation in Kabul had changed many times in the past. The Northern Alliance said it is willing to share the power but there was no one with whom to share power with.

Other BBC correspondents who were with the Northern Alliance troops went ahead of them (!?) into Kabul on foot. One of them said that over night Kabul seems a different place; many of the things forbidden by the Taleban reappeared quickly. Kabul radio was broadcasting music for the 1st time in 5 years and some shops were playing music on loudspeakers. Many young men had shaved off the beards and removed the turbans required by the Taleban. Others were seen wearing western inspired clothes.

Troops from Turkey, Indonesia, Bangladesh and Jordan. France called to accelerate the efforts for establishing interim government. Russian deputy foreign minister Vladimir Vassilyuk called the change in Afghanistan a

50

positive event but warned any foreign military force not to take advantage of the change. Russia who is traditionally a staunch ally of the Northern Alliance offered money and armament to support it. Pakistan insisted on demilitarization of Afghanistan saying it was not correct for the Capital to be in the hands of only one fraction. It insisted on broad based government and called for UN troops in Afghanistan. Pakistan was already earlier nervous about the situation in Kabul fearing a political vacuum and chaos and that it might loose the Taleban regime with which it maintains friendly relations. That is why already in the weekend Pakistan had asked assurances from the White House that the Northern Alliance will not enter Kabul before a political settlement was reached; but this promise was broken and Pakistan was very angry.

There were signs of disagreement between supporters of the former King and supporters of the former President Rabbani who is also acknowledged by the UN. An advisor to the former King said the Northern Alliance has broken an agreement (?) with the Monarch by entering Kabul. The advisor told the Reuters news agency that the former King Zahir Shah had wanted Kabul first to be demilitarized and have a political process in place. He said there was concern about the security situation in the Capital and the safety of civilians. The former Afghan monarch who lives in exile in Rome is seen by many as an important figure of Afghan unity though transitional.

The British government adopted new anti-terrorist measures allowing to detain terrorist suspects without trial up to six months; the charges and the trial could also be kept secrete. Human Rights and civil liberties groups protested.

At 14:50 GMT British Prime Minister Tony Blair gave a press conference praising the heroism of the British ground troops in Afghanistan. At 15:45 GMT the UN Security Council gathered in New York to discuss the present situation in Afghanistan. The meeting was scheduled long before; they heard a report from the UN special envoy to Afghanistan Lakhdar Brahimi-who later on-became a UN special envoy to Iraq after the end of US-Iraq war in April 2004.

The foreign minister of the Northern Alliance Abdullah Abdullah said the Northern Alliance had asked formally the UN to establish broad based multiethnic government in Afghanistan. George W. Bush was pleased with the development in Afghanistan and called the Northern Alliance to observe human rights there. Later this day it became clear that American Special Forces were operating in Kabul. The former president Rabbani gave an interview in the Arabic TV Al Jazzera in which he said that in the new Government the former King had an important role to play.

14 Nov 2001

In Kunduz the Northern Alliance encircled 20,000 Taleban fighters from Chechnya, Dagestan,Egypt and Pakistan. An UN food convoy managed to reached its destination in Afghanistan, said the UN in Geneva.

Until now the Taleban have lost 12 provinces but still posses 31 further provinces.

The Northern Alliance has not full control over the country said the German Intelligence Service, which expects the Taleban to fall back to guerrilla tactics. US defense Secretary Donald Rumsfeld said there were fierce fighting in and around the southern city Kandahar-the Taleban stronghold .

As the Northern Alliance consolidates its position in the Capital Kabul the situation in crucial eastern provinces remains fluid.

There is report that the former Mujahedeen group had taken the eastern town of Jalalabad which used to be a Taleban stronghold. Peshawar-based ex-Mujahedeen commanders were trying to restore their authority in the east say they are poised to re-enter the country and assume control but local officials say local uprising has ended Taleban rule in the east.

The Pakistan Army and extra border guards are on duty after reports large numbers of Taleban fighters and foreign Islamic militants were trying to cross into the lawless tribal areas across the border from Afghanistan. Pakistani newspapers said the Taleban are planed to conduct a guerrilla campaign from bases in the tribal areas.

Official in Pakistan said they wouldn't allow that. Kabul remains calm after the arrival of the Northern Alliance troops with the streets full of people and the shopping bazaars busy. There were guards outside all government buildings and troops were manning main roadblocks. Music, which was banned as un-Islamic under the Taleban rule, can once again be heard in the city. Radio Afghanistan was broadcasting again and the female presenters sacked by the Taleban had returned to work. There were long queues at barbershops as men lined up to have their beards trimmed but women were still wearing their all-enveloping clothing. The Northern Alliance has entrenched its position as the only power in the Capital.

Despite of the dramatic events of the few days the British Prime Minister Tony Blair said there is still a lot of work to be done before the work of the international coalition against the Taleban was completed:" We still have to make sure that Afghanistan cannot be used to export terrorism round the world; that the Al Qaida terrorist network is shut down and that Osama ben Laden and his associates were brought to justice"

The British Prime Minister Tony Blair said also there was a diplomatic challenge to create a broad-based government to take over from the Taleban and there will be a concerted effort to make sure that humanitarian aid was distributed.

The UN Security Council was meeting to consider a resolution endorsing a plan for a broad based transitional government in Afghanistan. The UN special envoy Lakhdar Brahimi who hopes to organize a meeting of all Afghan factions within a week was drawn up the plan. This indicates that the UN continues its efforts to find a future settlement in Afghanistan.

Later in the day Afghan refugees and aid workers said that the Taleban still hold the key southern city of Kandahar but their position was becoming increasingly fragile. At the border point of Shaman Taleban soldiers and refugees from Kandahar were crossing into Pakistan.

The border crossing point at Shaman was extremely tense. The BBC correspondent there Adam Brooks saw Taleban fighters and frightened refugees making their way into Pakistan. The Taleban were keen to persuade the BBC that in Kandahar-the city that controls southern Afghanistan-their comrades are still entrenched and ready to fight but refugees told a different story. They said there were noticeably fewer Taleban in the city than in previous weeks and a group of aid workers who had left Kandahar only hours previously said moral among Taleban fighters was low and several of their commanders had left the city to seek refuge in the surrounding mountains. The picture is very confused but reports from the border suggest that the Taleban grip on the city was starting to erode.

Reports were coming in that the Taleban started to lose control in provinces all over Afghanistan although not exclusively to the opposition Northern Alliance. Councils of tribal Elders who oppose the Alliance said they controlled various provinces in the east of the country. Several were calling for the return of the former King of Afghanistan Zahir Shah.

One of the leading factions in the Alliance, the Jemaah Islamiya, took power on 13th November in the Afghan Capital Kabul from where the BBC correspondent Kate Clark said at 17:00 GMT most of Afghanistan had fallen under the control of the anti-Taleban forces but they come from different parties, tribes and ethnic groups. In the east 5 provinces appeared to be ruled by tribal Elders who opposed the Northern Alliance. One of them, Jamah Ath, took control of Kabul on 13th November.

The Elders were calling for the return of the former King of Afghanistan. The Capital Kabul was calm with Jamah Ath police patrolling the streets. The Jamah Ath leader Burhanuddin Rabbani is due to fly from Tajikistan in a deeply symbolic act. At least one more member of the Northern Alliance had already set up defensive position in the west of Kabul.

As Taleban central control unravels Afghanistan was fragmenting. Heavy fighting was reported from the town of Kunduz; there were no signs that the Taleban were going to lay down their arms; there are some 20,000 foreign fighters in the town, which is on the strategic road linking the Tajik and the Afghan capitals. Reports from Jalalabad said the city had fallen to the Northern Alliance but no one could confirm this.

The city of Kandahar remained firmly in the hands of the Taleban. Mullah Muhammad Omar-the Taleban supreme leader-phoned up the BBC and told the Pashtun service that they are firmly in control of Kandahar; if necessary they will fight on from the surrounding mountains. The Taleban had a big plan Mullah Omar said but declined to elaborate. The fate of Kandahar remained uncertain.

The British Prime Minister Tony Blair said British troops were set on 48 hours notice and he did not exclude the possibility of engaging British troops in Afghanistan while at 21:00 GMT American special troops were already operating in Kabul.

15 Nov 2001

A senior Pashtun leader in opposition to the Taleban said a heavy fighting continued around the spiritual Taleban stronghold in the south city of Kandahar. The leader, Hamed Karzai, said there was a popular uprising in the area against the Taleban who were withdrawing heavy equipment from the city. There was no independent confirmation of this. Taleban sources in the Pakistani city of Quetta said the Taleban were withdrawing from the Central Afghan province of Guzny but aid agencies said key south city of Kandahar remained in Taleban hands. Guzny lies halfway between Kabul and the southern Taleban stronghold of Kandahar. It is strategically significant because it straddles the main Kabul-Kandahar highway.

It was not clear whether the pullout was an organized withdrawal or the Taleban had simply collapsed but it means that another large swape of Afghanistan might lack any recognizable political control. Aid agencies said that the key southern city of Kandahar remained in Taleban hands; relief workers in the city confirmed that Taleban fighters were still in evidence on the streets but one aid agency's spokesman described the situation there as "confused and fluctuating", said the BBC correspondent in the area Adam Brooks.

Taleban troops led by Arab and Pakistani fighters were reported to put fierce resistance to Northern Alliance forces around the northern Afghan city of Kunduz. From nearby Taloqan BBC correspondent Rupert Winfred Haze reported:" After a week of stunting advances in which after city had fallen with hardly a fight Northern Alliance forces now appear to be facing a real struggle! Along the dusty road between Taloqan and Kunduz columns of Northern Alliance troops could be seen moving towards the front. Heavy Armour including new tanks supplied by Russia, were sent in to try to dislodge Taleban from its last stronghold in the north of the country. But after 4 days of fighting Northern Alliance forces were still too nervous to allow foreign journalists to visit the front. There were even reports that Alliance's forces were pushed back towards Taloqan". The UN deputy representative to Afghanistan Francesc Vendrell told the BBC he will go to Afghan Capital Kabul very shortly as part of efforts to convene the council of Afghan groups aimed at setting up of broad-based transitional government. He said he was confident that the Northern Alliance would cooperate fully with efforts to form a Government in Afghanistan. He said the former King had a great role to play. He told the BBC that the UN aimed to start with small presence in Kabul and will expand its operations as conditions improve. He said that the Northern Alliance, which controlled Kabul, had consistently indicated that it was of favor of relinquishing power to a broad-based government. Meanwhile the US-envoy to Afghanistan James Dobbin was heading talks in Pakistan on the plans of transitional government. He arrived from Rom where he met the former King of Afghanistan Zahir Shah. The King himself made a pre-recorded speech for the Ramadan celebration saying he wanted to return to Afghanistan but not as a ruler but as an ordinary citizen serving his country.

American Special Forces brought eight aid workers who were detained by the Taleban on charges of preaching Christianity out of Afghanistan. President Bush said it was incredibly good news. The 2 Americans, 2 Australians and 4 Germans were arrested 3½ months ago along with 16 Afghans.

American officials said their 3 helicopters picked up the 8 aid workers in a high-risk operation from a field south from Kabul. They were flown to Islamabad's military airport and than to their respective embassies The operation began after a local military commander in Guzny-province contacted the international Red Cross saying he had the foreign aid workers and wanted assistance to get them out. The Taleban said this was one of their commanders; he called the Red Cross because he feared the aid workers could be killed. The Taleban deputy representative in Islamabad Zaher Shahin said not a single bullet was fired, reported the BBC correspondent Suzanne Price from Islamabad.

Western aid workers said the Taleban lost control over Jalalabad and it was now in the hands of local anti-Taleban militia. Pakistan increased control over its frontier with Afghanistan; armored vehicles, tanks and troops arrived at the border town of Shaman and checkpoints established at key border crossing points.

Officials were concerned that refugees and fighters from Afghanistan might try to cross into Pakistan Anti-Taleban forces had captured also the town of Tarrin Kowt-native town of the Taleban spiritual leader Mullah Omar.

A top American military official was visiting Kabul to access humanitarian needs there. At the Pentagon the American Defence Secretary Donald Rumsfeld said Osama ben Laden might try to slip out of Afghanistan while the American Commander for Afghanistan General Tommy Franks stated the hour was coming when Osama ben Laden and his Al Qaida associates would be caught; this was only a matter of time. 100 British troops arrived at the Bagram airport in Kabul at 21:44 GMT.

Crown Prince Abdullah of Saudi Arabia urged the country's senior Islamic clerics to exercise caution in their public statements saying they had responsibility towards their faith and governments.

The Crown prince told the clerics that Saudi Arabia was going through difficult times and they should not allowed themselves to be swept away by emotions.

China released information, which links ethnic Viga separatists in the northwest province of Shin-Xiang to international terrorist networks; a foreign ministry's spokesman said several hundreds Viga separatists were trained in Afghan camps linked to Osama ben Laden. He also named several groups responsible for attacks in Shin-Xiang in the 1990s and the bombing of the Chinese Consulate in Istanbul in 1998.

16 Nov 2001

Start of the Muslim holy month of Ramadan; in a hypocritical speech US President George W. Bush congratulated the Muslim world and its desire for peace. At 12:37 GMT in BBC-Newshour the BBC-moderator Alex Prody said:" I cannot understand is there (in Afghanistan) a crisis or not?"

Elite British troops secured the Bagram airport 25km north of Kabul; Bagram has the longest runway in Afghanistan. Their mission is to prepare the airport for flights and for possible arrival of further military forces. The British government said Bagram would be used for humanitarian operations. But the food aid need in Afghanistan requires truck convoys rather than planes coming into a single airport. The British government could have other unstated aims and the Northern Alliance troops in Kabul were uneasy at the British presence, said the BBC reporter in Kabul Kate Clark.

The Capital Kabul is held only by one faction of the Northern Alliance, the Tajic Jemaah Islamiya, while further factions' press for a large international presence. Their spokesman said they were not consulted about the arrival of the British troops. The BBC correspondent in Kabul said there were mixed feelings about their presence in Kabul. But elements within the leadership of the Northern Alliance in Kabul were uneasy about their arrival especially if presages larger missions.

Russia sent governmental delegation to Afghanistan for talks with the "legitimate government of Afghanistan" which comes to imply that Russia supports the Northern Alliance rather than the former King. Announcing the move the defense minister Sergey Ivanov said the mission would include representatives of the ministries of foreign affairs, defense and emergencies. The delegations was due to meet representatives of the "lawful government in Afghanistan" The BBC Moscow correspondent Steve Rosenberg said this was a clear reference to Northern Alliance, which Russia had continued to recognize as legitimate administration of Afghanistan throughout the years of Taleban supremacy.

American planes carried out further heavy bombing raids on the Taleban southern stronghold of Kandahar. The Afghan Islamic Press Agency said that the Taleban foreign ministry was hit, a mosque was destroyed and a number of civilians killed. Ethnic Pashtun leaders in Pakistan said Taleban forces were rapidly building new defensive positions in Kandahar. In a BBC from Kandahar Muhammad Tayab Aga-spokesman for Mullah Muhammad Omar-said the Taleban will not give up the city but the leadership was considering pleads by local tribal groups for the city to be handed over peacefully.

In the eastern city of Jalalabad local militia commanders were discussing the appointment of a new government following the departure of the Taleban but they failed so far to reach an agreement on how to share power. A

BBC correspondent in Jalalabad said there was an increasing concern among residents over the failure of the representatives of different factions to reach agreement. There were hundreds of heavily armed gunmen in the streets and it is feared shooting may erupt if talks break down. Some militia commanders had already established roadblocks in areas they control. BBC correspondent said those involved in the meeting described it as one "of high stakes" as they have to find agreement not only on governor of Jalalabad but also of all the provinces in eastern Afghanistan. thousands of Taleban including many foreign volunteers remained entrenched in the northern city of Kunduz. In Mazar-e Sharif the Northern Alliance continued executing surrendered Taleban fighters. As Taleban rule weakens there were fears that Afghanistan was rapidly disintegrating into a patchwork of warlord's fields; local leaders were taking control in the areas they ruled before the Taleban appeared and imposed a rough unity on the country. Soldiers hold the Capital Kabul are from just one faction of the Northern Alliance, the ethnic Tajiks of Jamaah Islamiya; they said there was no need for international peacekeepers. The international aid agency Oxfam called for an immediate food aid for Afghanistan because thousands of people could be dying from lack of food following the worst draught in living memory. Germany is about to send 4,000 German troops into Afghanistan; the German Chancellor Gerhard Schroeder had narrowly survived a vote of confidence in the Parliament at the end of the debate on the plans to deploy German troops in Afghanistan. The vote was 336 "for" to 326 "against". The majority of 10 in the vote on which it staked the future of Schroeder's social-democrat green-red coalition. The plans to deploy 4,000 German troops had lead to a descend within the coalition; Gerhard Schroeder survived after 8 Green MP's opposed to the deployment decided to split their votes so as not to bring DOWN their government. The issue had not gone away; opposition to the troops deployment is likely to surface again when the Greens held party conference next weekend. Then they can try to topple their own leadership by passing anti-war resolution. Japan was also preparing troops to send in for logistical support in Afghanistan.

French troops had arrived already in Afghanistan.

The US defense secretary Donald Rumsfeld said American Special Forces were active in Afghanistan shooting Taleban forces that did not surrender and members of the Al Qaida network moving around the country. Donald Rumsfeld said there were hundreds of American troops on the ground. Donald Rumsfeld revealed that American troops in Afghanistan had moved beyond the liaison of targeting and supply role, which was previously ascribed to them. Brandishing photos of US Special Forces in Afghanistan: American troops were killing Taleban who would not surrender and members of the Al Qaida network trying to move about the country. At times American forces have been OVERRUN, Donald Rumsfeld said, and air strikes have been called up to provide air support. The leadership of the Taleban and Al Qaida are the focus of the US attention. "They bob and weave and move, the defense secretary said but we are clearly reducing the square mile of geography that they have to function in", reported the BBC correspondent in Washington Johnnie Diamond.

Meanwhile the Pentagon said the bombing of targets in Afghanistan had continued despite the start of the Muslim holy month of Ramadan. The Americans said they have killed in the air raids the second person after Osama ben Laden -Muhammad Attaf who was designated to succeed Osama ben Laden if he was killed in the battles. He was distinguished military commander. Muhammad Attaf was initially pronounced dead in the suicidal plane attack on the World Trade Center in New York on 11th September 2001 but it seems now not to be so.

Muhammad Attaf was described by CNN and the BBC, as Taleban Chief of staff. His pronunciation dead took a great pride to the Americans. Later this day Mullah Omar agreed to leave peacefully Kandahar and to give over the power to Mullah Nagib and Hadji-2 Pashtun tribal leaders described as former Mujahedeen. The US said it does not believe the reports.

17 Nov 2001

The Afghan President deposed by the Taleban 5 years ago Burhanuddin Rabbani returned to Kabul and promised that his Northern Alliance would not cling to power. Speaking at a news conference in the Capital Professor Rabbani said he would welcome a broad based government in Afghanistan as soon as possible. The Northern Alliance would respect the will of the traditional Loya Jirga or Grand Assembly of tribal Elders or faction Chiefs to decide on the future administration.

The UN deputy envoy Francesc Vendrell also arrived in Afghanistan to open diplomatic moves on the future of the country. Correspondent said the lightening military advances of the Northern Alliance had left politicians and diplomats scrambling to establish a new government.

A spokesman for the faction of the Northern Alliance which controls Kabul demanded the withdrawal of the British troops deployed at the strategic air base to the north of the city. The spokesman of the Jamaah Islamiya said that just 15 of the 100 or so (!) British soldiers at Bagram could stay. He said they were deployed without consultation. A British Government spokesman said the British troops at Bagram were discussing the situation with the local commanders. The British said they were securing the air base to bring in humanitarian supplies. Jemaah Islamiya troops went into Kabul on 13th November despite assurances they would halt their advance on the Taleban at the outskirts of the city. The BBC correspondent in Kabul said ordinary Afghans welcome the security of international military presence there .

A spokesman of the Taleban leadership in Kandahar Muhammad Talib Aga said the Taleban had no intention of abandoning the city and will continue to defend it. He said that any information to the contrary amounted to Western propaganda. In BBC interview from Kandahar Muhammad Talib Aga said that bombing had continued around the city. There was no fighting and the Taleban leader Mullah Mohamed Omar was still in the area under their control. Across the border in Pakistan a Taleban official in the town of Quetta denied earlier reports that a deal was made to hand over Kandahar to 2 former Mujahedeen commanders.

Thousands of Taleban soldiers trapped in the Northern Afghan town of Kunduz have been exchanging artillery and rocket fire with the Northern Alliance units surrounding them. The Mayor of Kunduz asked the Northern Alliance troops to delay any advance while he negotiated with the Taleban. The dead line for their surrender runs up on 17th November. Kunduz straddles a strategically important road between Tajikistan and Kabul. Many of the Taleban fighters trapped there were foreign volunteers-Arabs, Pakistanis, Chechens and Indonesians. A Taleban official confirmed that a senior Taleban commander Muhammad Attaf was killed in an American bombing raid on 14th November 2001. The official did not say where the raid took place.

At 16:04 GMT BBC broadcast a statement of the Taleban Ambassador to Pakistan Abdul Salam Zaif that Osama ben Laden had fled Afghanistan with his family but the Americans countered this statement they had no evidence to believe this was true.

18 Nov 2001

American aircraft have been intensifying their bombing raids around the Northern Afghan town of Kunduz-the last northern stronghold of Taleban forces. Witnesses said planes attacked Taleban positions in hills close to Hanabad about 20km from Kunduz. Northern Alliance commanders whose troops surround Kunduz said they tried to negotiate a peaceful surrender but time was running out. They said they would attack unless Taleban give themselves up today. If that happens the fight is likely to be bloody; several thousands highly committed foreign volunteers were in Kunduz and they were more likely than their Afghan Taleban comrades to fight to the death.

At the same time diplomatic efforts to form new administration in Afghanistan were under way. The UN deputy envoy Francesc Vendrell has been holding talks with the Alliance leader and ousted Afghan President Buhanudin Rabani who said he wanted broad-based government as soon as possible. He was holding talks also with rival groups within the Northern Alliance whose forces were now in control of large parts of Afghanistan. So the UN is keen to establish a broad based government before the Northern Alliance settled in. The Russians were also sending a delegation to Kabul. The Russian defense minister Sergey Ivanov described the Northern Alliance as the legitimate Government of Afghanistan.

More than a week after the last independent journalist made contact with Osama ben Laden there was growing speculation as to his whereabouts. A spokesman for the Northern Alliance said Osama ben Laden was still in Afghanistan. The Americans said they had no reasons to believe he is not in Afghanistan and they were still looking for him. A Pakistani journalist last interviewed Osama ben Laden. Donald Rumsfeld said Osama ben Laden was running out of places to hide in Afghanistan and USA does not believe he was out of the country but it will hound him down.

The Northern Alliance was reported to negotiate a peaceful surrender of Kunduz but the Taleban said they would surrender only if they were guaranteed a safe passage, which was denied by the Northern Alliance. Americans keep asking themselves whether they won the war or not.

19 Nov 2001

American aircraft have made new attacks on Taleban forces holding out the town of Kunduz-their last stronghold in northern Afghanistan. B-52 bombers circled above the town and the BBC correspondent saw huge explosions among the Taleban hilltop positions. The Taleban commander in Kunduz Mullah Dardula was trying to arrange safe passage for his men out of the town. In Kunduz Taleban were said to kill their comrades who were willing to surrender to the Northern Alliance.

A Family of 7 was killed in American air raids at the town of Gardez south of Kabul. The Family had taken refuge in a destroyed UN building of a mine-clearing agency. Gardez had fallen to the Northern Alliance a week ago but the Americans continue to bombard and destroy the town.

Foreign envoys were at work in Afghanistan trying to influence the political outcome of the situation there. The UN, Russia, Britain and Iran either sent diplomatic teams to the Capital Kabul.

The UN special envoy Francesc Vendrell was hoping to arrange a meeting of Afghan faction leaders within the next few days to discuss the formation of an interim government. The UN said it does not want to recognize any particular group or faction as the legitimate government of Afghanistan. UN official said that recognition should come as a result of a collective decision of the Afghan people. But since most countries never recognized the Taleban government the former President of Afghanistan and Northern Alliance leader Prof. Rabani does still hold Afghan seat at the UN. The UN had said that issue would have to be revised at some stage in the future.

European Union ministers were meeting in Brussels to review EU foreign and defense policy concentrating on events in Afghanistan and the Middle East. They also assess plans to form a EU rapid reaction force by the year 2003.The ministers will be briefed on the continuing visit to the Middle East by a EU delegation, which was seeking to boost the peace process. Donald Rumsfeld said the US stepped up its hunt for Osama ben Laden and will not negotiate with Mullah Omar the surrender of Kandahar. More special US forces were deployed in Afghanistan and Washington said it would not allow any foreign fighter to slip out in the neighboring countries. Meanwhile Pakistan closed the Taleban consulate in Peshawar.

20 Nov 2001

The UN special deputy envoy to Afghanistan Francesc Vendrell completed 4 days of talks with factional leaders. His spokesman said he hopes to make a positive announcement shortly. Vendrell was trying to arrange a conference outside Afghanistan at which the factions would discuss the creation of a broad based government. The Northern Alliance, which controls the Capital Kabul, said the Taleban should not be invited to the conference, which will take place in Germany on 24th November 2001.The US said that thousands of Taleban fighters trapped in the town of Kunduz in northern Afghanistan have only one option: to surrender. The American spokesman in Pakistan Kenton Keat said there were about 12,000 Taleban in Kunduz including some of their best forces along with some 3,000 foreign volunteers; besieged by the Northern Alliance they have been bombed heavily by American aircraft. The Northern Alliance was trying to negotiate an agreement under which the Taleban would surrender their weapons but it said any amnesty would apply only to Afghans not to foreigners; the US government said it wants to see the foreign fighters killed or captured. Along with the Taleban there were 30,000 civilians trapped in Kunduz who were desperate to escape the fighting; as the Americas bombed on the Taleban positions the casualties among the civilians amounted to 500 a day. Refugees fleeing across the frontline said American raids have hit civilian as well as Taleban targets and there was a growing panic inside the besieged city. Some families said they were forced to flee by the Taleban; other Taleban were selling their guns to pay drivers to take them out of Kunduz. Independent Western journalist obtained first hand evidence of the extent of the refugee crisis in southern Afghanistan. A group went in into a Taleban controlled area on the border with Pakistan a saw for a first time a camp occupied by 60,000 displaced Afghans; all those spoken to said they were forced to leave their homes by American bombing. Many complained of malnutrition and shortages of food and medicine; some said they have not eaten for 10 days. Meanwhile the first consignment of UN aid from Pakistan to Kabul for a week was heading for the Capital in a convoy of nearly 50 trucks. Drivers had until now refused to go in from Pakistan because of the unstable situation.

As the fighting goes on talks on the reconstruction of Afghanistan have begun in Washington; the meeting has been chaired by the US and Japan with 12 other countries attending as well as institutions such as the World Bank, the EU and the Islamic Development Bank. The American Secretary of State Colin Powell said there was a need for reconstruction program, which would take many years. Colin Powell also said the US had increased the reward for information leading to the capture of Osama ben Laden:"I have the authority which I will use to authorize an award of up to $25,000,000 for the capture of Osama ben Laden". The Pentagon broadcasted this message several times from a plane flying over Afghanistan and distributed leaflets with that message too.

21 Nov 2001

Taleban authorities in Afghanistan said they intend to fight on despite losing so much territory to the Northern Alliance. A spokesman of the Taleban leader Mullah Omar said they retained control of 4 or 5 provinces. The spokesman Tayab Aga dismissed reports that the Taleban have been negotiating to hand over their main center Kandahar and said they had a duty to defend it: "This is a compulsory from our Almighty Allah that we should fight until we are alive to secure our religion and to secure our innocent nation from the looting and robbing and killing of the people who want to enter the city". The spokesman repeated that the Taleban were no longer in contact with Osama ben Laden. The General leading the American military campaign in Afghanistan said he was prepare to use all means of his disposal against the Taleban and Osama ben Laden Al Qaida network; General Tommy Franks said that could include the deployment of additional ground troops. General Franks revealed that he visited Afghanistan on 20th November 2001 although nothing was reported on his visit to meet leaders of the Northern Alliance; he said he wanted to hear their assessment of the overall situation and discuss coordination between their fighters and US Special Forces. General Franks said he would stop the bombing of Taleban positions if the Northern Alliance asked him to do so. UN officials said many of their offices in Afghanistan have been looted; an UN spokesman Eric Fout said the UN premises have been ransacked and a convoy with 200 tons of food was hijacked while under way to the northwestern city of Herat. Tens of thousands of people in Afghanistan are in desperate need of assistance and leading aid agencies have said the lack of security is the main obstacle to delivering food and other supplies.

22 Nov 2001

Taleban forces encircled in Kunduz-their last stronghold in Northern Afghanistan-were reported to be ready to give up the fight. After intense negotiations the Taleban commander Mullah Feysal said his troops would lay down their arms. A spokesman for the Northern Alliance also confirmed that an agreement has been reached but it was unclear whether it covered the thousands of foreigners-mainly Pakistani-fighting with the Taleban in Kunduz. A BBC correspondent in the region said the foreign fighters may choose to fight on because of fear over their faith should they fall in the hands of the Northern Alliance. The Taleban leadership in Kandahar in southern Afghanistan has denied reports of a deal. Fighting has broken out in the Afghan Capital Kabul where the Northern Alliance was trying to dislodge pocket of a Taleban forces; 700 Taleban fighters and 400 foreigners were holding out in ridge overlooking a village Midensharh 30km southwest of Kabul. Other reports said the Taleban were 2,000 dug in into mountain positions. The attack started after peace talks collapsed. The local Taleban Commander Gula Mohamed is said to have accepted money to defect but than stayed in the hills apparently fearing reprisals because of his reputation of brutality when he controlled the area. Tanks backed the Northern

Alliance troops but latest reports said they met stiffer resistance than expected and retreated. The Northern Alliance had asked the US in vain for air support to bombard the Taleban positions.

The British foreign Secretary Jack Straw was in Iran for talks about the future of Afghanistan; Iran called against foreign troops in Afghanistan, which would complicate the situation. Jack Straw said British troops wouldn't remain longer than necessary. He had also talks with the foreign affairs spokesman for the Northern Alliance Abdullah Abdullah's BBC correspondent in Teheran said. The British Foreign Secretary Jack Straw called the meeting very constructive and reassuring. Abdullah Abdullah said they talked at length about the need of broad based government to which he said the Northern Alliance was fully committed. Asked if that would include moderate elements of the Taleban Abdullah Abdullah replied that there was a contradiction in terms. Jack Straw was to have talks with senior leaders in Iran later and than goes on to Pakistan ahead an UN conference on the future of Afghanistan, which begins in Bonn-Koenigswinter in Germany on 26th November 2001.

Pakistan said it ordered the closure of the Taleban Embassy in Islamabad; a foreign ministry's spokesman said the decision was taken yesterday and communicated to the Taleban today. Staff were given a reasonable time to wind up their affairs. A BBC correspondent in Islamabad said the move brings to an end the close relationship between Pakistan and the former Afghan rulers. The Pakistanis have already announced the end of the diplomatic ties and a spokesman said they allowed the Embassy to remain open as the only official channel for communicating with the Taleban. The closure came after the US said it saw no reason for the office to remain open and disclosed that it will be discussing the matter with the Pakistani authorities. The Taleban Ambassador expressed disappointment at the decision of the authorities to close the last Taleban diplomatic outpost. The Ambassador Abdul Salam Zaif said the move would complicate humanitarian relief efforts in Afghanistan by making contacts with world organizations involved more difficult but he said the move was no surprise-the closure followed pressure from the US. The Embassy had provided an international platform for the Taleban to give their version of the fighting and aerial bombing of Afghanistan.   After fall of darkness the Northern Alliance began the long waited assault on Kunduz where thousands of Taleban remained surrounded by the forces of the Northern Alliance; the attack started despite frantic last minute efforts to negotiate a surrender and conflicting reports said Taleban leaders inside the city had agreed to lay down their weapons. Taleban troops responded with mortar rounds. But the returning fire was soon drawn out by the thunder of bombs raining down on Taleban positions from American bombers high above. Even as the advance began northern commanders continued to insist that surrender is still possible. But with tanks and troops pushing their way down the road to Kunduz it appears that time for a talking has come to an end. Local UN officials in Afghanistan have asked the Americans to stop dropping food packets in certain areas. A person was blown his head and others maimed after mistaking unexploded yellow cluster bomb for the food packets, which are the same bright yellow color.

23 Nov 2001

The Pakistani foreign minister Abdul Satar has called for special efforts by the international community to end the fighting in Afghanistan and promote reconciliation. He was speaking after a meeting in Islamabad with the British foreign minister Jack Straw. He said a humanitarian disaster was possible in the besieged city of Kunduz.

Jack Straw said that the Northern Alliance should accept the surrender of those Taleban fighters who wanted to give themselves up but for those who had been fighting for the Taleban could not expect to get free. Jack Straw also met the Pakistani President General Pervez Musharraf and both expressed their support for the rapid establishment of a broad based government in Afghanistan. Northern Alliance forces in Afghanistan said they gained some ground in the battle for Kunduz where thousands of Taleban fighters were surrounded. Alliance commanders said they have driven the Taleban out of hilltop positions around Kunduz and 100 more Taleban soldiers have give themselves up. But Taleban resistance was continuing and American B-52 bombers have been back in action in the besieged city. The continuing fighting came as some Northern Alliance commanders said they're still trying to negotiate the Taleban surrender. Kunduz occupies a strategic position controlling links to neighboring Tajikistan. There were fears of heavy casualties of the Taleban and their foreign allies fight to the finish in the city. Northern Alliance forces have also renewed their assault on Taleban fighters dug in along the hills round Midensharh 30km south from Kabul. The fighters have stayed there following the general withdrawal from Kabul by the Taleban 2 weeks earlier. Alliance forces first launched their attack on 22nd November but were beaten back. A BBC correspondent said there was some 1,000 Taleban dug in round Midensharh but it was not clear whether Alliance forces surrounded them. One Alliance commander told the BBC that the Taleban had a supply route open to the south, which they can use as a mean of escape.

24 Nov 2001

There were growing indications that the siege of Kunduz-the Taleban last remaining stronghold in northern Afghanistan was coming to an end; to the applause of the besieging Northern Alliance troops jeeps and tanks driven by Taleban soldiers crossed the frontline east of the city. Northern Alliance forces surrounding Kunduz were predicting a general surrender of the city within 24 hours. BBC correspondent Rupert Winfield Haze reported from just outside Kunduz, that after days of speculations and rumors the surrender of Taleban troops inside Kunduz has finally began. On the front 20km east of the city a column of 20 Taleban vehicles streamed across the lines; Northern Alliance troops waved and clapped as the Taleban vehicles beat their horns and flashed their lights. It was less surrender than a wholesale defection. Northern Alliance commanders said around 1,000 Taleban surrendered. On the other side of Kunduz Alliance commander general Abdul Rushed Dostum said another 600 Taleban surrendered to his forces including some foreign fighters. A confrontation between Taleban troops and Northern Alliance forces around Midensharh South-West of Kabul had ended peacefully with an estimated 2,000 Taleban handing over their heavy weapons to the Alliance. A Taleban commander told the BBC his fighters would be allowed to go home.

Meanwhile clashes have been reported between Taleban forces and Pashtun tribal fighters on the essential supply route between the Taleban stronghold Kandahar and the Pakistani border. The Taleban denied that they have lost any territory. Eyewitnesses said 8 people were killed in an air strike in a village close to the border. The Green Party in Germany was debating the government decision to offer military support to the US war in Afghanistan. Senior Party members warned that failures to back Chancellor Schroeder's offer would certainly lead to a government's collapse. But the Green Party co-leader Claudia Roth was told the BBC she was unsure how delegates would vote. In a demonstration in London the British Foreign Office minister Ben Bradshaw was sprinkled with blood by angry anti-war protester. Food convoy with 40 tons of food reached the Capital Kabul and was distributed there among the population. A Swiss-Air plane crashed near Zurich; the reasons for the crash are still unknown.

25 Nov 2001

The siege of the Taleban-held city of Kunduz in Northern Afghanistan appears to be in its final stage. Today 100 more Taleban soldiers defected crossing the lines into Northern Alliance territory. The Alliance forces were moving towards the city. It took shorter than many expected but the collapse of the Taleban control in the city of Kunduz appears now a virtual certainty. Late this afternoon a long column of Northern Alliance tanks and armored personnel carriers began rolling towards the city. News came from further up the road that links the small town of Hanabad 20km north of Kunduz had fallen without a shot. Hours earlier hundreds of Taleban defectors had poured across the frontlines in jeeps and pick-ups surrendering themselves to the Northern Alliance. Reports from the north of the city said a thousand more Taleban gave themselves up. Northern Alliance commander said they are prepared to enter the city on Monday morning 26 Nov 2001.

The Northern Alliance leader and former Afghan President Buhanadin Rabani said fears that captured foreign fighters would be massacred were baseless. The statement follows concern from the Western coalition of a possible bloodbath in Kunduz. He said he had ordered his commanders around Kunduz not to harm any foreigners who surrendered or were captured, reported the BBC correspondent in Kabul Peter Greste. "It is a great lie we want to kill them", he told a news conference in the Presidential Palace in Kabul," we will investigate them and than hand them to the UN for repatriation". This statement was not true because there were no UN troops in Afghanistan.

This repatriation occurred even despite an incident in which one Arab prisoner reportedly blew himself and one senior Alliance commander up with a hidden grenade instead of being prisoners to the Americans: "The Northern Alliance would disarm and send Afghan Taleban fighters to their homes", said Buhanudin Rabbani further. However reports from Mazar-e Sharif said that revolts of captured Taleban prisoners and foreign Arab fighters had continued all night long at the Kala-Jungi prison complex and American planes and Special Forces were called in to suppress them. Mazar-e Sherif was under the control of the Northern Alliance General Abdul Rushed Dostum. Two senior Alliance commanders were killed and another injured after the Taleban broke into ammunition depot and armed themselves; heavy fighting with the Northern Alliance ensued for several hours. A spokesman said there were large numbers of dead on both sides. The Pentagon confirmed its warplanes bombed parts of the complex Kala-Jungi in which the Taleban prisoners were kept in support of the National Alliance forces. A BBC correspondent in Mazar-e Sharif said the revolt began after one prisoner threw a hand grenade killing his guards. Other reports said that all 800 prisoners at Kala-Jungi prison near Mazar-e Sharif were killed and no captives taken. At Kunduz itself Northern Alliance commanders said they were preparing to take control of the city after the surrender of hundreds of Taleban fighters. Aid agencies will follow them in the city where were several thousands civilian casualties after 10 days of US air strikes. Early reports said that the Commander Daud took Kunduz but this was later contradicted; Commander Daud took the town of Hanabad. Kandahar is still under Taleban control, reported BBC correspondent Daniel Lakh in Quetta. "The Western media does not cover this war sufficiently", said Guram Farukhazam, former minister of Buhanudin Rabani, now living in exile in London and chairman of the Afghan Forum in London.

26 Nov 2001

1,500 American Marines have taken control of an air base 100km southwest from Kandahar-the main Taleban stronghold. As helicopters rolled in with men and equipment residents of Kandahar heard loud explosions. Additional marines are expected to be sent in over the coming days to support anti-Taleban forces. BBC correspondent reported from the Pakistani city of Quetta, that this deployment came rapidly over night; waves of American helicopters carrying armored vehicles in slings ferried in 1,500 US marines. There was fierce American bombardment of Kandahar beforehand and later reports spoke of renewed air attacks. However it is difficult to confirm any information coming out from southern Afghanistan at the moment. But the marines have certainly established the most significant beachhead of this conflict 7 weeks after the war began and seems to be almost over. US officials said the deployment of US forces would continue in the next few days with additional 1,500 men eventually on the ground in south Afghanistan. President Bush said the troops were part of the operation to hunt down those linked to the September attacks on the US.

In Pentagon briefing the defense secretary Donald Rumsfeld said this hunt would not end in Afghanistan: "Our job does not end in Afghanistan and with the Taleban and with Al Qaida or even with Osama ben Laden; Afghanistan is only the beginning of our efforts in the world. We are committed to a war on terrorism and this war will not end until terrorists with global reach will be found and stopped and defeated". The US troops destroyed column of 15 Taleban vehicles near the airport where they landed. President Bush said the risk of American casualties has risen but he did not believe they would capture Mullah Mohamed Omar: "He is not the kind that will surrender!" he said. The next target will be Saddam Hussein, if he does not let in US weapon inspectors, President Bush announced. Asked by journalists what will happen if he does not, he answered:" Saddam Hussein will find out".

Fighting was still going on in fort Kala-Jungi near Mazar-e Sharif where hundreds of Taleban prisoners staged a revolt against their captors. A leading figure in the Northern Alliance in Mazar-e Sharif Dr. Abdul Rahid told the BBC that Taleban prisoners were still holding out in the southern wing of the fort. He said the revolt began when the prisoners who still were carrying hand grenades started killing their guards indiscriminately. The city of Kunduz-the Taleban's last stronghold in Northern Afghanistan-has finally fallen to the Northern Alliance. BBC reporter Rupert Winfield Haze arrived in the city and reported from there, in the main bazaar huge crowds of curious people, soldiers, tanks and armored personal carriers. Local people said the Taleban left late last night so that the Northern Alliance could enter the city in the morning **unopposed**. Another journalist however said that the forces of General Daud met fierce resistance. A large group of foreign Taleban retreated to the south of the city near the city's air port and were airlifted by a large number of Pakistani aircraft coming into the airport over night which were believed evacuating the foreign Taleban to Pakistan. It was impossible to confirm this reports but the situation in the center of Kunduz was so far calm and the Northern Alliance was reported to be in complete control. Later reports however said that wounded Taleban soldiers were beaten, kicked, punched, lashed and executed in the streets. Many of them were also dragged on the backs of trucks. Flies were buzzing over their lifeless bodies. General Abdul Rushed Dustman told the BBC that 6,000 Taleban fighters were captured. He again offered assurances that prisoners' rights would be respected and said it was up to the UN to decide what to do with them.He did **n o t** say what would happen to those Taleban soldiers who did not surrender. An US bomb fell astray the fort of Kala-Jungi killing 6 Northern Alliance soldiers and 5 Americans. The Pentagon said the bomb was dropped to try to suppress a revolt by hundreds of captured Taleban soldiers. The US soldiers were trying to guide the bombers to the part of the fort still controlled by the Taleban. A BBC correspondent said at 20:00 GMT that the fighting was still going on and there have been hundreds of casualties among the Taleban prisoners and the Northern Alliance. Summary executions also took place. In Kandahar anti-Taleban Pashtun tribes captured the main road between Kandahar and Spin-Boldak close to the Pakistani border. 14 men were arrested in Belgium on suspicion for the assassination of Northern Alliance Commander Ahmed Shah Masood on 9th September 2001. The prosecution said the killers traveled on stolen Belgian passports. The EU Arab league demanded the dismissal of the Belgian Justice minister Verwighen because he issued a racist report.

27 Nov 2001

Egyptian foreign minister Ahmed Aga visited the US for talks with the US foreign minister Colin Powell. The riots in Kala-Jungi prison complex near Mazar-e Sharif still continued; special US and British troops were called in to suppress the rebellion. US aircraft were bombing the prison complex all night long. Meanwhile Russian troops arrived in Kabul. They said their mission was to establish a mobile field hospital. Their arrival wakened sensitive feelings; 12 Russian airplanes with equipment arrived at the Bagram airport near Kabul. The Russians held Afghanistan under occupation till 1989.

Rival tribal leaders arrived in Germany for talks. The meeting was held in Koenigsberg near Bonn. The German foreign minister Joschka Fisher addressed the participants in broken English. He spoke at length about the German role in Afghanistan and the way the Germans are going to help Afghans. The BBC Newshour covered the conference, journalist Alex Prody and the BBC Pashtun service journalist Baka Moan among others. The landmark conference will discuss the shape of an interim government for Afghanistan. In an address the UN Special Envoy to Afghanistan Lakhdar Brahimi read out a message from the UN secretary general Kofi Annan urging the Afghan delegates not to repeat the mistakes of the past. He told them to prove the skeptics wrong and choose the path of compromise over conflict.

The representative of the Northern Alliance Eunice Khanuni made also a very eloquent speech about the mistakes of the past and the way they want to keep Afghanistan united and to move towards democracy and human rights. The King's representative talks about Islam and democracy. Altogether the delegates were very optimistic that this conference will bring about a transitional period for Afghanistan in which reconstruction and proper government and Constitution will be the start. All sides agreed over the creation of a broad based government after the collapse of the Taleban. The former governor of the Western Afghan city of Herat Ismail Khan has issued an appeal for urgent international help "to stay off eminent humanitarian disaster". Ismail Khan told the BBC that some 100,000 refugees from the highlands of the Khor and Badris provinces north and east were heading for Herat in hope of survival.An estimated 100,000 people were on the road trying desperately to get to Herat. The city and the nearby refugee camps have been already swamped by hundreds of new arrivals every day. The camps were full there were no facilities for the newcomers. Ismail Khan said that if an immediate international relief operation were not forthcoming a humanitarian disaster would be inevitable. "People are already dying," he said. Gunmen killed a Swedish TV cameraman covering the conflict in Afghanistan; Wulf Strongberg was shot by a group of armed robbers who broke into the house where he was staying with other Swedish journalists in the northern town of Taloqan. The Canadian journalist Malcolm Hicks was kidnapped and held for ransom near the south Afghan town of Spin Boldak.

The mutiny of the Taleban prisoners in the Kala-Jungi prison complex near Mazar-e Sharif ended in a bloodbath after the last Taleban fighters were killed by tank fire. British and American Special Troops were also called in to suppress the mutiny. The Guardian-journalist Luke Harding saw the Taleban surrounded by hundreds of lifeless corpses of their comrades, said he in a phone interview for the BBC. Amnesty International said it would launch an investigation into the blood bath of Kala-Jungi prison complex; only yesterday General Abdul Rushed Dustman vowed the prisoners would be handed to the UN, although there were no UN troops in Afghanistan. The US continued re-enforcing their troops at a military base 100km southwest from the Taleban stronghold of Kandahar. Additional 600 US marines arrived their "to hunt down terrorists", as Donald Rumsfeld put it. The US started a formal procedure to get the Algerian born pilot Lofty Raici extradited from the UK; the British authorities accused him of falsify ing a pilot's application while the Americans consider him directly involved in the September attacks.

27 Nov 2001

Afghan delegates attending a conference in the German city of Bonn-Konigswinter said they all accept the principle of broad based government in their country following the collapse of the Taleban regime there. The UN spokesman of the conference said that it was encouraging to hear that they were all speaking with one voice. The BBC diplomatic correspondent reported from the conference, the UN spokesman Ahmed Fousi said the Afghan parties had set themselves the aim of reaching an agreement within 3-5 days. The agenda they have adopted covered the arrangements for a transition to a new broad based government together with measures to ensure security of the people of Afghanistan. The UN would like the conference to approve the establishment of 2 bodies that would run the country within the next 2 months: the small interim administration or cabinet and a large interim council or parliament. Ahmed Fousi said that at the end of this period a traditional assembly in Afghanistan-the Loya Jirga-would approve an administration and a council to hold office to up to 2 years. The UN called this longer lived bodies "transitional".

Afghan delegates at a conference in Germany on the political future of their country were expected to get down to hard bargaining today on the strategy for placing government forces in Kabul. Delegates representing the Northern Alliance and only 3 other factions were meeting the UN official in charge of the talks Lakhdar Brahimi. A BBC correspondent at the conference said the Alliance, which was already in Kabul and one other delegation are less in a hurry to install a government there than the other 2. The UN deputy envoy to Afghanistan Francesc Vendrell warned that full agreement might not be reached on the future of Afghanistan. He said the atmosphere at the conference was positive but difficult negotiations lie ahead especially on whether the UN must send in multinational UN peacekeeping force. He said the 4 delegations were still holding separate meetings to get to know each other; all the parties had to accept that when elections get under way in 3-years time there would be winners as well as losers, he added.

A mutiny of Taleban prisoners in fort Kala-Jungi near Mazar-e Sharif ended after a 3 days of battle described as the bloodiest yet in the Afghan war; a series of detonating explosions was heard when the revolt was finally quelled as the last 2 prisoners still holding out were killed by a tank fire. Red Cross officials and journalist were allowed in fort Kala-Jungi near Mazar-e Sharif to see the carnage left there after a 3-day revolt by Taleban prisoners. A BBC journalist-one of the first to go in the compound saw hundreds of dead bodies thrown around. thousands of pieces of grenades and bombs covered the ground. The Red Cross was assessing how many Taleban were killed as Northern Alliance forces backed by American airpower and special US ground forces tried to put down the uprising. The human rights organization Amnesty International called for an inquiry into the deaths. General Abdul Rushed Dustman who was in the charge of fort Kala-Jungi denied the prisoners were ill-treated. He said the blood bath began when one of them blew up a grenade at a general who'd been sent to assure that the prisoners were well looked after. The British government denied any responsibility for the massacre in Kala-Jungi but a senior Labor MP said an inquiry was necessary.

One CIA agent died in the battle of Kala-Jungi; it is not clear what role-played the American Special Forces there. The Americans said their planes bombed a compound used by the Taleban leadership and Al Qaida network during action in Kandahar area yesterday. The Taleban last Ambassador to Pakistan Abdul Zaif Salam said the Taleban leader Mullah Omar was still safe. He said the attack were to the north and east of Kandahar and hit a Taleban convoy rather than a training camp. Abdul Zaif said the situation inside Kandahar was now normal although the city's airport was under heavy bombardment by the Americans. US helicopters and transport planes have been flying more men and equipment into the airstrip base established outside Kandahar at 25th November 2001 just 100km southwest from Kandahar. Truck drivers between Herat and Kandahar refused to drive food supplies after American planes hit and destroyed by rocket fire 40 trucks loaded with food and blankets; the supply was import from Iran into Afghanistan. Germany and France warned the US not to extend its campaign to other countries such as Somalia, Iraq or Sudan. German Chancellor Gerhard Schroeder warned that Germany will not join any action in these countries; the French defense minister Alan Richard said there was no evidence these countries were involved in terrorism.

29 Nov 2001

Afghan delegates to the conference in Germany on the future of their country have expressed optimism about the prospects of reaching agreement. One report quotes a Northern Alliance official said a deal was reached in principle with the team representing the ex-King Zahir Shah on the shape of an interim administration. However the BBC correspondent on the talks said the difficulty would come with the fine details. It was not clear if the delegations will be able to agree on who should be represented on the body and who should lead it. UN official said the quicker the parties can make progress the more it will encourage the international community to start putting in massive funds for promised reconstruction. The Taleban leader Mullah Omar called on his fighters to continue resisting the American forces in Afghanistan. In an address to his men over military radios Mullah Omar said there was no need for negotiations and no question of surrender. The Taleban were reported to be still firmly in control of their southern stronghold Kandahar despite the increasing military pressure in the area. There was some overnight bombing in and around the city but no word of the targets was said: were they civil targets? Additional US marines were sent to the airstrip they were holding 120 southwest from Kandahar raising the number there from 600 to 800. The Americans said they would now concentrate on try to break the coordination of the Taleban and Al Qaida network by cutting off the leaders from their troops. The Taleban have hanged publicly a man accused of spying for the Americans; he was accused of directing the American bombers by his satellite telephone.

30 Nov 2001

The Beatles-musician Sir George Harrison died in Los Angeles aged 58. Very little attention was paid to his death, his work and his funeral although he's a knight to the Queen.

As delegations from 4 Afghan factions met a senior UN official at the start of a key conference to determine the country's political future the British foreign secretary Jack Straw said there was more progress than anticipated at the meeting.

The Northern Alliance who led the military campaign against the Taleban said all delegation at the Bonn conference now agreed that the country's former King Zahir Shah should play a leading role in any future interim administration. An Alliance spokesman also confirmed that they were prepared to accept the UN peacekeeping force. However one delegate walked out of the conference: Hajji Abdul Kadir said the Pashtuns were underrepresented. The 4 delegations were yet trying to reach an agreement on the specific details of an interim administration for the country. A BBC correspondent at the conference said that the delegations have still to agree on the compositions of the interim bodies that will run the country. The former Afghan President Buhanudin Rabani questioned the legitimacy of the Bonn talks; he argued that only the principal should be agreed in Bonn and that the final details should be debated in Kabul.

In Afghanistan itself American warplanes have been bombing Taleban sheltering in bunkers at the airport of Kandahar-the last city held by Taleban troops. BBC correspondent Suzanne Price sent this report from the border city of Quetta in Pakistan: "A spokesman for anti-Taleban fighters backing the former governor of Kandahar said they were about 6km from Kandahar airport. He said American planes were bombing the airport but there was no fighting on the ground. The anti-Taleban forces in the South a group to various Mujahedeen commanders and clan leaders have yet to form a united coalition. The all come from the largest ethnic group-the Pashtuns-and none of them wants to see the Northern Alliance who come from different ethnic backgrounds expanding into that area". A tribal commander outside Kandahar said today's raids were among the fiercest since the start of the war. He said US planes were targeting a large number of suspected Taleban and Al Qaida sites in and around Kandahar including 2 garrisons and weapon depots to the west. Several thousands Pashtun fighters opposed to the Taleban are amassed close to the airport south of Kandahar but said they have no immediate plans to advance. More than 1,000 US marines have been now flown into the desert airfield outside of Kandahar, which was seized, from the Taleban on 25th November. A spokesman for the Americans confirmed that a suspected leader of Osama ben Laden's Al Qaida network has been captured in Afghanistan by the Northern Alliance

68

forces and will be handed over to the Americans shortly. Ahmed Abdul Raman is the son of the blinded Egyptian cleric Omar Abdul Raman currently in jail in the US for his role in the bombing of the World Trade Center in 1993.The American spokesman Kenton Keat said Ahmed Abdul Raman had close links with al Qaida; American media reports said he was involved in training recruits to the Al Qaida network. Tribal Pashtun leaders were surrounding Kandahar before they make their final push on the city.

The foreign ministers of Pakistan and Iran gathered to discuss the situation in Afghanistan after the removal of the Taleban; they said relations between the two countries would improve by the overthrow of the Taleban regime in Afghanistan. The Pakistani foreign minister Abdul Satar said that a shadow that had clouded ties between Islamabad and Teheran had disappeared. His Iranian counter part Kamal Kharazy said both countries could now play an important role in an establishment of a new government in Afghanistan and in the reconstruction of the country. The BBC Islamic affairs analyst said relations between Shiite Muslim Iran and mainly Sunni Muslim Pakistan have long been tainted with suspicion as they fight for influence in Afghanistan.

Iraq recalled his Ambassador to Turkey because of his alleged contacts to the Al Qaida network. After the fall of Saddam Hussein in April 2004 there was no American confirmation of his alleged contacts to Al Qaida . Iraq was a colony of Turkey till 1915.

01-12-2001

Talks on the future of Afghanistan have gone into their 5th day but the problem of sharing out power among the various factions of the country is still unresolved. The delegations have agreed in principle on political structures for an interim administration, a parliamentary stile supreme council and a cabinet but the delegates meeting in Koenigswinter still could not agree who gets which portfolios. Delegates at the conference said the emphasis now had switched to the composition of a small interim executive. Discussions on a larger parliament have been put aside among with disagreements within the Northern Alliance. BBC correspondent Burnaby Mason reported from Bonn: "It is hard to say whether the change of direction in the negotiations is a good or a bad sign for the outcome of the conference. The UN was still hoping for a deal on power sharing sometime today its original target. But the talks have been bobbed down in the problem of getting agreement on the composition of a large interim council of some 200 members. Things were made worse by blocking tactics of the older Northern Alliance leaders in Kabul to the evident exasperation of the head of the Alliance delegation Eunice Khanuni. In a reference to these divisions British government officials have criticized saying Britain would give no support to anyone seeking to hold up the process.

Progress has been held up by the failure of the Northern Alliance to provide its list of names for 2 proposed interim bodies: a small executive and the much larger supreme council. They would run Afghanistan for the next few months; the list was apparently blocked by elements of the Northern Alliance leadership in Kabul in particular by Burhanudin Rabani-the president in the old Alliance government. Now Reuters was quoting the leader of the delegation there Eunice Khanuni has saying he would seek popular support to strike a deal if Mr. Rabani continued to block the list".

A week after the revolt of Taleban prisoners at fort Kala-Jungi near the Afghan city of Mazar-e Sharif a number of survivors have been found alive in the basement of the complex,said the Russian Radio The Voice of Russia. A photojournalist from the New York Times James Hill told the BBC that many of the prisoners were seriously wounded with bullet wounds to the legs or to the chests. "Several of the Taleban prisoners need operations; I spoke to Red Cross officials and they told me many of them need operation many have lost limbs hit by bullets or shrapnels. Nearly all of them are in very serious state. I would say that probably a third of them are seriously wounded" James Hill said that most of the prisoners were mostly non-Afghan Taleban fighters. Their faces were charred and blackened after Northern Alliance forces poured oil into the basement and set it alight. Yesterday the UN Human Rights commissioner Mary Robinson backed calls for an inquiry into the mass assassina tion. Hundreds of Taleban prisoners died in the riot as Northern Alliance backed by American Special Forces fought to regain control of fort Kala-Jungi. 90 Taleban fighters surrendered today after the Northern Alliance flooded the basement of Kala-Jungi with water to expel the non-Afghan Taleban fighters. Nearly a third of them need medical treatment for injuries and wounds inflicted by Northern Alliance troops.

02-12-2001

American warplanes continued air strikes on the remaining Taleban position in their stronghold Kandahar; forces opposed to the Taleban say they were continuing to advance towards the city. The Pashtun militia said they were just outside the airport and they have clashed with Taleban fighters. BBC correspondent Suzanne Price reported from Kandahar:"The area around-the last Taleban stronghold Kandahar-was once again subjected to heavy bombardment by American warplanes. But there was still no sign that the Taleban was willing to surrender. There have been various reports of civilian casualties. One man who arrived in the Pakistani border town of Shaman said American bombs hit his village between the city and the airport killing 15 residents including 5 of his children. More than 1,000 American marines were stationed at the airstrip southwest of Kandahar. They have been carrying out patrols but have not been so far involved in any fighting. Donald Rumsfeld said that all Taleban who will not surrender would be killed".

The UN said it hopes to finalize an agreement on Monday between the Afghan factions who negotiate the country's political future. A UN spokesman at the conference in Germany told correspondents the interim authority of some 30 representatives to run Afghanistan for 6 months affirmed a draft plan presented to the factions. The spokesman said all that was missing was the agreement of the main factions to a list of names of who should serve on this interim executive.

03-12-2001

Anti-Taleban forces took parts of the Hatkliz-province in which is Kandahar. They took also parts of Kandahar airport.Anti-Taleban commander Mohamed Zeman said 100 civilians were killed in the past 3 days after US planes hit the wrong targets near Tora-Bora.

Delegations from Afghanistan's 4 main factions were preparing to meet the UN special representative Lakhdar Brahimi to discuss the draft document on the political future of Afghanistan.

A BBC correspondent at the conference near the German city of Bonn said now follows the most difficult part of the talks-the allocation of posts in the cabinet which would govern Afghanistan for the next 6 months.2 possible candidates to head the body are the leader of the former Afghan King's delegation Professor Abdul Zatar Zirat and an influential Pashtun tribal leader Hamed Karzai, whose forces are fighting the Taleban. Conference sources said the increasing weary delegates and officials were now in the last stages of negotiations. Forces loyal to Hamed Karzai said they have taken the district of Hahriz from the Taleban as they advanced from the North on Kandahar. Other anti-Taleban forces said they have now captured part of Kandahar airport and were engaged in a fierce battle for the main terminal building. US planes have continued heavy bombing close to Kandahar but Taleban official said their defenses have not been severely damaged. American planes also conducted raids on the mountain range south of Jalalabad where Osama ben Laden was reported to have sought refuge.

04-12-2001

Taleban forces round Kandahar formed a body trying to persuade Mullah Omar to surrender Kandahar. Talks on the future of Afghanistan resumed today in Bonn after a session produced agreement late on Monday on the formation of an interim government for the next 6 months. Today's remaining task is denominating members of the participating factions to specific government posts with a view of overall accord on Wednesday. The top job of the interim administration may go the Pashtun leader Hamed Karzai who was currently fighting the Taleban near their stronghold in Kandahar. Hamed Karzai became later president of Afghanistan. The draft document reached on Monday includes provisions on the deployment of international security force in the Capital Kabul and a symbolic role for the exiled King Zahir Shah. 150 names were submitted for 29 posts. The UN began an emergency food distribution scheme for 1,000,000 people in the Afghan Capital Kabul. The UN World Food Program said it employed over 3ooo men and women to help carry out the distribution; they will be visiting the poorest areas of the city to determine how many people are in each household and to assess their needs. They were also distributing food coupons. British journalist Richard Lloyd Parry said there were 120 killed civilians and anti-Taleban fighters in villages south of Jalalabad where American planes missed their targets despite the boasted American smart bombs.

The journalist said there were no indications that Taleban or Al Qaida members were in the area and the killed were civilians rather than Taleban. Donald Rumsfeld said already this were manipulated rumors. Anti-Taleban fighters retreated from the Kandahar airport after they met fierce resistance from Arab fighters.

05-12-2001

Among the prisoners in Kala-Jungi prison complex was discovered John Walker-young American who fought for the Taleban in Mazar-e Sharif. His Father was Irish Catholic, his Mother Buddhist. He converted to Islam when he was 16. Donald Rumsfeld said a secret anti-terror military court would try him. An American aircraft has accidentally bombed US Special Forces killing 3 American soldiers and wounding 19 others. A number of Afghan anti-Taleban fighters working together with the US soldiers were also killed or injured. The Defence Department in Washington said it was investigating the cause of the incident, which happened north of the city of Kandahar. It said the attack involved a guided bomb equipped for a special navigation system but it was not clear why it fell in the wrong place. Hamed Karzai was also hurt in the raid after a B-52 missed its target. Five Americans were hurt when a similar weapon went astray in November in Northern Afghanistan; this is the first time we learnt for the accident. The Pentagon said it was not clear if it was an equipment failure or the bomb went astray.

The French Agency Medicines sans Frontier said in the past 4 days 80 civilians were killed in American raids near Tora Bora mountain base; the Agency transported 50 other wounded bodies. The Pentagon denied this report saying that ALL BOMBS hit their targets.

Reports from eastern Afghanistan said anti-Taleban forces including American Special Forces had launched an attack on Tora Bora mountain base where is believed Osama ben Laden may be hiding. Tanks fired repeated volleys into the mountainside complex. The anti-Taleban fighters were supported by American planes, which were bombing the base for days; this was reported only now. Else where Taleban fighters resisted an offensive on the airport at Kandahar -their last stronghold.

After 8 days of intense negotiations an agreement was finally signed in Koenigswinter on the transitional government to run Afghanistan following the collapse of the Taleban. The delegates agreed that the Pashtun tribal commander Hamed Karzai would head the 29-members administration. Eunice Khanuni was elected for interim interior minister; the Northern Alliance got 17 seats. The new government will take power on 22nd December 2001. The UN special envoy to Afghanistan Lakhdar Brahimi said delegates must leave up to their commitments to reconciliation, human rights and the rule of law.

BBC diplomatic correspondent reported from the conference, "Eunice Khanuni said the result had proved, the Afghans had proved they cannot only fight they can make also and compromise.

Hedayat Amin Afsala became the new finance minister; he is from the group centered on the former King of Afghanistan Zahir Shah. He said it will be a tough job but he was looking forward to it.

From the German Chancellor Gerhard Schroeder there was pure delight; he said that time takes some credit for the successful outcome and he stressed that it have shown the role the UN should and could play in resolving this these kind of conflicts". Hamed Karzai said his main priorities would be peace and stability. He told the BBC he thought that Taleban would hand over power to local tribal chiefs and clergy in those provinces still under Taleban control. He also said he could foresee a role for an UN-led peace keeping force. Under the agreement the Northern Alliance will hold the defense, interior and foreign ministries with ministers Rabani, Khanuni and Abdullah. Many will see the interim body as a puppet administration working for the Americans.

06-12-2001

09:00 GMT The man named as Afghanistan's new leader Hamed Karzai is due to make an announcement on the faith of Kandahar-the last city held by the Taleban in the south of the country. A Taleban spokesman was quoted to say the Taleban leader Mullah Omar has agreed to surrender Kandahar but there was no confirmation. Hamed Karzai who was in Southern Afghanistan for a number of weeks to negotiate with tribesmen said that he would offer an amnesty for Taleban fighters but not for Mullah Omar himself and he will not be awarded the Medal of Freedom, as Donald Rumsfeld put it. Hamed Karzai was as a leader chosen for Afghanistan's new interim government, which is due to take power in Kabul later in December.

17:00 GMT:A deal was made for the surrender of Kandahar. Speaking from Kandahar a Taleban spokesman told the BBC Taleban would surrender the city to opposition forces led by the man named as Afghanistan's new leader

Hamed Karzai. Hamed Karzai said that the surrender would be unconditional. He said he had assured the Taleban of their safety if they lay down their arms. But he refused to be drawn on the faith of the Taleban leader Mullah Omar saying that he would be treated as other Afghans. Some reports have suggested that the handover could take place on Friday; Hamed Karzai said the practicalities of the Taleban surrender were still worked out. The American Defence Secretary Donald Rumsfeld said that the US would not be in favor of any deal with the Taleban that would allow their leader Mullah Omar to remain free and live in dignity; he said he did not want Mullah Omar be awarded the medal of freedom as he put it. Donald Rumsfeld said the US wanted justice but there were different ways it could be achieved. The British Prime Minister Tony Blair said the Taleban's agreement to surrender Kandahar was a total vindication of the strategy worked out from the start by the Western Alliance. Other reports said however that Kandahar would be surrendered to Pashtun tribal leader Mullah Nagibulla and the Taleban will retain their weapons. There will be amnesty also for Mullah Omar if he denounces terrorism and dissociates from his friends. However Americans prefer to see him dead rather than put on trial. At 23:30 GMT a report came in that the Taleban lost the airport of Kandahar; it did not say to which forces.

Reports from Afghanistan suggest there is a split in the Northern Alliance following the multiparty agreement on a new interim administration. One of the Alliance's leading military commanders Abdul Rushed Dustman had said he would not take part in the new government. His complaint in a BBC interview was that he was promised control over the foreign ministry as award for his army efforts in capturing Mazar-e Sharif from the Taleban. "That was the beginning of the downfall of the Taleban", he said. General Dustman is not the only Alliance member said to be unhappy with the Bnn agreement. Other factions complained that Jemaah Islamiya-the largest party with Indian lines-has the bulk of the top jobs including the 3 power ministries. There are further signs of disaffection within theNorthern Alliance over the multi-party agreement on new interim Afghan administration. The former governor of the western city of Herat Ismail Khan who controls most of western Afghanistan accused delegates at the conference in Bonn of negotiating positions for themselves. He said the allocation of posts within the new government failed to take into account realities on the ground. Another prominent Alliance commander-Abdul Rushed Has-has also angrily denounced the Agreement and threatened to boycott the new government; he commands a large military force in the north of Afghanistan.

UNHCR officials expressed concern over reports that Pakistan is planning to move Afghan refugees out of urban areas into refugee camps-a move widely seen as a first step towards repatriating them. The UNHCR said it opposes any plan, which involves forcibly picking out refugees from existing communities and moving them against their will. A BBC correspondent in Pakistan said the plan could be an attempt to appease growing public impatience there as many Pakistanis see the refugees as a growing financial burden at time of economic hardship.

A court in London has found 9 Afghan men guilty of hijacking a plane from Kabul to Britain. They were part of a group that took over in Afghan Airlines plane in February 2,000 and forced it to fly to Stansted airport near London. The men said in vain they were fleeing Taleban persecution .

07-12-2001

The surrender of Kandahar-the last Afghan city held by the Taleban-is under way. Fighters were been giving their weapons to a commission of clerics, tribal elders and opposition commanders. Some Taleban had fled from Kandahar with their weapons.

The man who was taking over as Afghan Prime minister Hamed Karzai told the BBC they were heading for the mountains. The Americans have said their ground troops of marine commandos based nearby Kandahar intercepted Taleban convoy near the city over night and killed 7 Taleban. The surrender of the Taleban was accompanied with looting, skirmishes and chaos. BBC correspondent Suzanne Price reported from Quetta "The Taleban forces are quietly leaving the city which they held for the past 7 years. Afghanistan's new leader Hamed Karzai who brokered the surrender of the city said they have begun handing over their weapons. The Taleban said they would give Kandahar to a former Mujahedeen commander and his forces are already on the streets. The atmosphere is tense, shops are closed and there are few people outside their homes. The Taleban are handing over their weapons in other areas in southern Afghanistan and the town of Spin Boldak close to the Pakistani border has been given to tribal leaders. One of the opposition commanders, a former governor of Kandahar-whose forces captured the airport, said he had not been kept informed about the talks."

As the Taleban left Kandahar the security situation there has become increasingly confused and hazardous. Rival factions have taken charge of parts of the city and an armed force remains of 300 Arab Taleban fighters; it has been surrounded at Kandahar airport; they refused to surrender. Shooting was reported where checkpoints were set up.

Control of Kandahar changed hands somewhat chaotically. There have been reports of violence and looting as the Taleban withdrew and anti-Taleban forces moved in. Other reports are of some skirmishes between the two sides. A key question for the coalition is where is the Taleban leader Mullah Mohamed Omar. The newly named leader of the interim administration in Afghanistan Hamed Karzai who also led the fight for Kandahar said he is missing but he should be brought to justice; that will please the Americans. But the situation in Kandahar itself is still clearly volatile; there were tension between the anti-Taleban forces with some said to be unhappy over their shares over the spoils victory and there have been already reports over clashes between some anti-Taleban groups. American planes strafed defenses around Kandahar looking for emerging targets as a Pentagon spokeswoman put it but there was no sign of Osama ben Laden.

In eastern Afghanistan efforts were continuing to hunt down Osama ben Laden; there were fierce fighting in the mountainous Tora Bora area where he fled to a complex of caves occupied by hundreds of Arab fighters. Northern Alliance units helped by US Special Forces attacked the caves and now control large part of it but there was no sign of Osama ben Laden. With the fall of Kandahar attention has now switched to the continuing search for Osama ben Laden-head of Al Qaida network and chief suspect on the attacks on the US in September 2001.

There were speculations that he had retreated to a mountain fortress-a complex of caves in an area in eastern Afghanistan known as Tora Bora occupied by hundreds of Al Qaida fighters. Fighters of the Northern Alliance helped by US Special Forces have been attacking the complex and said they now control many of them. Electra Naysmith reported:" Throughout these 2 months military campaign American officials have been careful not to identify the specific area they believed Osama ben Laden to be hiding. But just last week the head of the US Central Command general Tommy Franks confirmed that the mountains South of Jalalabad were "very

74

interesting", as he put it. And that the in ground attacks were increasingly focused on these mountainous hideouts. Tora Bora -deep in the wild mountains is an elaborate network of caves and tunnels developed in 1980ies by anti-Soviet Afghan Mujahedeen. The underground complex is said to extend several hundred meters into the hills; equipped with power supply and ventilation systems it is told to be able to hold up to 1,000 people within its fortified walls". Hamed Karzai told the BBC Mullah Omar was given a last chance to denounce terrorism and dissociates from it and now after he did not made any use of this proposal he will be brought to justice. Hamed Karzai did not specify whether he would be brought to American or Afghan court of justice. The US defense secretary Donald Rumsfeld made it clear that the US would not accept any deal that allows Mullah Omar to go free. Latest reports however said that Mullah Omar was under the protection of a local Mujahedeen commander Mullah Nagibulla, who was sympathetic to the Taleban. Mullah Omar was born 1959.

08-12-2001

Afghan tribal leaders occupying the southern city of Kandahar after the Taleban surrender have formed a local council to help end the conflicts between their rival militias; there have been armed arguments between the tribal leaders over their share of power and over the faith of the Taleban leader Mullah Mohamed Omar who has disappeared, as BBC correspondent Peter Greste reported from Kabul the search for Mullah Omar and Osama ben Laden was continuing: "They may be missing without a trace but Afghanistan's new leaders believe that the world's most wanted man is still inside Afghanistan. The Taleban supreme leader Mullah Mohamed Omar vanished as his forces handed over the last stronghold of Kandahar to the anti-Taleban factions on 7th December 2001. Although intelligence reports suggest that Osama ben Laden was hiding in Tora Bora cave complex in the eastern mountains, a thorough search of the captured side has found nothing. The designated leader of Afghanistan's new interim government Hamed Karzai said he does not know where either man is but he is convinced that both are still inside Afghanistan".

Pakistan has stepped up surveillance of its lengthy border with Afghanistan to prevent the escape of Osama ben Laden's Al Qaida network. A Pakistani spokesman said hundreds of soldiers have been deployed at key points along the border since the fall of Kandahar and armed helicopters were patrolling the area. A vital bridge linking Afghanistan with Uzbekistan that has been closed for 5 years is expected to re-open tomorrow in a new move to increase humanitarian aid across the frontier. The Uzbek President Islam Kharimov said the bridge would be reopened after a final technical assessment. He was speaking at joint news conference with the visiting American Secretary of State Colin Powell who was been working at consolidating US relations in the region. Colin Powell said America is looking for a permanent change for the better in its relationship with Uzbekistan: "We are looking for relationship that will stay long after that crisis is over. I applauded Uzbekistan and the President personally for the political courage shown to assist US in this war and we will respect their courage by continuing to remain engaged with them long after the war is over".

09-12-2001

The US have carried out wave after wave of bombing raids on the Tora Bora cave complex in the eastern mountainous region of Afghanistan. It is thought that Osama ben Laden and his supporters could be hiding there. BBC correspondent Nick Childs reported from Quetta on the Pakistani border:" As the Americans appear to be stepping up their pressure on the Tora Bora caves from the air local tribal fighters say they are preparing for a new assault on the ground with reports of reinforcements arriving by truck. One commander said Osama ben Laden was personally leading some 1,000 of his fighters in the area. Others said the Al Qaida leader was in southern Afghanistan where the hunt is also on for the Taleban leader Mullah Mohamed Omar. But the coalitions 2 prime targets remain elusive". General Richard Myers said the Americans have no absolute proof of Osama ben Laden's whereabouts but they believed he was in Tora Bora .

The UN Secretary General Kofi Annan warned the US not to attack Iraq "because it will be unwise and will lead to complications". He spoke in Oslo where he was awarded the Nobel Peace Prize.

The US Vice-President Dick Cheney said American official has found videotape in Afghanistan showing the involvement of Osama ben Laden in the September attacks on New York; the video tape was found in an abandoned house in Afghanistan. Dick Cheney restated Osama ben Laden must be handed over to a special US military court to be tried if captured alive.

The interim leader of Afghanistan Hamed Karzai has held talks in the southern city of Kandahar to try to diffuse a bitter dispute between 2 rival local commanders which has led to clashes into the surrender of the last Taleban stronghold 2 days earlier. Hamed Karzai held the talks between the former governor of Kandahar Gul Aga and his rival Mullah Nagibulla who took control of Kandahar following the Taleban surrender. Hamed Karzai told the BBC that the talks went well; further discussions were expected in the next few days.

The World Food Program said the threat of thousands of Afghans going hungry this winter was declining. A spokesman, Mike Huggins said Uzbekistan's opening of a bridge over the river on its frontier with Afghanistan meant relief supplies could now reach more people than ever before. Mike Huggins said the World Food Program was this month well ahead of its target for moving supplies into Afghanistan but were still not reaching all those it wanted to: "We are trying to reach 6,000,000 people and we believe we are getting close to these toll; we are moving the food more than ever", he said. The WFPO said it has enough food stockpiles to last throughout the winter.

10-12-2001

US marines with armored vehicles and helicopters support have moved closer to the southern Afghan city of Kandahar as they reinforced their search for Al Qaida and Taleban fighters. There have been no sightings that the Taleban leader Mullah Omar whose forces lost Kandahar last week but he's believed to be moving around the Kandahar area with a small group of followers. Marines have been already manning roadblocks on possible escape routes in Kandahar but a spokesman said they were not planning to enter the city. Kandahar itself is reported to be tense despite a power sharing agreement between rival local commanders. The Pentagon in Washington said the US bombers have dropped daisy cutter bombs-the largest conventional weapon in the US arsenal-on the mountainous Tora Bora area of eastern Afghanistan. That is where Osama ben Laden and other Al Qaida members were believed to be hiding. A Pentagon spokesman said forces on the ground were not able to assess the damage because of FIGHTING IN THE AREA. The deputy US Defence Secretary Paul Wulfowitz said many Al Qaida fighters were still at large and the job to find them was likely to be very long and difficult.

Meanwhile the leader of the anti-Taleban forces in the Tora Bora area said his troops had captured a strategic area about 2km from Tora Bora . End 2003 Paul Wulfowitz-who has Serbian background-narrowly escaped an assassination attack on him in US occupied Iraq.

US marines have moved back into the American Embassy in Kabul for the first time since it was abandoned 12 years ago. The marines were there to provide security for State Department officials who have come to assess prospects for the Embassy's re-opening. The marines' arrival marks the first known American military presence in Kabul where the interim government is due to assume power later in December 2001 under the UN supervised accord. However in an apparent setback for the accord a spokesman for the Afghan defense ministry said that international peacekeepers would not be allowed to patrol the whole of the city. Correspondents said the officials' remarks indicate nervousness over the arrival of the peacekeepers for it was not clear how much weight they should be given. Pakistan has reinforced its boundary with Afghanistan to prevent Al Qaida fighters from crossing over into Pakistan; some 20 Al Qaida fighters were captured while they crossed the border into Pakistan.

11-12-2001

There were signs that some fighters of Osama ben Laden's Al Qaida network in its last big stronghold of Tora Bora were preparing to surrender. After more than a week of fighting in the mountainous eastern region an anti-Taleban commander called the cease-fire to allow negotiations to take place. He said the Al Qaida fighters would hand over their weapons tomorrow. There was no independent confirmation of this; other reports suggest there was disagreement within Al Qaida command. Anti-Taleban fighters who have got into power in Tora Bora cave complex have found many bodies of Al Qaida 's fighters their defense oppose devastated by intense American air raids. The group's leader Osama ben Laden was said to be leading the resistance and TRUCKLOADS OF US SOLDIERS have been seen in the area. Aid agencies said they were increasingly worried about the humanitarian situation the southern Afghan city of Kandahar. There were no humanitarian convoys into the city for several weeks. The aid agency OXFAM said it was concerned that 60,000 Afghans living in a make shift camp near the Pakistani border lack food and water. Meanwhile there have been conflicting reports about the security situation in Kandahar itself. A spokesman for the city's new governor said Kandahar was calm. However local residents said looting was continuing and the Reuters news agency said hundreds of local armed men had been entering the city demanding a share in its administration.

The American Secretary of State Colin Powell indicated that Britain is likely to lead an international peacekeeping force in Afghanistan. Colin Powell said a head of talks in London for the next step would be for the UN to authorize the deployment of the force. Britain said its troops were ready for a possible operation but agreement is still a long way off. Colin Powell arrived in London from Paris where the French said they were prepared to take part in an international force in Afghanistan. French officials said talks on the operation were underway with EU partners.

12-12-2001

Anti-Taleban forces in Afghanistan were still waiting to see whether fighters from Osama ben Laden's Al Qaida movement will give up there mountain stronghold in the east. American bombers attacked positions in the Tora Bora area after members of Al Qaida failed to meet a deadline for their surrender. BBC correspondent Peter Greste reported from Tora Bora :" There may well be talks of surrender for the Al Qaida forces but on the ground there has been no sign of it happening. Instead of the expected waves of foreign Al Qaida troops marching off the mountains with their hands in the air the only people to come down so far were wounded anti-Taleban fighters caught in the ongoing battle. The talk on the capitulation began on late Tuesday 11-12-2001 after the Al Qaida fighters lost key defense positions lower on the Tora Bora mountains in a FIERCE BATTLE.A local commander-Hajji Imam-said that they apparently agreed to quit at 8 o'clock on Wednesday morning local time; just before the dead line US B-52 planes underscored the time marking a GIANT FIGURE OF 8 with their contrails in the sky. And as the dead line passed the bombers dumped payload after payload of bombs on the mountain top filling the sky with a cloud of acid smoke and dust".   Anti-Taleban commanders in Afghanistan were continuing their negotiations with Al Qaida fighters who were under siege in Tora Bora cave complex. American B-52 planes used giant bombs known as green humor and daisy cutters in an attempt to flush out Osama ben Laden's fighters. But it is not clear if Osama ben Laden himself was there. His Taleban hosts were in former days controlled by the Pakistani Intelligence service-the ISI. The man who ran the ISI, as the Taleban rose to power was Hamed Gul. The BBC asked him if he knew whether Osama ben Laden was in Tora Bora : "He may be there or he may be not there", he answered. "The more chances are that he is not there because Tora Bora was targeted...therefore why should be he there in case he wishes to escape arrest; than he should be somewhere else in Afghanistan."

The US raised fears that Osama ben Laden may have slipped into Pakistan but Hamed Gul said he won't be a welcomed guest there: "In Pakistan the tribes may be not very sympathetic to him because tribes are very friendly with the Government at the moment; secondly Pakistan has a very long history of picking up any body was wanted by America and than handing them over even beyond thebale of Pakistani law. don't think he could not take the chance of getting in to Pakistan."

The Pentagon said one of its supersonic B-1 bombers crashed into the sea near the base of Diego Garcia in the Indian Ocean. All 4 crewmembers were killed.

A senior American official described the complex of caves in Tora Bora area as "the last effective Al Qaida stronghold" The fact that the remaining Al Qaida fighters have managed to hold out under heavy American bombing with anti-Taleban fighters advancing up the valleys is a sign of the difficulty of this terrain. The mountains always have been the strongest defense of any one resisting authority in Afghanistan. The Tora Bora caves are located in the White Mountains, which were among the highest peaks in this part of the country. The border with Pakistan lays among the top most ridges. During the war against the Soviet occupation Mujahedeen fighters used remote valleys as an escape route to Pakistan and American officials fear that senior Al Qaida leaders could do the same. There is no definite word of the whereabouts of the Al Qaida leader Osama ben Laden but the Americans say their best guess is that HE IS in the Tora Bora region. Pakistan sent thousands of troops to guard the border to prevent any Al Qaida fighters crossing over. But apart of the harsh terrain the situation is further complicated by the fact that the Pashtun tribes in this part of Pakistan are semi-independent and always lived according to their tribal customs. There are many supporters of the Taleban among them and some might be willing to give Osama ben Laden shelter for a time regardless of the wishes of the Pakistani government. But if he is here and if his escape is impossible it is quite likely that Osama ben Laden and his most committed followers will simply fight to the death. They know they can expect no mercy from the enemy who surround them.

At the other end of the country the Taleban's former stronghold of Kandahar is now returning to some semblance of normal life; the Taleban surrendered the city a week earlier after negotiations with the new interim leader Hamed Karzai.

On an enormous volcanic outcrop known as Elephant's mountain the Taleban anti aircraft defenses remain intact. There is a large green and yellow painted mosque built on Osama ben Laden's orders as gift for Mullah Omar. The assumption is the Special Forces are helping guaranty Hamed Karzai's security and participating in the search for Mullah Omar and Osama ben Laden.

The US Attorney General John Ashcroft has hold talks in London with the British Home Secretary David Blunket on NEW LEGAL MEASURES to combat terrorism. Britain is the first stop of John Ashcroft's tour of Europe where he will be holding with law-enforcement officials on legal means to curb Osama ben Laden's Al Qaida network. The German Government has banned 20 Islamist groups that it calls extremists. The main one is a Cologne based organization the Caliphat State whose aim is to establish a theocratic state in Turkey. German authorities have also carried out house searches at some 200 premises including a number of mosques. The action is one of the largest in Europe in pursuit of radical Muslim groups since September suicide attacks in the US. The German interior minister Otto Schilly announced the ban on the Caliphate of Cologne and related organizations. The ban and wide spread police searches followed a new law in removing the groups protection. The Caliphate is one of the most outspokenly aggressive Islamist organizations in Europe committed to the overthrow of the secular government in Turkey. Turkish community leaders warned that overzealous police actions in the name of security will harm race relations. But the German Government said it was investigating possible links between the Caliphate and Osama ben Laden's Al Qaida network.

Afghanistan's foreign minister designate Abdullah Abdullah began a 2 days visit to India for talks with Prime minister Atal Behari Vajpee and other key politicians. A spokesman for the government in Delhi said Mr. Abdullah's trip highlighted the important role India had to play in the reconstruction of Afghanistan.

13 December 2001

The head of Afghanistan's interim administration Hamed Karzai has been meeting members of his new cabinet in Kabul. It is Hamed Karzai's first time in the Afghan capital since fellow Afghans at a meeting in Bonn appointed him. He also held talks with the former President Burhanudin Rabani. Mr. Karzai told the BBC the talks were friendly. He reiterated a call for international forces to deploy in the country ahead of his official swearing in on 23rd December. Mr. Karzai denounced the ousted Taleban regime saying it had destroyed the values of Afghanistan. US aircraft have resumed heavy attacks on the Tora Bora area in Eastern Afghanistan after the deadline passed with no sign of Al Qaida fighters agreeing to a conditional surrender. As American planes bombed mountain positions held by Al Qaida fighters local anti-Taleban commanders said they had given up attempts to negotiate.Videotape has been released by the US government, which it says shows compelling evidence that Osama ben Laden knew in advance about the attacks in New York and Washington on 11th September. The videotape was found in Jalalabad. In the 1-hour long videotape transmitted by the CNN relaxed and cheerful Osama ben Laden is seen discussing how the attacks were planned. Osama ben Laden in a white turban and deep-gray jacket is sitting cross-legged on the floor of a bare room with 3 other men. They chat and laugh recalling the events of 11th September. The sound is muffled but something is clear-Osama ben Laden says he knew the exact timing of the attacks 5 days before they happened but adds grinning that the hijackers themselves did not know this was a suicide mission. He describes listening the news on the radio on being delighted that destruction of the World Trade Center in New York was far more devastating than he had expected. He explains to his companions that some of those who had carried out the suicide attacks were only told the details of the operation in the last moment. The POOR QUALITY TAPE is said to be found by American intelligence officers in Afghanistan. A BBC correspondent in Washington said President Bush took the decision to release the tape in the hope that it would convince American allies of Osama ben Laden's guilt. Britain says the videotape leaves no room for doubt about the involvement of Osama ben Laden in the 11th September attacks. A spokesman for the Prime Minister Tony Blair said there was also no doubt about authenticity of the tape. A senior member of the US Congress Senator Richard Shelby said, "It offered damning evidence of Osama ben Laden's complicity". Washington Arab journalist Attaf Abdul Gawa said: "In certain moments I have the d o u b t this words are coming from Osama ben Laden's lips". The biographer of Osama ben Laden Hamed Mir said, "this tape was deliberately left by Osama ben Laden to make the Pentagon broadcast it across the world". Many Arab journalists said the tape was faked; others said it was at least manipulated. The Taleban defense minister said Osama ben Laden couldn't be so naive to say such things on a record. But a leading Saudi dissident in London said the tape was genuine because of its topic. The United Arab Emirates information minister said it was authentic. The tape has been called "bin Laden's smoking gun" and its releasing has been controversial but the White House hopes that the sight of Osama ben Laden will consolidate support among the Arab nations.

In Afghanistan US bombers and Afghan militia fighters have stepped up their efforts to capture Tora Bora-the last substantial stronghold controlled by Osama ben Laden's Al Qaida movement. A BBC correspondent near Tora Bora said that despite air and ground attacks and bad weather the Al Qaida fighters were putting up strong resistance. The defenders of Tora Bora have refused an offer of protection if they surrendered. A local militia commander-Hasrat Ali-said that he believed that many of the Al Qaida leaders who are believed to be at Tora Bora had fled the area but that he hope to capture alive any who remained.

14-12-2001

American air and ground forces have stepped up their activity in the Tora Bora area in eastern Afghanistan amidst reports that Osama ben Laden may be hand in there with hundreds of his Al Qaida fighters. Reports have say heavy bombing over night and again after dawn has forced Al Qaida fighters to abandon some of their positions and take cover in caves. More American Special Forces have been sent to the area to take part in the fighting. The US said the fierceness of the fighting reporting sightings by anti-Taleban forces and intelligence information all pointing to Osama ben Laden being in the Tora Bora area. The American aircraft have been supported by an increased number of Special Forces on the ground. Sources at the Pentagon said they believed Osama ben Laden may still be in the area. BBC correspondent Damian Grammaticas has been watching the bombing and reported about the devastating supremacy of the Americans.

Meanwhile American marines have taken control of the heavily damaged airport outside the Taleban stronghold of Kandahar; when repaired the airport will be handed over to new Afghan authorities and there is hope that food aid will be delivered more easily. BBC correspondent Suzanne Price reported from Quetta across the border with Pakistan: "A week after the Taleban surrendered Kandahar city the American marines are now moving in. A convoy traveled to the area and cut off routes as helicopters brought in more marines. Officials said they would clear the airport of any Booby-traps or mines and bring in air traffic controllers. They said part of the runway was still Usable and they can bring in some cargo planes. However there are still many large bomb craters as well as shrapnel and debris scattered round the area. The Americans said they would hire local contractors to help rebuild the airport which can be also used to bring in international humanitarian aid".

All 15 EU countries agreed to contribute EU multinational peacekeeping force which to take part in international peace force in Afghanistan. The news was given at the EU summit at Laaken near Brussels. Military officials from several EU countries together with the USA, Jordan and Turkey held a separate meeting in London to discuss the formation of the Afghan force. It is hope that the first elements of this force will be in place in Kabul when the Afghan interim government takes office in just over a week's time. The defense minister of the interim government Mohamed Fahim said he does not want a force larger than a 1,000 men. 10,000 anti-war protesters surrounded Laaken to protest against the escalation of the war in Afghanistan. Police used water cannons and DOGS to disperse the protesters, which braved the bitter cold of minus 5 degrees. MEP Caroline Stuart joined the protesters in an anti-war demonstration .

The yesterday released hour long video tape was watched by thousands of people round the world; some Arab commentators doubted the authenticity of the tape. The BBC-correspondent in Islamabad Suzanne Price said, "it is a common view here that the tape is a fake manufactured by the Americans". But in Afghanistan itself televisions are rare. BBC correspondent Ion McWilliams was in Kabul where he was gauging reactions: "American officials said the video was proof that the chief suspect Osama ben Laden was responsible for the attacks on 11th September. Most people in Kabul don't have satellite dishes necessary to receive international TV channels. But foreign radio stations broadcasting in Persian and Pashtun chiefly the BBC are widely listened to and important news generally spread quickly by the word of mouth. Even so many people in Kabul have yet not heard of the video. And there is some skepticism among those who have. It is a common view in Afghanistan that Osama ben Laden was simply not powerful enough to organize the attacks on New York from his Afghan hide-away. Taleban opposers think Osama ben Laden had close contacts with international terrorists and may have been responsible for the World Trade Center attacks; but those who think he was not responsible won't be necessarily be convinced by this video. Most people here are pre-occupied with the return to normal life after the Taleban's departure and are getting ready for the eat festival after the end of Ramadan today when day-time fasting will end. Even while the search for Osama ben Laden continues in eastern Afghanistan and bombing continues round Tora Bora the events in New York 3 months ago are not the main concern in Kabul".

81

President Bush said the videotape of Osama ben Laden released yesterday amounts to a devastating admission of guilt for the attacks against New York and Washington on 11ᵗʰ September. Speaking in Washington Mr. Bush said it was pre-posteriors that any one could think THE TAPE HAVE BEEN FAKED by the Americans. He said:"It's a feeble excuse to provide weak support for an evil man!" The President repeated his determination to get Osama ben Laden: "It might be tomorrow, in a month or in a year", he said "but we will get him". And he again said he did not care if he was dead or alive. But in Newshour at 21:20 GMT Judy Swallow said Osama ben Laden knew of the attacks 4 days in advance while yesterday's message was Osama ben Laden knew 5 days in advance. Audio forensic expert Dr. Peter French said the present level of science and technique allows the tape to be doctored; it could be the latest Hollywood achievement. How could Osama ben Laden know of the attacks and the CIA not supposed that his phone was permanently bugged? Abdul Aturak-a translator of an Arab newspaper-said there were gaps in the translation and the translation itself was inaccurate.

15-12-2001

The Americans said their Special Forces and Afghan allies were engaged in a grim fight against Osama ben Laden's Al Qaida movement in the mountainous Tora Bora region of Afghanistan. The US defense secretary Donald Rumsfeld said -being in Azerbaijan- "a very energetic battle was under way". A local militia commander Hajji Zahir said important peaks were captured over night; with the coming of day light B-52 bombers resumed their attacks on Al Qaida positions. The Americans said some Al Qaida members were captured and will be interrogated; they did not show the captured fighters on TV. BBC correspondent in Tora Bora Damian Grammaticas reported: "Several hours after Al Qaida and Taleban fighters had apparently offered to surrender there was no sign of any of them handing in their weapons. A local commander from the eastern Shura forces fighting alongside with the Americans said he believes it may have been a diversion designed to allow to Al Qaida men to flee. Small groups were attempting to escape by riding donkeys over the high mountain passes towards Pakistan. Of the main target-Osama ben Laden-there was still no sign. Hazrat Ali-leading the ground assault-said Osama ben Laden may be trapped in a cave with a 100 of his men. The Americans though admit they do not know where Osama ben Laden is." Donald Rumsfeld held talks in Azerbaijan as part of the mission to bolster the US coalition against Afghanistan. Mr. Rumsfeld said the US is grateful for Azerbaijan's continuing support for the campaign and that he hoped the two countries would enjoy closer military cooperation. Mr. Rumsfeld was going to Armenia and will travel on to Georgia and Uzbekistan.

Chapter 6

USA (PART6)

16-12-2001

Afghan militia commanders in Eastern Afghanistan said they have taken the last Al Qaida positions in the Tora Bora region and that Osama ben Laden was not there. They said all tunnels and caves in the Tora Bora Mountains where Al Qaida guerrillas have been holding up for weeks have now been overrun. There was no independent confirmation of the reports. A local commander of the EASTERN ALLIANCE anti-Taleban forces said that more than 200 Al Qaida fighters in the Tora Bora hills have been killed and 35 have been held prisoner. A BBC correspondent in the region said this means that 2,500 Al Qaida fighters are on the run in the forest. Local anti-Taleban commander Hazard Ali warned local villagers that if they harbor these Al Qaida fighters they would be punished by death. British and American Special Forces continued the chase of defeated Al Qaida fighters.

The American defense secretary Donald Rumsfeld has had talks in Afghanistan with the country's new interim leader Hamed Karzai. Mr. Rumsfeld is the most senior member of the US administration to visit Afghanistan since the Taleban fell from power. He told Mr. Karzai that the US did not cover any territory in Afghanistan and that American troops were there for the sole purpose of expelling terrorism. The troops will not exceed 5,000 and will be in Afghanistan by the end of the year 2001. Mr. Karzai thanked the US for its help in overthrowing the Taleban. The 2 men met at Bagram air base North of Kabul where Donald Rumsfeld also spoke to American troops. A team of British troops also arrived in Kabul under the leadership of the British General Donald Coal.

For the first time in 7 years the people of Afghanistan are celebrating the Ede al Fitah festival, which marks the end of the Ramadan fasting period without the restrictions imposed by the Taleban. In the Southern city of Kandahar which the Taleban surrendered less than 2 weeks ago shops blared up the latest popular songs and Hindi film tunes following the ending of ban on film and music. Many of the men in the crowds also had clean-shaven faces and bare heads throwing the Taleban rulings that they must grow beards and wear hats. But few women embraced the new freedoms to show their faces and discard the all-enveloping burka.

Several US marines were injured in an explosion at Kandahar airport. The explosion occurred at the end of a runway where US forces were clearing explosives left by retreating Taleban fighters and unexploded devices dropped by US planes.

American forces moved into Kandahar airport on Friday 14th December 2001.

India arrested Mohamed Afsal-leader of the terrorist Jashi Mohamed group who organized the killing in the Indian Parliament on 13th December 2001 in which 13 men were killed; with him were arrested 5 other men all from

83

Pakistan. India blamed Pakistan for the assault saying Jashi Mohamed took orders from Pakistani intelligence officers. Pakistan said India must provide evidence of its allegations.

17-12-2001

Afghan anti-Taleban forces have been parading some of Osama ben Laden's men which they have captured during battles in Eastern Afghanistan in the past 24 hours. The anti-Taleban fighters have taken more prisoners as they moved to clear areas where Al Qaida mountain bases fell over the weekend. BBC correspondent Damian Grammaticas reported from Tora Bora : "The Al Qaida prisoners have been held in a small mud-walled compound at the base of Afghanistan's White mountains."

Local Afghan commanders said the captured another 19 of Osama ben Laden's men in battles over night. About a dozen Arabs and Taleban men were led out and put on show; their faces cast to the ground in humiliation. They bagged their captors not to parade them in public and said they'd rather be shot than degraded in this way. But the anti-Taleban forces were reveling in their triumphs. Some of the Al Qaida prisoners were bandaged and limping others looked exhausted, dirty and tired". Osama ben Laden himself managed to cross the border and slipped away into Pakistan. But Kenton Keith-the spokesman of the US led-coalition-said, "he has not found a safe haven there".

Meanwhile the US special envoy to Afghanistan James Dobbins said he expects to see a foreign security force in the Capital Kabul by the time the new interim government takes power on 22nd December. Speaking in Kabul in the compound of the old US Embassy James Dobbins said the number of forces would not be very large; it was a psychological and symbolic move to make the city's people feel that the current tranquility will last:" I anticipate that at least lead elements of it will be here although it would take longer for it to be fully deployed. The defense minister put it very well yesterday when he reiterated the request for international security force and indicated that he hope that eventually it might be deployed not only in Kabul but elsewhere". Mr. Dobbins's comments came, as preparations will be made to re-establish US diplomatic presence in the Afghan Capital where the American flag was raised after 12 years of absence.

The British Prime Minister Tony Blair said Britain is ready to send 1,500 British troops to the Afghan Capital Kabul. He was very careful not to say "peace-keeping forces. "Instead of this he said, "defense assistance troops".Tony Blair has been giving details to the British Parliament of the international security force in Afghanistan that Britain was expected to lead. He told Parliament that Britain is likely to contribute 1,500 troops and the lead elements of the force were likely to be on the ground of Afghanistan shortly. A Pentagon spokesman Admiral John Stufflebeem has said that some senior Taleban officials have escaped capture by doing deals with opposition commanders. He said there were evidence that the Taleban have bartered weapons and territory for safe passage particularly in the southern Afghan city of Kandahar. He said he believes that Mullah Omar was still in southern Afghanistan but Osama ben Laden's whereabouts "were anybody's guess."

Tensions between India and Pakistan have escalated with both side threading threats and accusations in the wake of the last week's attack on the Indian Parliament building; India blamed the suicide attack on 2 Pakistan based militant groups and said it is prepared to take military action against them.

84

There have been more fierce clashes in Afghanistan's mountainous Tora Bora region between anti-Taleban forces and remaining Al Qaida fighters but despite this most consider large-scale military operations against the Taleban forces to be largely over. Now US military planners begin to think about where the next battle against Al Qaida will be fought.

The US defense secretary Donald Rumsfeld was warning that the battle in Afghanistan itself was by no means over. But President Bush is likely to wants to move to the next stage of the campaign "against terrorism of the global reach" as quickly as possible. BBC defense correspondent Jonathan reported,one phase of the operations in Afghanistan is drawing to a close. But the men hunt for key Taleban and Al Qaida leaders could continue for months if not for years ahead. That is going to require some long term US military presence in Afghanistan, as this will involve Special Forces units and elements of the CIA rather than large combat formations. It's going to be a difficult task requiring some skilful handling of America's Afghan allies. Up until now they have been marching in step with Washington. But with the war against the Taleban won it's increasingly likely that some Afghan factions would not take kindly to protracted US operations on Afghan soil. But the frontline struggle against terrorism could extend elsewhere; a number of countries has been identified by US officials as harboring Al Qaida groups or other organizations linked in some way with Osama ben Laden: Somalia, Sudan, Yemen, Indonesia, the Philippines have all be mentioned. But the diversity of these different countries underlines that the US administration is likely to pursue a variety of strategies to tackle Al Qaida and its offshoots beyond Afghanistan. In some cases there may be increased military support to legitimate governments battling local insurgence. But it is the failed states like Somalia with no single unchallenged authority that pose the greatest problems. In some cases the US may well pursue military action against training camps or other installations Washington have a battery of legal, financial, diplomatic and military tools at its disposal. But the wider struggle against the terrorism cannot just be a unilateral battle by Washington. Allies will be needed and that's going to force the Bush team to weigh its next steps carefully.

18-12-2001

A gun battle started in Yemen between tribal Al Qaida supporters and government forces. The government put in tanks and helicopters to flush out the rebels from a village in the northeast of the country in the remote province of Mahreb.

There were no reports of US troops involved but this may mark phase 2 of the US war on terrorism worldwide. The newly appointed governor of the southern Afghan city of Kandahar said his forces have arrested up to 80 Al Qaida fighters and announced their search for the Taleban spiritual leader Mullah Omar. The Governor Gul Agha Sherza told the BBC he'd turn over to the international community any Taleban leaders they captured. BBC correspondent Suzanne Price reported from Kandahar: "When the Taleban surrendered the city less than 2 weeks ago it was agreed that ordinary fighters who gave up their weapons would be allowed to go free. More than 1,000 weapons have been handed in so far. However the Governor said they have sent out search parties to find the Taleban spiritual head Mullah Omar and would hand over any leader they captured to the international community. There has been NO KIND OF AMNESTY FOR THE AL QAIDA FIGHTERS.

Most residents in Kandahar city agreed ordinary Taleban fighters should not be detained. But they wanted to see their foreign supporters-such as Arabs, Pakistanis and Chechens-being put on trial." Reports from Kandahar say 2 American military transport planes came under fire from ground-to-air missiles over Southern Afghanistan early today but were not hit. A US marine spokesman said the missiles might have been "Stingers" which the US provided to Afghan Mujahedeen fighting Soviet occupation in the 1980s. BBC correspondent Ion McWilliams in Kabul said: "A spokesman for the US marine said the 2 American planes were fired at in 2 separate incidents during the night about half an hour apart. He said the planes might have been fired at by shoulder-launched Stinger-missiles although this is yet to be confirmed. Washington gave a large number of Stinger-missiles to Afghan Mujahedeen groups when they were battling occupying Soviet troops in the 1980s. Some Stingers are thought to still be in the hands of Taleban fighters before they were finally defeated. The incidents suggests that small pockets of Taleban supporters may still exist in the area around Kandahar although the city which was their main stronghold is now under the control of local anti-Taleban forces."

The new interim leader of Afghanistan Hamed Karzai is in Italy for talks with former Afghan King Mohamed Zahir Shah.

The 2 men were expected to discuss the return of the former monarch to Afghanistan; Zahir Shah is expected to preside over a Loya Jirga or meeting of tribal groups to decide how power will be shared.Hamed Karzai who is due to take over the reigns of power in Kabul on 22nd December 2001 in accordance with international agreement reached in Bonn earlier in December arrived in Rom in the early hours via London. Mr. Karzai held brief talks with British Foreign Office officials at Heathrow airport before continuing his flight to Rome. His first call will be upon the Italian Prime minister Silvio Berlusconi Than-in the early evening-he will travel to the villa just North of Rome where the former King of Afghanistan has lived with his Family since he was overthrown by his cousin in a coup d'etat in 1973. The ex-king's son Mir Vise had said that the new leader of Afghanistan would discuss logistical, political and organizational details of the King's return to his native country that could take place early 2002. Mohamed Zahir Shah has made it clear that he has no ambition to play any future political role in Afghanistan although he is anxious to see his native country once more before he dies; he is now 87 old and in frail health. Mohamed Zahir Shah's main task will be to preside over the Loya Jirga or traditional meeting of Clan Chiefs, which will take place to authorize the holding of eventual elections when the 6-months' term of Karzai interim government runs out.

The spokesman for the incoming Afghan defense minister General Mohamed Fahim has denied reports that he has agreed to an international security force of 5,000 soldiers. He said negotiations over the number of troops are continuing. The new Afghan defense minister has always opposed the idea that large numbers of foreign troops should be based in Afghanistan. General Mohamed Fahim said last week there should be no more than a thousand soldiers. Defence ministry officials told journalists this morning that a 5,000 strong force has now been agreed. But General Fahim's spokesman is denying that. He said negotiations are still continuing over the size and the location of the force. That shows how sensitive the issue is in Afghanistan. It won't be a formal UN peacekeeping force but it is designed to provide stability in a country where a war has become a way of life. Any force needs to be assembled quickly; the new interim government takes power on 22nd December 2001. The incoming administration credibility inside and outside Afghanistan depends on whether peace returns to the country. Despite the lack of political consensus in Kabul on the question of the peacekeeping force in Afghanistan it has been confirmed in Britain that the country is ready to lead an international contingent. Up to 1,500 British soldiers could be inside Afghanistan by 22nd December 2001. Because the exact role of such a force in Afghanistan is not yet clear there is concern in Britain over the safety of the troops.

The British defense secretary Jeff Hoon told the BBC measures will be taken to ensure that the force would be able to defend itself: "This is a security assistance force", he said "this goes beyond peace keeping; any British force deployed will have robust rules of engagement to ensure their own safety. "Meanwhile British General John McCall is in Kabul assessing the ideal make-up of an international security force. It is expected to be formally authorized by the UN later this week. A row broke out between Germany and Britain as to who is going to lead the peacekeeping force in Afghanistan:Germany wanted separate command structure. British officials said that 200 royal marines-the first contingent of the international security force should be in the Afghan Capital Kabul by Saturday the 22nd December 2001 when the country's interim Government takes office. Many of the marines are already in the Bagram airport outside the city. But a spokesman for the Prime minister's office said that plans were not yet complete and he stressed the importance of the meeting in London on 19th December 2001 of all the countries offering to join the security force.Differences have emerged between Germany and Britain over the structure of the force. The BBC Berlin correspondent said which has offered to contribute to the force wants to have a separate command structure from that of the American led military operation. Britain dismisses this as result of domestic political pressures in Germany .

The US Defence Secretary Donald Rumsfeld warned the EU Nato allies of further terrorist attacks in Europe. He was speaking at Nato meeting in Brussels. He warned NATO itself to brace for more surprises from terrorist organizations. He told the NATO meeting in Brussels that after the destruction unleashed in America the Alliance had to accept that European cities were also at risk from adversaries with increasing power and range: "In particular I emphasize the threat posed by terrorist movements and terrorist states that are seeking weapons of mass destruction". Donald Rumsfeld said that advanced conventional missiles or even nuclear, chemical and biological weapons were all emerging dangers, which cannot be ignored. He urged European NATO members to spend more and cooperate on developing the region's defense capabilities.

The St. John Divine church in New York caught fire and was partly destroyed. The reason for the fire is not known but this is yet another blow to the spirit of the city. The Christmas services were abandoned.

19-12-2001

Security forces in Pakistan have been involved in a fierce clash with Al Qaida prisoners from Afghanistan that has left 6 men on each side dead. The prisoners-Al Qaida fighters supporting Osama ben Laden-were arrested on 18th December after crossing the frontier to escape the latest American bombing. They were taken to a prison in Peshawar in a convoy of busses when several of them overpowered the driver, seized weapons from their guards and opened fire. In the fighting and confusion which followed the bus overturned and more than 40 prisoners managed to escape. Meanwhile the new interim leader of Afghanistan Hamed Karzai has said that Taleban prisoners who have committed crimes will be punished according to Islamic law. Immigration officials in Britain have detained at least 8 foreign nationals suspected to having links to international terrorism. Those held are reported to be North Africans mainly Algerians. They won't be named but reports say that they are from a list of radical Islamists drawn up by the police and intelligence agencies. The move came only days after British Parliament approved new anti-terrorists laws including the right of the authorities to detain non-British suspect without charge or trial. Civil liberties groups have said they intend to challenge the new powers.

20-12-2001

An international conference on the reconstruction of Afghanistan has been told that the country's warlords wer putting the program in jeopardy with their continued looting of aid convoys. The EU Commissioner for external affairs Chris Patten said the activities of these local armies were the most worrying aspect of the task ahead. H described Afghanistan as a failed state with no working institutions, its infrastructure in ruins and many of it best people in exile. The EU Commissioner for developing aid Paul Nielsen said donors must send local armies clear message: reconstruction will only take place in areas in Afghanistan where they are providing security and stability.

A bomb went off on the market in the northern Afghan city of Mazar-e Sharif; 50 people were injured.

The Pakistani authority said they were questioning a senior Taleban official who was detained trying to enter the country from Afghanistan. He is Eminal Amin-the former Afghan security chief in Spin Boldak in the southern border area. Pakistan has made efforts to tighten security along its long and poor border with Afghanistan to keep fleeing Taleban and Al Qaida fighters out of the country.

Pakistani forces pursuing the group of detained Al Qaida fighters who staged a violent escape yesterday said they killed 2 of them and recaptured all but 5.

21-12-2001

50 British marines were beginning work in Afghanistan as a vanguard of an international force that's supposed to ensure security in and around the Capital Kabul. Their first task will be to escort political figures such as diplomats taking part in the inauguration of the new Afghan government. Speaking in Kabul the UN deputy envoy to Afghanistan Francesc Vendrell said he was pleased with the progress so far in transferring power to a new interim administration: "The only difficulties have been logistical in terms accommodating the people who are coming in both Afghans and non-Afghans and foreign guests. Problem is the transportation but in terms of security I am extremely glad that things are very much moving in the right direction as we agreed in Bonn."

The American Ambassador to Kabul Kenton Keat said there were 7,000 Taleban and Al Qaida prisoners in Afghanistan kept in IS captivity. This is the first time the official number of these detainees has been announced. He did not say where they were kept but it is largely believed they are in makeshift camps at Kandahar airport and in Mazar-e Sharif. Kenton Keat told reporters in Islamabad that the search for more Taleban fighters and Al Qaida members would continue.

Zafar Abas, BBC correspondent, said from Islamabad, the coalition spokesman did not give a break down of Taleban and Al Qaida prisoners but said a clear picture emerged once the clearing process is over. Kenton Keat said the situation was changing by every passing day and more suspects have been detained for questioning. He said it would be wrong to categorize all this prisoners as terrorists or Al Qaida members. Once all of them have been

88

properly screened he said only than the coalition will be in a better position to know how many of them were Al Qaida members and how many were just sympathizers of the terrorist group. Though the spokesman Kenton Keat did not say where these prisoners were kept; it is widely believed that most of them have been locked up in makeshift detention centers near the Kandahar airport and in Mazar-e Sharif. Kenton Keat described Islamabad's performance in blocking the escape route for Al Qaida members as impressive and said there was no need to involve the US forces in tracking down the suspected terrorists who have slipped into Pakistan. On the whereabouts of Osama ben Laden and the Taleban leader Mullah Omar the spokesman said there was no credible information to suggest that they have left Afghanistan and said the search for them will still going on inside the country." Meanwhile the American bombing raids over Afghanistan continued. A food aid convoy has been persistently bombarded by US planes; 65 civilians were reported to have been killed and 40 injured. Other reports say the Americans hit a convoy of tribal elders traveling to Kabul and over 100 people were killed. Afghanistan will need help of estimated $900,000,000 said Michael McBrown speaking at the EU-summit in Brussels.

The German Defence minister Rudolph Scharping said Germany would contribute 1,200 German soldiers to Afghanistan. The move was approved the next day by the German Bundestag. Later on Rudolph Scharping was dismissed from his post for his lavish and exuberant life style.

22-12-2001

Ceremonies have been taking place in the Afghan Capital Kabul to usher in the new interim government led by Hamed Karzai following the defeat of the Taleban. First to be sworn in was Mr. Karzai himself; in an address to the gathering he paid tribute to all those who have died in decades of conflict in the country. Hamed Karzai acknowledged his country's bloody past after 23 years of war but spoke of his happiness that the sun of peace as he said was rising in Afghanistan. He told the urgent tasks ahead to eradicate factionalism and reconstruct the country. Afghanistan he said had become a land of terrorism but now the country was ready to retake its place alongside the international community. The 2,000 gathered dignitaries from different ethnic groups in the country listened in respect for silence occasionally applauding the country's new leader. The peaceful transition of power from the outgoing President Burhanuddin Rabbani to the interim administration opened a new page in Afghanistan's political history.

A delegation of tribal leaders in Afghanistan has repeated allegations that American aircraft bombed a convoy of dignitaries who were on their way to Kabul for today's ceremony. They said 65 people died and 40 were injured. An US official admitted that convoy of vehicles was fired on but insisted that they fired at American planes first. The delegation from eastern Afghanistan came to Kabul for the inauguration ceremony from the town of Gardez. Members of the group have repeated reports that a second delegation of tribal leaders from the nearby town of Khost was attacked by American planes. According to the Gardez leaders the Khost delegation had been prevented from taking the main road by armed men and were traveling by round about route to the mountains when American planes attacked their convoy. The Gardez group told the news and went on to Kabul while the Khost tribal leaders went home to see the death and the wounded. The American Defence Secretary Donald Rumsfeld has said that a series of heavy air strikes have destroyed many vehicle and killed many people near

Khost-an area where Al Qaida had training camps but the Pentagon said the convoy they hit was of Taleban fighters but not tribal leaders. The cover-up continued few days.

23-12-2001

Officials in the US were questioning a man who is suspected of trying to detonate explosives on board a passenger airliner in midair. The man was restrained by aircrew and passengers before being sedated by police narcotics.. The American Airlines from Paris to Miami was diverted and escorted by fighter aircraft for an emergency landing in Boston. The officials are trying to identify the man who was traveling on a false British passport. The explosive in his shoe was C4.

Afghanistan's interim cabinet has held its first meeting in Kabul as it faces up the task of rebuilding the shattered country. The new leader Hamed Karzai described the atmosphere among the various factions as "excellent".He said the main themes have been security and re-establishing the civil service. A Pashtun tribal leader Gul Bedin warned that he will take up arms against the new Afghan administration if there is a repeat of the last week American air attack in the East of the country in which 65 people were killed and 40 injured. The victims are told to be tribal elders on their way to Kabul. But the Americans said they still believed they were either Taleban or Al Qaida leaders. Meanwhile the UNHCR said that some Afghans who fled to Pakistan during the war are returning to the country. A UNHCR spokesman Mohamed Adar said there is been a steady trickle of refugees going back over the border. Mr. Adar said he has just returned from a large refugee camp on the edge of Peshawar from where reported the BBC correspondent Rachel Right. He said many of the refugees there told him they are ready to return home. But it is only the poor who have nothing to lose who will go home immediately. Those Afghans who have made a life for themselves in Pakistan will want more time and more evidence that the new interim government will do what it has promised to bring peace and stability to the country.

The former Taleban Ambassador to Pakistan Mullah Abdul Salam Zaif said he asked Pakistan for political asylum. Mullah Zaif became the best-known public face of the Taleban during the American military campaign against Afghanistan holding frequent news conferences broadcasted round the world. Pakistan was the last country to have diplomatic relations with the Taleban before its fall from power. Mullah Zaif told the Reuters news agency that he was awaiting a reply from the Pakistani government.

24-12-2001

Afghanistan's new leader Hamed Karzai stressed that the first priority are security and rebuilding of civil service structure. British soldiers were patrolling areas around government ministries at the start of "necessary move towards larger peace keeping force" as Hamed Karzai put it. Mr. Karzai has appointed the Uzbek war lord General Rushed Dostum to the post of deputy defense minister. The country's new cabinet ministers have been taking up their full responsibilities today after their inauguration on 22nd December. General Dostum was initially to support the new government because he thought his faction was underrepresented. The Pakistani leader General Pervez Musharraf said he will act against 2 militant groups accused of attacking the Indian Parliament earlier in December if evidence is found linking them directly to the shootings. Speaking during a visit to China General Musharraf said Pakistan was already taking measures against all groups involved in any form of terrorism. The Indian government has demanded that Pakistan arrests the leaders of the groups involved.

25-12-2001

British, American and other Western soldiers in Afghanistan have been marking Christmas as preparations continue for the arrival of further contingents of peacekeeping troops who'll form the international security assistance task force (ISATF). At Bagram air base North of the Capital Kabul the British and the Americans celebrated with special Christmas rations and a FOOTBALL MATCH. The have been insuring the smooth running of Bagram which Kabul's lifeline to the outside world. In Southern Afghanistan a larger American force has continued preparing Kandahar airport for use by humanitarian and OTHER FLIGHTS.

26-12-2001

An UN relief agency said armed militias and inter-factional fighting hampered the aid delivery to the Southern Afghan city of Kandahar. A spokesman for the World Food Program Jordan Day described Kandahar as a "no go area for the UN."Speaking to the BBC he said there was a lack of authority, security and control surrounding the city with reports of armed groups demanding tolls from drivers. But he said in Afghanistan as a whole things were going well and more than 6 million people were receiving food aid. The head of the interim Afghan administration Hamed Karzai said after a meeting of the incoming cabinet there was unanimous support throughout the country for the international security force to help guarantee a peaceful transition of power.

The Qatar based satellite television al Jazzera broadcasted excerpts from the new videotape fromOsama ben Laden. Al Jazzera said the wording on the video tape indicated it was recorded within the last 2 weeks; it says Osama ben Laden stated the video was made to mark 3 months since the attacks on New York and Washington. In the recording he condemns the WEST for excessive bombing of Muslims in Afghanistan referring specifically to an attack on a mosque during Ramadan prayers a few weeks ago. He accused the WEST of hating Islam and referred directly to the attack on America on 11th September. He called it "an act of benevolent terrorism" and criticized bitterly the US for its military and political support for Israel.

The US said it formally placed 2 Kashmiri militant groups based in Pakistan on its list of foreign terrorist organizations. The American Secretary of State Colin Powell named the groups as Lashkar Itaiba Jashi Mohamedi.

27-12-2001

The interim government in Afghanistan has rejected an assertion by Osama ben Laden in his latest videotape that the American bombing campaign against the Taleban showed the West's hatred for Islam. In the tape broadcasted by the Arabic TV station al Jazzera Osama ben Laden justifies the September attacks as a "response to injustice". The Defence Ministry's spokesman Mohamed Abil said the Afghan government strongly rejected Osama ben Laden's message in his latest video released to the Qatar based Al Jazzera satellite TV station .In the video Osama ben Laden described the American bombing campaign in Afghanistan as an attack against Islam but Mr. Abil rejected this accusing Osama ben Laden of being behind the assassination of the Northern Alliance's charismatic military commander Ahmed Shah Masood who was, he said, " a great Muslim". The top leaders of Afghanistan's new interim government have repeatedly described Osama ben Laden's Al Qaida network as terrorists and have vowed to bring them and the main Taleban leaders to justice. However they denied Osama ben Laden is Afghanistan and said he sought refuge in neighboring Pakistan. In Press conference for the Pentagon Donald Rumsfeld acknowledged "Osama ben Laden may be still in Afghanistan, in some other country or dead." Donald Rumsfeld confirmed also that Taleban and Al Qaida prisoners were kept at the American naval base Guantanamo in Cuba.

Afghan defense ministry said Osama ben Laden is no longer in the country but has taken refuge in Pakistan. A ministry spokesman said it was not clear exactly where Osama ben Laden was but believed he was under the protection of a radical Pakistani Islamic group led by Molano Fazlo Reman. Mr. Reman who is currently under house arrest by the Pakistani military government dismissed the suggestion as a joke. The Afghan defense ministry statement follows the broadcast of a new videotape of Osama ben Laden by the Arabic TV station al Jazzera. The tape appears to have been recorded several weeks ago possibly before the start of the heavy US bombing of the Tora Bora mountains where Osama ben Laden was thought to be hiding. The tape was broadcast by al Jazzera TV station in its full 33 minutes version; Donald Rumsfeld dismissed the videotape saying he had not watch it.

28-12-2001

President Bush admitted THEY HAVE LOST Osama ben Laden's TRACES.The Afghan defense minister general Fahim said he might be in Pakistan in the Peshawar area. General Fahim is a prominent Northern Alliance commander but he opposed strongly Pakistani and US influence in Afghanistan.

29-12-2001

Some 100 FBI agents were questioning the captured Al Qaida prisoners about the location of Osama ben Laden. It is not clear under which law they preceded. British and Afghan soldiers are patrolling jointly the streets of Kabul; it is expected that such patrols will become a regular feature for the international security assistance force once a final agreement is reached on the force's mandate. At the same time American forces in Afghanistan are continuing their search for information on the leaders of Al Qaida network. BBC correspondent Ion McWilliam reported from Kabul:"British troops appeared on the streets of Kabul in the first joined patrol with Afghan police. A small group of royal marines and Afghan police in white helmets drove through the city and walked side by side along the busy street in an experimental patrol as a British Embassy spokesman put it.The spokesman said further joint patrols would be arranged, as required although there are no planes yet to carry them out on a daily bases. Talks are still going on with the Afghan authorities to draw up a formal agreement on the exact duties of the international force, which is eventually expected to total between 3,000 and 5,000 foreign troops. Elsewhere American forces in Afghanistan have been continuing their search for more information on the Al Qaida network. An US military contingent sealed off a prison in the northern town of Shipigan and removed a number of Al Qaida prisoners; they have been take to American detention centers in the Southern city of Kandahar for questioning. Shipigan is the hometown of the ethnic Uzbek war lord Abdul Rushed Dostum, who is now Afghanistan's deputy defense minister. General Dostum told the Uzbekistan TV station that thousands of Taleban of various nationalities WILL BE HELD IN HIS PRISONS, DESPITE THEIR WOUNDS. He said the UNO should decide what to do with this prisoners". In fact their destiny was decided by the Yankees who kept them illegally imprisoned in their Guantanamo Bay base in Cuba in 2x2m cages.

30-12-2001

The Pentagon said it carried out a strike on Afghanistan on Saturday 29th December on what it said to have been a building used by the Taleban. The Afghan Islamic Press Agency said at least 15 civilians were killed in a bombing raid by American planes on Shikan-a village in the eastern province of Paktika. It quoted eyewitnesses have saying there was sign of Taleban or Al Qaida fighters in the area. The new Afghan government has said it plans to rebuild the historic Buddha statues in Bamian destroyed by the Taleban. The giant 50m high Buddhas were shelled by the Taleban regime in March 2001 that viewed them as an affront to Islam. The destruction caused international outrage at the time. According to Richard Myron in Kabul, the new minister of information and culture Raheen Makhdoom said that his government would like to rebuild the destroyed statues of Buddha as soon as possible. He said that while the rebuild Buddhas would not be exactly what they once were it was necessary to reconstruct them. The two statues situated in the central Bamian region stood between 40 and 50m high and were over 1,500 years old when they were shelled by the Taleban in March 2001. Afghanistan's minister of culture also said that he'd like to attract tourists back to his country but with minimal infrastructure and with uncertain security situation that may be some way off.

An agreement governing the operation of the international security assistance force for Afghanistan has been concluded in the Capital Kabul. It is expected to be initiated shortly. The agreement opens the way for the arrival of further troops from Britain as well as contingents from other countries that are contributing to the force. From Kabul reported the BBC correspondent Richard Myron:" Afghanistan's foreign minister Dr. Abdullah Abdullah has said an agreement has now been reached and the multinational force should begin its task as soon as possible. The agreement is due to be initialed later today by Afghanistan's defense minister and the British officer leading the force General John McCall. A further 50 British troops were expected here this evening and the bulk of the British contingent is than due to arrive in the coming few weeks. The multinational force is charged with helping the Afghan government impose security in Kabul but in an indication of a possible larger role for the force in the future Dr. Abdullah said his government was willing to see its duty extended to elsewhere in the country". Later this day was announced that the agreement was not signed because the both countries could not agree on the size of the peacekeeping force.

The head of Afghanistan's official women's movement has called on women to remove their all enveloping covering-the burka-which was made compulsory by the Taleban. Speaking on Afghan radio Armina Azali said the Koran did not insist on women covering up completely. She said that even through their harsh pilgrimage they did not cover their faces.

31-12-2001

Reports from Eastern Afghanistan say that about 100 villagers were killed in an American bombing raid early on 30th December.

There was no word from the Americans. BBC correspondent Ion McWilliam reported from Kabul: "American planes were reported to have bombed the village of Niazi Kaleh in Paktika province on 30-12-2001.Villagers say that up to 100 people may have been killed. One report said that as many as 90 bodies have been pulled from the ruins of houses. Communications are very difficult in this remote area and the number of casualties can be much higher. The village near the town of Gardez is in a region of Eastern Afghanistan where American planes earlier this month bombed both a compound and convoy of civilians, which the Americans thought were Taleban and Al Qaida leaders. This area is a location of many Al Qaida training camps and the US forces have been continuing their search there for senior Taleban and Al Qaida leaders.

Reuters news agency quoted a resident saying the raid was carried out by a B-52 bomber, fighter plane and 2 helicopters; other report said a missile was fired at the planes but the question is what were doing the planes in this area?

An US military spokesman said American planes have bombed a compound of Taleban or Al Qaida leaders to the northwest of Gardez. He said the operation was extensively researched beforehand, no mistake was made and he was confident they stroke a legitimate target. The BBC correspondent in Kabul said some confusion might have been caused by the fact that many local leaders have only recently switched their allegiance from the Taleban to the new interim government.

01 Jan 2002

American military officials confirmed that a mission is under way to capture the fugitive leader of the Taleban Mullah Mohamed Omar. Reports from the southern city of Kandahar said American troops took off from their military base near the airport. Afghan officials said Mullah Omar might be hiding in a remote area near the border between Helmand and Oruz gun provinces originally his home region. A BBC correspondent in Kabul said the search for the reclusive Mullah will be all the more difficult, as he never allowed his photograph to be taken. However they denied earlier reports that the operation was under way. The Pentagon called the operation "aggressive gathering of information"; it is largely assumed that Mullah Omar is hiding at sympathizer near Kandahar. In eastern Afghanistan one American vehicle was attacked by angry protesters and destroyed; one American soldier was injured. The protesters escaped unidentified.

Meanwhile in the eastern Afghanistan pictures of the American bombing of the compound at Niazi Kaleh showed stacks of ammunition in the area suggesting it was used to store weapons.

The WHO said it started a vaccination program in Afghanistan; 9,000,000 children under 12 will be immunized against measles, which kill some 35,000 Afghan children each year. The campaign will last until end of March.

02 Jan 2002

Zacarias Moussaoui appeared in a court in Virginia where he said: "In the name of Allah I have nothing to plead". The next court trial is scheduled for the 14th October 2002.

An advanced contingent of peacekeeping forces arrived in Afghanistan.

The Americans continued their search for Osama ben Laden amid reports that he and some of his top associates may have escaped to neighboring Pakistan. But now as he had lost his sanctuary in Afghanistan what is the future hold for Osama ben Laden and his Al Qaida organization? In the messages the Al Qaida leaders have managed to send to the outside world a recurrent scheme is what ever the faith of individuals the struggle must go on. That was the message of the video tape broadcast last week by the Arabic TV station al Jazzera in which Osama ben Laden urged Muslims to go on striking at America regardless of his own faith.The same theme is echoed in a book written by Osama ben Laden's Egyptian deputy Ayman al-Zawahri that was smuggled out of Afghanistan in December 2001. "Should the movement face defeat", he wrote, " it must pull out as many of its members as possible to a safe place; those who remained could than confront death in the knowledge that their brothers would live to fight another day." This seems to be what happened last month when Al Qaida fighters in the mountains in Eastern Afghanistan realized they could not hold out for long under a furious American assault. While many remained or were killed or captured it seem likely Osama ben Laden and the hard core of followers managed to escape. The US military thinks he probably slipped across the border into Pakistan and has found refuge with sympathizers".

A secret document was revealed in London after expiry of the 50 years law saying that London intended partition of Afghanistan between Russia and Pakistan under the form of reunification. A senior Taleban leader was killed in an American air raid last week. He is named as Karry Ama Dula-head of intelligence for the Taleban said to have been killed along with 3 associates in a village in Paktika province in eastern Afghanistan. Afghan government officials have backed the continuation of the American air strikes.

The American defense department said a number of Taleban forces in Afghanistan were negotiating with anti-Taleban units for a possible surrender but the Pentagon spokesman Admiral John Stufflebeem said this talks were not on behalf of the Taleban leader Mullah Omar. From Washington the BBC correspondent John Line said: "The Pentagon has been perhaps deliberately obscure about a military operation that was going on in Central Afghanistan; there are increasingly wide spread reports that Mullah Omar has taken refuge near the town of Bagram North-West of Kandahar. He is thought to be guarded by more than a 1,000 supporters. At the same time reports on the ground have seen increased activity by US marines based at Kandahar airport. At first the Pentagon denied they were doing anything; now it says the marines were checking out locations where Al Qaida and Taleban forces had been based. But the US authorities were playing down any suggestion that they have launched a new hunt for Mullah Omar".

03 Jan 2002

The BBC correspondent Richard Myron confirmed the reports of the destruction and the civilian casualties in Niazi Kaleh. Reports from eastern Afghanistan said that some 300 Taleban prisoners were freed as a part of the reconciliation program; western TV pictures showed the prisoners boarding specially chartered busses to take them home. Tribal and village elders who'd come to Kabul to ask for the prisoners' release accompanied them. Some of them were kept prisoners by the anti-Taleban forces for several years. Reports were also made for negotiations with the Taleban to surrender their fugitive leader Mullah Omar if the Americans stop their

95

bombardments in the area; reports from the southern city of Kandahar said they had talks with fighters in the neighboring province of Helmand where Mullah Omar is believed to have sought refuge in the mountains.

BBC correspondent Ian McWilliam reported from Kabul:" Officials in the Southern city of Kandahar say they've been negotiating with Taleban fighters in the Bagram region of neighboring Helmand province. Bagram lies in a poor, remote and mountainous region, which would have difficulties to support large numbers of fighters at the best of times.

It would appear that the extra ordeal of prolonged American bombing has convinced many local people that the presence of the Taleban is no longer worth to trouble. Kandahar officials have also said that some of the Taleban might go free if they hand in their weapons a condition, which might not please the Americans. The Afghan government has previously said that Mullah Omar should be arrested and put on trial; but such surrender deals often take days to finalize and there is no certainty yet that Mullah Omar's faith is settled if he is actually in Bagram". A Pentagon spokesman Rear Admiral Greg Quake said in a BBC interview with Judy Swallow the Pentagon will not stop bombing southeast Afghanistan. No statistic is led on the casualties in this war.

UN said it has credible information that civilians were killed in Niazi Kaleh; among the victims were 50 women and 25 children said the spokeswoman Stephanie Bunkerk. The planned surrender of Mullah Omar may no take place, as the local leader probably is not in position to hand him over.

04 Jan 2002

Reports from Afghanistan say that more than 30 civilians have been killed were killed in American bomb raid in eastern Afghanistan. The Afghan Islamic Press said 32 people have been killed during the raid on villages near the eastern town of Khost. Earlier the Pentagon confirmed that it had resumed air attacks on Afghanistan after a break of several days.

The Head of the US military General Richard Myers said the target in one raid was a military compound in Eastern Afghanistan where Al Qaida fighters have been trying to regroup. The Pentagon has defended itself against criticism of a bombing raid in the same region last week in which the UNO said it has reports that more than 50 civilians including many women and children were killed.

The interim government in Afghanistan signed a document allowing for peacekeeping contingent to enter the country. The document was signed by the interior minister Eunice Qanuni and the British General John McCall who will lead the force. The ISA Force amounts to 4,500 soldiers. The USA intensified its recognizance flights over Somalia, which might be the next target of the US aggression. One US soldier from the Special Forces was killed in Afghanistan in the Khost-Gardez area. This is the first American casualty in this war. The soldier was shot with a small arms fire weapon very precisely. His death comes to underline the danger of underestimating Al Qaida fighters.

05 Jan 2002

The former Taleban Ambassador to Pakistan Abdul Salam Zaif was deported to Afghanistan; there he was intercepted by American forces and imprisoned to the camp near Kandahar where some 270 Taleban prisoners were kept. The Americans gave no further details neither what would happen to him now. Mr. Zaif is the most senior Taleban official to be held by American troops. He became well known in the early days of the US bombing attack on Afghanistan for his televised news conferences in Islamabad becoming the main international outlet for the Taleban point of view. Mr. Zaif's detention came after Pakistan denied him political asylum and deported him to Afghanistan. Later on he was imprisoned on an American ship in the Arab sea. The Pakistani Human Rights Commission protested against his deportation and said he was entitled to receive political asylum in Pakistan.

A senior Taleban leader was arrested in Afghanistan. The man was identified as Evanal Sheikh Alibi, said to have run Al Qaida training camps. Mr. Alibi has been detained in the Southern Afghan city of Kandahar where hundreds of Al Qaida and Taleban captives are under American military control. The new US envoy to Afghanistan Zermay Harrizad told reporters on his arrival in Kabul that the thread posed by supporters of Osama ben Laden meant that the US bombing campaign would continue; he said: "We do not like to bomb, it is with reluctance and with great deal of concern about possible civilian implications and costs but we also understand that the remnants of Al Qaida and the Taleban leaders are dangerous not only for US but also for the Afghans so we'd like to continue with the of war until we achieve our objectives."

But even as US forces continue the hunt for Osama ben Laden and for the former Taleban leader Mullah Omar a small British led force is in the Capital Kabul to back up the government that replaced them. The forces are known as ISAF. Its commander General John McCall has been speaking to the BBC about his plans. BBC correspondent Elizabeth Blunt reported: "The problems facing General McCall's force so far have been more diplomatic than military. He had to sort up his relationship with would-be troops contributors, with the various Afghan groups in Kabul and with the American led coalition forces elsewhere in the country. The faction leaders involved in the interim government have not been used to any constraint on their activities. Some of them are deeply suspicious of any foreign involvement and have succeeded in the limiting the size of the new force. But general McCall was not complaining: "Our mission is focused on Kabul-city and therefore I think we will be able to have a significant patrol presence around the city." So far most of the troops in Kabul are British. This puts Britain in the unusual position of having military personnel taking part in the American offensive elsewhere in Afghanistan at the same time as heading the peace keeping force! And General McCall himself comes under the overall command of General Tommy Franks-the American leading the whole Afghan war !

06 Jan 2002

15 years old Charles Bishop stole a plane and flew it into the Bank of America block in the center of Tampa in Florida. Investigators found a note in his pocket in which he expressed sympathy for Osama ben Laden and the events on 11th September. There was nothing the connect Bishop with any terrorist organization and the hand written note said that he was acting alone.

07 Jan 2002

The British Prime Minister Tony Blair visited Afghanistan at 20:00 GMT 23:00 local time. During his stay at Bagram air base near Kabul he spoke amid tight security with the Afghan leader Hamed Karzai. Tony Blair met also

British troops at the Bagram air base and flew back to London. He is the first Western leader to visit Afghanistan since 23 years.

He said he came to reaffirm the long-term commitment of the international community to Afghanistan. He said that although Afghanistan had been an exporter of terrorism in the past there is now real prospect of progress and stability under the new interim government. He also paid tribute to the British troops who are there as the advanced guard of the international peace keeping force.

American delegation of Senators also arrived in Bagram for talks from the US base in Uzbekistan and flew later on to India.

The USA has begun to send extra military personnel to its base in Guantanamo Bay in Cuba to build a maximum security jail which could hold up to 3,000 Taleban and Al Qaida prisoners from Afghanistan. They are currently some 300 prisoners in US custody in Afghanistan who could be eventually transferred to Cuba. There was no indication when and where they might be put on trial; President Castro of Cuba continues to oppose the existence of the American base in Guantanamo but in recent talks with US officials raised no objections to have been used to house the Afghan prisoners.

American plane raids began over night on suspected Taleban and Al Qaida positions around the Eastern Afghan town of Khost. Reports from the area said some bombs have landed very close to the border with Pakistan. They also suggest that 6 US helicopters landed American troops overnight in the Sawara area near Khost. According to the Pakistan based Afghan Islamic Press the US forces were pursuing fighters loyal to the former Taleban commander in the area Jalalaldin Harkani. The Americans renewed their raids on Eastern Afghanistan on Saturday with attacks South of Jalalabad.

In Singapore several people were arrested on charges of planning to blow up the US Embassy and American owned businesses. The home affairs ministry said raids on the homes and offices of 15 people arrested last month found information on bomb building, photos of targeted buildings and papers related to the Al Qaida network. The authorities said most of those detained belong to a militant group linked to similar organizations in Malaysia and Indonesia.

08 Jan 2002

Reports from Afghanistan said 3 prominent members of the Taleban have given themselves up. A local official in Kandahar said the Taleban Justice minister Mullah Turabi, the defense minister Mullah Abidula and the industry minister Mullah Sadun Ean have surrendered. During his time in power Mullah Turabi was responsible for the strict enforcement of Taleban strict social and religious codes in the Capital Kabul. The new interim Afghan leader Hamed Karzai said war in Afghanistan is over but "the pursuit of terrorist remnants would go on." He told the BBC "West must stay committed to future stability in Afghanistan". If necessary he would ask for the British led international security force to be expanded. A spokesman in Kandahar said the Taleban who had given themselves up would be released under the general amnesty unless they were accused of a specific crime.

Turkey has formally protested to Saudi Arabia over the demolition of an historic Ottoman fortress in the city of Mecca. Turkey has also lodged a complaint at the UN cultural organization UNESCO. The Al Jihad castle was torn down recently to make way for a housing complex and a shopping center catering for pilgrims of the

98

Muslim holy sites. The BBC correspondent in Turkey said feelings in Turkey were running high. The Turkish cultural ministry issued a statement likening the demolition of the fortress to the blowing up by the Taleban of the giant Buddha's statues in Afghanistan.

09 Jan 2002

The interior ministry in Afghanistan said all Afghan military units in the Capital have been ordered to withdraw to barracks outside the city within 3 days. The move is intended to normalize conditions in the city where security will now be the responsibility of an international force. BBC correspondent Richard Myron reported from Kabul: "According to the interior ministry Northern Alliance soldiers will be withdrawn from the city within 3 days. The move is in line with the military technical agreement signed between the government here and the International Security Assistance Force, which states that all Afghan forces will be confined to barracks situated on the edge of the city. They must seek the agreement of the interim administration and notify the multinational force if they move around in large groups. Troops belonging to the multinational force have already begun patrolling and many people here are looking to it as a guarantee against factional fighting which caused wide spread damage and loss of life in Kabul during the 1990s".

The Chief of the American defense staff General Myers required the delivery of all 3 surrendered Taleban ministers for interrogation. At the same time the value of the Afghan currency-the Afghan-has fallen from 25,000 to 33,000 for a Dollar. The head of the Afghan interim administration Hamed Karzai made his first televised speech in which he pledged to restore law and order, freedom of the press, democracy and free market economy, to improve the domestic production, control of the inflation and the creation of new national army.

An American military aircraft with 7 marines on board crashed in Pakistan. The US Central Command said KC-130 refueling plane crashed as it was coming into land at a base near Shamsi in the west of the country; the aircraft burst into flames. There is no word on casualties or what caused the crash. The US Defence Department said the KC-130 tanker aircraft was coming into land at the Shamsi air base when it hit a hill top and burst into flames. There were 7 crewmembers on board but the Pentagon has not yet disclosed whether any of them survived. Pakistani and US military vehicles raced to the scene and eyewitnesses said the area around the crash site was on fire. It's thought that the plane came down in an unpopulated area though. The Pentagon said it would not give any further details until relatives of those on board had been informed on the incident.

10 Jan 2002

American warplanes launched an attack on the cave complex Jalala Khali in the Khost area where Taleban and Al Qaida fighters are suspected to be regrouping. No word of casualties was said. The Defence Department confirmed the death of all 7 marines involved in the plane crash yesterday. No reason for the crash was given.

President Bush accused Iran of harboring defeated Taleban and Al Qaida fighters after they managed to escape to Iran; Iran harbored them to destabilize the interim government in Afghanistan and weaken the American influence.

Bush said Iran must join the campaign again terrorism and hand in all Al Qaida members. Iran rejected the accusations and said its borders are firmly sealed against any Al Qaida intruders. Iran said also that Washington was pursuing a special regional agenda under the cover of the fight against terrorism. At the same time President Bush admitted the war against Afghanistan had generated $24,000,000,000-budget deficit that must be covered by the taxpayers.

A batch of 20 Al Qaida and Taleban prisoners held in American US marine base near Kandahar has been flown to a detention center at Guantanamo naval base in Cuba. The prisoners were put on board of US military cargo plane under extremely tight security. They were hooded, shackled and chained to their seats during the 20-hour flight. There were reports of shooting near the runway when the plane took off but it is unclear where the gunfire came from. More prisoners' air lifts are expected over the next few days; there were over 350 Al Qaida and Taleban fighters held in Kandahar most of whom have been turned over by Afghan forces. The International Committee of the Red Cross said it regards them as prisoners of war. It said the men have all the rights and privileges of the PoWs under the Geneva Convention while American officials described them as detainees. They say they will be held in Guantanamo for interrogation and some of them could be put eventually on trial. It's reported they had their beards shaved for reasons of hygiene prior to the 24-hour journey-a measure the Red Cross said might constitute a breach of their human dignity under the Geneva Convention. The Red Cross plans to visit Guantanamo early next week and to inspect the conditions of the prisoners as it did in Afghanistan. The delegation includes medical doctors and officials who speak Arabic and other local languages.

12 Jan 2002

The interim government in Afghanistan said it would maintain 1,500 troops in the Capital Kabul despite the agreement to remove all soldiers belonging to Afghan militia groups from the city by today. The administration said most of the 10,000 fighters who entered Kabul after the defeat of the Taleban in November would be redeployed to provinces in the south, west and east to the city. thousands of troops have been in Kabul since the fall of the Taleban, most of them belonging to one faction of the Northern Alliance. Commanders have taken over houses and make shift barracks and the upsurge in violent crime has been widely blamed on the presence of so many armed men. However a spokesman for the defense ministry said the men have been now evicted from 70% of the houses, which they've taken over. He said only ministers and about 10 senior commanders would be allowed armed bodyguards all of whom would have to carry permits.

Other commanders entering Kabul would have to leave weapons at the city's limits.

13 Jan 2002

The Australian Broadcasting Corporation ABC has shown a 6 hours video showing Al Qaida fighters training in their training camp. The fighters were shouting commands in English obviously training for kidnapping and hostage taking at a golf tournament. Northern Alliance forces provided the videotape.

Many people in Afghanistan were celebrating the return of heavy rains bringing relief from the severe drought. A government's spokesman said Afghans could now try to revive what is left from their agriculture after years of war and drought. Senior US Senator on a visit to Afghanistan has called on the West to release about $100,000,000 of frozen Taleban funds to allow the interim administration in Kabul to function. Joseph Bidon-the head of the

Senate Foreign Relations Committee said the Afghan authorities needed money to pay staff and buy essential materials in days not weeks or months. The Afghan planning minister said Afghanistan's finances currently stood at zero.

Another 30 Taleban and Al Qaida prisoners have left Afghanistan on a military transport air craft bound to US naval base at Guantanamo Bay in Cuba. They'll join 20 detainees who arrived at the high security facility on Friday. As before each prisoner was shackled and flanked by 2 US soldiers. About 400 prisoners were waiting transfer from Kandahar in Afghanistan to the base in Cuba and more are been rounded up. The US has refused to treat them as prisoners of war.

4 Jan 2002

American planes continued bombing places in Eastern Afghanistan where suspected Al Qaida members were sheltering.

Powerful blasts rattled windows up to 35km from the target and over the nearby border in Pakistan. Witnesses said a number of cave mouths and buildings have been destroyed. Others spoke of people fleeing their villages and said a number of civilians have been killed. US ground troops were also involved in operations in the area. The US is sending 650 soldiers to the Southern Philippines. The Philippines are former US colony.

The UN said the interim government in Afghanistan needed immediate injection of money to save it from bankruptcy. The spokesman of the UN political mission in Afghanistan Ahmed Fowsy said the government needs several million Dollars immediately and a hundred million Dollars in the next few days. He said almost a quarter of civil servants haven't been paid for six months.

5 Jan 2002

A group of bereaved Americans who lost relatives in the September attacks on New York and Washington have gone to Afghanistan to meet the families of civilians killed by American bombing. The Americans are taking message of reconciliation with them on their visit, which has been organized by a human rights organization called "Global Exchange".

Among the American group are a music professor who composed a piano piece in memory of his daughter killed on one of the hijacked planes and a sister of a man who died in the World Trade Center where he stayed to help a friend. Their first meeting will be with a family in Kabul whose 5-year-old daughter has been killed in American air raid.

US officials said American planes were seeking new targets in Afghanistan in their hunt for members of Al Qaida network and remnants the Taleban. The officials did not specify exactly where their planes will be operating. The Pentagon said the change of focus followed the completion of several days of air strikes in the Zawa-Killi area of eastern Afghanistan, which has sealed a complex of caves and flattened about 60 buildings.

16 Jan 2002

The UN High Commissioner for Human Rights Merry Robinson accused the US of mistreating the Taleban prisoners, beating them, housing them in roofless buildings, hooding, shackling, intoxicating them etc. The US

101

refused to acknowledge them prisoners of war. The Pentagon called them unlawful combatants. Amnesty International said holding them in cages with the flow size of 2 double beds is far below the minimum standards for humane treatment. The US said the detainees were treated in a humane way. The Pentagon described them as unlawful combatants, which it said means they did not need to receive the full protections accorded to prisoners of war under the Geneva Convention. At the same time a new group of Al Qaida prisoners arrived at Guantanamo bringing the total to 86.

The interim government in Afghanistan banned the production of opium. The ban covered the trafficking of opium and all opium derivatives including heroin. Since the fall of the Taleban farmers in the main opium growing areas have already been growing opium seeds for the next year's crop. The decree renewed an order issued by the Taleban authorities in 2,000 when Afghanistan was the world's major producer of opium. That Taleban ban was strictly enforced with opium production virtually eradicated in areas under Taleban control.

17 Jan 2002

The American Secretary of State Colin Powell visits Afghanistan for few hours and pledged long-term commitment for it. He also promised big money help for Afghanistan and than flew to India as he did not dare to stay longer in Afghanistan. This is the first visit of American Secretary of State to Afghanistan for 25 years; he had spoken for the long-term commitment of his country there. Speaking after talks with the interim Afghan leader Hamed Karzai Colin Powell said the US would support the country in its current crisis and in the future.

Hamed Karzai praised Colin Powell for taking the risk to come to Kabul. Inevitably his brief visit was surrounded by most intense security. After their talks in the Presidential Palace Colin Powell stressed American commitment to Afghanistan's reconstruction as well as to the pursuit of Al Qaida and Taleban fugitives. But he would not put a figure on the funds he'll pledge on next week's Afghanistan donor conference in Tokyo. The interim government in Afghanistan has put a new figure on its own assessment of the cost of rebuilding the country over the next 10 years $30,000,000,000.

The International Committee of the Red Cross has been giving more details about its planned visit to the American military base at Guantanamo Bay in Cuba to inspect the conditions under which Taleban and Al Qaida prisoners were held. A spokesman in Geneva told the BBC that the 4 Red Cross delegates including a doctor would fly in from Florida around mid-afternoon local time (today) and probably get access to the prisoners tomorrow. A spokesman said the ICRC would make a confidential report on whether the conditions of detention were in accordance with the Geneva conventions. Presently the prisoners are kept in cages 6x8 feet each but receive 3 meals a day. If they are recognized as prisoners of war they have to tell only their names and their ranks but they will NOT be interrogated. By contrast Washington want to interrogate them and put them on trial subsequently- something which the Geneva Convention does not allow. Geneva conventions say that each soldier imprisoned during a war is a prisoner of war. American officials however argue these are illegal combatants, as they wear no uniforms.

18 Jan 2002

Islam bin Laden-the Brother of Osama ben Laden-who is living in Geneva was allowed to issue the trademark "Bin Laden" imprinted as a logo on jeans clothes in Arabic language. As for Osama ben Laden the Pakistani President General Pervez Musharraf said in an interview that he might be dead. He came to this conclusion as Osama ben Laden suffered kidney problems but was unable to have access to dialysis equipment. If he is not dead yet he might be hiding in Afghanistan or in Pakistan, General Musharraf said. Speculations about his kidney problems circulate since some time in the media.

The Senior Commissioner of the EU Xavier Solana criticized bitterly the conditions under which the Al Qaida fighters are held in the US military base at Guantanamo in Cuba and said they must be treated as prisoners of war. The Americans denied they are prisoners of war and insisted they must be treated NOT as illegal combatants and so deprived from their human rights. Pictures emerged about the conditions under which the Al Qaida prisoners were held at the American military base Guantanamo in Cuba. The pictures published by newspapers around the world show the prisoners in conditions of sensory deprivation, forced to wear goggles, ear masks and heavy gloves. They were housed in cages 6x6 feet open to the elements and were hooded and shackled. The human rights group Amnesty International said it was shocked by the photographs describing them as reminiscent of torture methods used in Eastern Europe in the 1970s. The US has repeatedly denied mistreating the prisoners and the BBC correspondent who visited the base said the prisoners were not kept under these conditions all the time; officials from the International Red Cross are being continuing to interview the prisoners later today one by one.

One of the most prominent Anglican clergymen in Britain said the war in Afghanistan was morally questionable. Dr. Williams is seen as a leading contender to become the next Archbishop of Canterbury he spiritual head of the Anglican Church. In his new book he accused Western leaders of failing to define the exact cause of the war and the use of antipersonnel weapons tainted the whole war. He also voiced unease about the treat of Al Qaida prisoners at the American base Guantanamo in Cuba.

An American military helicopter has crash-landed in a mountainous terrain about 60km from the Bagram military air base north of Kabul. There were 7 US marines on board. According to American officials 2 marines were killed and 5 others injured in the crash. Officials haven't yet given any details as to the likely cause of the accident but the spokesman for the US marines said there was no indication that the helicopter had come under hostile fire. The worst single casualty toll for the US war in Afghanistan occurred nearly 2 weeks earlier when all 7 marines aboard a refueling tanker were killed near Shamsi air base in south-western Pakistan.

22 Jan 2002

A US human right organization has brought to a court in Los Angeles the conditions in which Al Qaida prisoners were held at Guantanamo base in Cuba. It said the conditions under which the prisoners were held are in breach with international conventions and with the American constitution. The defense Secretary Donald Rumsfeld insisted again the Al Qaida fighters are not prisoners of war but illegal combatants. As prisoners of war they must not be interrogated but only have to say their names and ranks.

The UN special envoy Francesc Vendrell said some 30,000 international peace keeping forces are needed for Afghanistan. Speaking to the BBC to Islamabad Francesc Vendrell said problems existed across the whole of

Afghanistan. He said what was needed is the deployment of international security force in urban areas outside Kabul possibly involving 30,000 troops. Mr. Vendrell denied that Afghans would see the troops as occupiers. He said the Afghans he talked to wanted to see an end to the rule of Afghanistan's warlords. The interim government of Afghanistan said it would start the creation of new national army, which will comprise 200,000 men. Also from today the interim government started to pay salaries to governmental officials.

Chapter 7

USA (PART7)

23 Jan 2002

The US suspended the transfer of Al Qaida prisoners to the US military base at Guantanamo in Cuba among growing international concern and criticism at the prison conditions there. The US planes to delay the transfer for some 45-60 days during which time it will improve the conditions for prisoners there. The trial for the young American John Walker Lint who converted to Islam and fought for the Taleban is scheduled for tomorrow in Alexandria, Virginia. If convicted he might face life imprisonment.

25 Jan 2002

American officials said their forces have clashed with suspected Al Qaida fighters in Afghanistan killing up to 15 of them. An American soldier have been wounded during an American raid on compound thought to be holding leaders of Al Qaida and its former Taleban allies. American officials said 27 Al Qaida fighters were captured during the raid north of the city of Kandahar. The Commander of the American war in Afghanistan General Tommy Francs who is on a visit to Central Asia republics repeated that American forces would remain focused on hunting down Taleban and Al Qaida fighters. "We'll root them out until we have the very last one", he said.

There have been UN calls for a larger scale expansion of the British lead international security force in Afghanistan to help stop the country sliding into further conflict. The UN deputy special representative Francesc Vendrell said in Kabul that a large security force was also essential to keep on pursuing supporters of Osama ben Laden's Al Qaida network. He said the crucial issue was deploying enough troops beyond he Capital because of the fragile situation in much of Afghanistan. And he suggested an expansion from the present 5,000 to as many as 30,000. The UN secretary general Kofi Annan who is due to visit the country on 25 Jan 2002 said he was encouraged by the show of international support.

26 Jan 2002

The UN Secretary General Kofi Annan who is in Teheran has praised Iranian leaders for supporting UN efforts to achieve in Afghanistan. Mr. Anan was speaking after talks with President Mohamed Khatami and the foreign minister Kamal Kharrazi. The Secretary General said he thanked to Iranians for "their great support for the Afghan people, their general pledges of financial contributions for reconstruction and their backing for UN peace process in Afghanistan." Kofi Annan's friendly and appreciative tone stood in stark contrast to recent accusations

105

by American officials that Iran is being stirring up trouble across its eastern border giving arms and money to dissident tribal leaders and allowing Al Qaida fugitives to slip across the border. The Iranian foreign minister Mr. Kharrazi said Iran had been giving arms to the Mujahedeen groups when they were fighting the Taleban but ALL arm supplies have been NOW halted.

The General in charge of American military operations in Afghanistan said the US is broadening the net of intelligence gathering there. He said the US is still keen to track down the head of the Al Qaida network Osama ben Laden and the Taleban leader Mullah Mohamed Omar and US forces are following every lead they've got. But he emphasized that finding the two fugitives was NOT the only priority. Even more important was gaining information that could help prevent further attacks like those of 11ᵗʰ September.

The only lion in the Kabul Zoo has died of liver and kidney problems after he had lost an eye to a grenade. He died half-blind, lame and toothless, said the BBC quoting animal rights organizations.

27 Jan 2002

15 civilians had died in an American raid at Hazar Kadan near Kandahar, said Hamed Karzai when he visited Washington. His talks with President Bush are mainly focused on how to limit civilian casualties in the US raids in south Afghanistan. The 15 were sent out to negotiate the surrender of the Taleban when the planes came and bombarded them. The US defense Secretary Donald Rumsfeld visit the prison in Guantanamo where the Al Qaida prisoners are kept and found the conditions there splendid. Colin Powell contradicted to him saying they must be considered as prisoners of war and not as illegal combatants, which is their present status.

The interim leader of Afghanistan Hamed Karzai is beginning a visit to the US with the future of the American campaign in Afghanistan likely to be the main focus. His trip comes amid reports that an American bombing raid has killed 15 civilians. The BBC correspondent in Kabul Mike Dunking sent the details: "What really happened when US Special Forces targeted Taleban compounds at Hazar Kadan north of Kandahar is now hotly disputed. The US insists its bombing raid 3 days ago killed 15 Al Qaida fighters but village elders said the 15 had been sent to the compound by a pro-government official to negotiate the surrender of weapons from Taleban hideouts. The controversy will cloud what other-wise would had been a very warm meeting in Washington between Hamed Karzai and President Bush. The White House has been impressed with and surprised by how the interim government has wielded now its first month.

The US defense Secretary Donald Rumsfeld was visiting later today the detention camp for suspected Al Qaida and Taleban prisoners at the American base of Guantanamo Bay in Cuba. The conditions under which the prisoners are held have come under international criticism but Donald Rumsfeld said they have been treated "humanely". The American Secretary of State Colin Powell argued they should be given the status of prisoners of war and not of unlawful combatants.

28 Jan 2002

President Bush finally accepted Hamed Karzai in the White House after he let him wait for 2 days. Before the meeting Hamed Karzai raised the old monarchist flag at the Afghan embassy in Washington. After the meeting President Bush was speaking at the White House. He said the US will train police forces and will help the creation of new Afghan army. President Bush said the US was committed to building a lasting partnership with Afghanistan and the major part of that was providing security in order to guarantee that the country remains peaceful. He said that helping rebuild and train its police and army was the better way to do this than peace keeping. But he stressed that the US will continue to provide logistical support to the international force already in the country. He also promised an extra $50,000,000 in credits to help private institutions rebuild Afghanistan. Hamed Karzai thanked President Bush and the American people for helping liberate his country and said that with international help Afghanistan will eventually be strong enough to stop terrorist returning to the country. Speaking at a press conference after the meeting President Bush the Al Qaida prisoners will not be granted the status of prisoners of war and they will be treated further as unlawful combatants.

There has been a day on battle in the southern Afghan city of Kandahar as American and Afghan forces finally moved against a group of Al Qaida fighters who have been barricaded in a wing of the main hospital for more than 2 months. All six of the Al Qaida fighters were killed in the attack and six of the Afghan government soldiers were injured. Afghan anti-Taleban troops began the assault before dawn after American Special Forces had sealed off the surrounding area. Later loud explosions were heard and smoke poured from the building as American soldiers went in to bring the siege to an end. Patients and staff of the hospital were trapped for days as the fighting continued.

Reports from Washington say the US Secretary of State Colin Powell will urge colleagues to reconsider the status of Al Qaida and Taleban prisoners at the American military base Guantanamo in Cuba. American newspaper reports say Colin Powell was arguing that a case-by-case assessment should be made of whether detainees should be declared prisoners of war. This will give them extra legal rights under the Geneva conventions covering for instance the conduct of any interrogations. The US administration has spoken of them as "unlawful combatants".

29 Jan 2002

President Bush said the US would continue to work with the international peace keeping forces in Afghanistan and help train an Afghan police force and Afghan National Army. He was speaking after a meeting with the interim Afghan leader Hamed Karzai at the White House. President Bush said the US was committed to building a lasting partnership with Afghanistan and a major part of that was providing security in order to guaranty that the country remains peaceful. He said that helping rebuild and train its police and army was a better way to do this than peace keeping. But he stressed that the US will continue to provide logistical support to the international force already in the country. He also promised an extra $50,000,000 in credits to help private institutions rebuild Afghanistan. Hamed Karzai thanked President Bush and the American people for helping liberate his country and said that with international help Afghanistan will eventually be strong enough to stop terrorist returning to the country.

Police in Florida said they have arrested the niece of George W. Bush after she tried to obtain a controlled drug from a pharmacy using false prescriptions. Noelle Bush aged 20 was charged and released pending a court appearance. Florida police said that Noelle Bush was attempting to obtain the anti-anxiety drug Xanax. She was arrested outside the pharmacy in the state capital Tallahassee. It's alleged that the woman phoned in the prescription to the pharmacy using the name of a local doctor. The pharmacy became suspicious because no quantity was specified. When it checked with the doctor's practice it was told that the doctor in question was practicing no longer and that the prescription was fake. The pharmacy duly alerted the police. In a statement Noelle's father-the Governor of Florida Jeff Bush-said that he was deeply saddened by the incident. "This is a very serious problem", he said. "Unfortunately substance abuse is an issue confronting many families across our nation".

30 Jan 2002

The interim leader of Afghanistan Hamed Karzai asked the UN to extend the mandate of the international security force. Hamed Karzai said that expanding the role of international peacekeepers beyond the Capital Kabul would signal a continuing commitment to the country's security. As he was speaking at the UN headquarters in New York there were reports from Afghanistan of clashes in the town of Gardez. Rival factions were said to have fired mortars and rockets at each other. The BBC correspondent in Kabul said it appeared to be a dispute over who should be Governor, the man appointed by Hamed Karzai's administration or the man favored by the local community.

31 Jan 2002

Visiting London Hamed Karzai received the cold answer Britain will not extend its contingent of peacekeeping forces in Afghanistan. As Tony Blair put it Britain's possibilities are limited. The same afternoon Hamed Karzai left London and flew to Kabul. At the same time the skirmishes in Gardez continued with some 50 killed on both side. The supporters of Pasha Khan took upper hand over the supporters of Xy Fula. The government troops watched the rocket and mortar battle but did not intervene.

01 Feb 2002

NATO Secretary General Lord Robertson said in the World Economic Forum in New York that USA must prove evidence against each nation that may be subject to American aggression. The Russian Prime Minister Victor Kasyanov said Russia has no such evidence. The French Prime Minister said President Bush's declaration was for domestic market. Madeleine Albright, the former Secretary of State, said President Bush's statement made the world believe the US has lost its mind.

03 Feb 2002

Reports from the eastern Afghan town of Gardez said the interim national government has received little cooperation from the newly appointed governor there who is locked in a bloody dispute with a rival law warlord. Mediators appointed by the new Afghan leader Hamed Karzai are making efforts to resolve the dispute. A delegation appointed by the interim government is to hold more talks tomorrow to try to solve the dispute over who should be governor of the Paktika province. The head of the delegation is the brother of one of the combatants, Pasha Khan Sadran. He was appointed provincial governor by the interim government in Kabul

108

but was rejected by people in the provincial capital of Gardez. Last Wednesday he tried to take the town by force but fighters loyal to the local Shura expelled his man; he responded by rocketing the before being force to withdraw completely. Earlier Pasha Khan said he had not given up his claim to be governor and his men were ready to do battle again. Local people said they would accept anyone but him.

It was a second day of interim fighting also in Mazar-e Sharif in north Afghanistan. No reports of casualties were released.

NATO Secretary General Lord Robertson made an urgent call for the NATO Alliance EU members to significantly improve their military capabilities. Lord Robertson told the Security Conference in Munich that without such improvement EU-forces will be unable to operate alongside the Americans and would loose influence. The BBC defense correspondent said that although the 11th September attacks on America were declared by NATO to be an assault on the alliance as a whole NATO largely has set out the war in Afghanistan.

09 Feb 2002

The former Taleban foreign minister Wakil Ahmad Mutawakel surrendered to the Americans who began interrogating him in breach with the Geneva conventions and their own decisions not to interrogate Taleban. Meanwhile the interim government in Afghanistan released 300 rank and file soldiers to return home paying them small amount of money. Mutawakel by contrast will be tried by American court. The International Red Cross continues to disagree about the faith of the Taleban prisoners arguing that only an international court not the glorious power may trial them.

10 Feb 2002

The Iranian authorities have closed down the offices of the Afghan faction Hezb-e-Islami that is headed by former Mujahedeen commander Gulbuddin Hekmatyar. Gulbuddin Hekmatyar has vowed to fight Western intervention in Afghanistan and to oppose the interim government in Kabul. Iran's action comes after recent accusation from the US that Teheran has been aiding fugitive and Taleban fighters. This action has been seen as a gesture of support for the interim government in Kabul and as conciliatory move towards the Americans. The Iranian authorities have closed down activities by the hard-line Afghan leader. Gulbuddin Hekmatyar has been resident in Teheran for several years. His Hezb-e-Islami had a number of offices around the country especially in towns and cities near the Afghan border. Mr. Hekmatyar himself is said to be still in the country but the Iranian interior minister has said that his expulsion has been considered. Last week the Iranian intelligence minister also accused Mr. Hekmatyar of abusing Iranian hospitality and breaching undertakings given to the government. Iran's policy, he said, was to support the Kabul administration and it was opposed to any activity that might weaken it.

The authorities in Afghanistan said they have detained 2 men they suspect in involvement in the shooting of 4 journalists in November. The interim interior minister Eunice Qanuni said they've seized documents from the two suspects, which link them to the murders. The four journalists-Australian, Afghan and Spanish men and an Italian woman, were ambushed and shot dead in Gorge, about 90km east of Kabul.

The head of the new Afghan Army General Mohamed Fahim arrived in Moscow with large delegation for 5-day talks with the Russian leadership and to buy military hardware for the new Afghan Army. They will discuss also Russian training for the emerging new Afghan army that will replace the local tribal militias in Afghanistan. As Afghans are already familiar with Russian weapons and Russian equipment, they shall discuss their sophistication further.

3 leading US newspapers reported that American military forces in Afghanistan imprisoned, beat and kicked Afghan villagers, which they had misidentified as Al Qaida and Taleban fighters following an American raid on 28 Jan 2002. The Washington Post said several of the 27 villagers who had been held after an assault on a school and a government office in the village of Uruz Gan claimed that they have been so harshly beaten that they lost consciousness during their beatings. 21 other civilians were killed in the raid and 1 US soldier was wounded. In BBC-interview Admiral John Stufflebeem said:" Our first aim is to secure the area and than to interrogate the civilians on the whereabouts of Al Qaida fighters so it is not excluded they have beaten the civilians". 300 Taleban fighters came to the southeastern Bulgarian border and asked for political asylum.

12 Feb 2002

The FBI warned that today is possible a terrorist attack against US targets. The FBI got this information from interrogated Al Qaida prisoners in Guantanamo base and placed the photo of the main suspect-the Yemeni Arabiya -on the FBI website.

13 Mar 2002

Many protesters gathered at the US Embassy in Kabul to protest against the civilian victims of the American war. The Pakistani President General Pervez Musharraf started his visit to Washington.

15 Feb 2002

A riot began and still continues when rioting mob lynched and assassinated the Afghan civil aviation minister Dr. Abdul Rahman. Turkey sent 230 troops to Afghanistan as a part of its future 25,000 contingent.

16 Feb 2002

The funeral of the civil aviation minister Abdul Rahman. Several hundred people attended. There is renewed concern about security in the Afghan Capital Kabul after a government minister was killed and trouble broke out at a football match. The interim government is opening a cabinet-level investigation into the death of the civil aviation minister Abdul Rahman who was beaten to death by disgruntled pilgrims at Kabul airport. The mob also attacked the head of the national airline Ariana who had to be rescued by foreign peacekeeping soldiers. In Kabul itself Afghan police fired shots into the air as thousands of Afghans tried to force their way into a football match between a local site and the international security force. The British foreign secretary Jack Straw is in Kabul would not comment on whether the peacekeeping force should be strengthened. Addressing the funeral the interim Governor Hamed Karzai said: "It is time for Afghans to stop killing each other; it is time for peace and reconciliation".

Members of the international security force in Afghanistan had come under fire for the first time. The British chief of staff of the force said gunmen had opened fire at six paratroopers in an observation post. The soldiers returned the fire but than withdrew to a safer position. Later a dead man and 5 injured people were found in a house near where the accident took place.

"We are the poorest, we are the most illiterate, the most backward, the most un-enlighten and the most unhealthy" said General Pervez Musharraf returning from Washington to Islamabad where he opened an exhibition on science and technology: "Islamic countries must embrace education and science", he added.

18 Feb 2002

Several countries sent airplanes to Kabul airport to help airlift the stranded pilgrims who expected transport to Mecca for the annual pilgrimage Hajj. It comes to show that the Taleban had a better grip and better control on the situation in Afghanistan than the present interim regime. Saudi Arabia sent a Jumbo Jet plane, Pakistan sent an Airbus, the United Arab Emirates UAE sent a plane and the British Royal Air force sent 4 planes to airlift the pilgrims to Mecca.

22 Feb 2002

The American defense Secretary Donald Rumsfeld acknowledged that a raid by US Special Forces in January 2002 on two compounds in Afghanistan did N O T strike Al Qaida or Taleban members as originally insisted. At least 14 civilians were killed in the compounds north of the city of Kandahar. The local Afghan authority said the OPERATION WAS A MISTAKE. In news briefing in Washington Donald Rumsfeld refused to accept this: he said the US special troops have acted in self-defense opening fire after being fired on and this was no mistake. He said the deaths were unfortunate BUT WAR WAS ALWAYS UNTIDY.

24 Feb 2002

The interim leader of Afghanistan Hamed Karzai was visiting Iran for wide ranging talks with senior officials there. The two countries will be examining a plan under which some 2 million Afghan refugees in Iran gradually be repatriated. Iran, which lies on a major drug smuggling route, is also extremely concerned by the upsurge of opium poppy cultivation in Afghanistan since the fall of the Taleban. Mr. Karzai arrived with a delegation of ministers and top officials from at least 10 ministries reflecting the full range of the detailed talks he expects to have with his Iranian counterparts before he leaves after 2 days. Iran is keen to support the Kabul administration by playing a strong role in efforts to reconstruct Afghanistan. Mr. Karzai's visit is warmly welcomed by Iranian newspapers, which support the reformist government headed by President Mohamed Khatami. But some Iranian hardliners regard Mr. Karzai as an American stooge. One of them newspapers said his administration had failed to get a grip on the country and that he had also failed to consolidate his position and to justify the American and British presence in Afghanistan. Later today Hamed Karzai started his first round of talks with the Iranian President Mohamed Khatami. In a press conference Mr. Khatami said his country is going to help Afghanistan and rejected American accusations that Iran was trying to destabilize the country. The Iranian talks are great success of recognition for the interim government that is considered by many as American puppet regime and American stooge. In his turn Hamed Karzai said that the close relations Afghanistan maintains to Washington should not worry Iran.

25 Feb 2002

The interim Afghan leader Hamed Karzai has had a meeting in the Iranian Capital Teheran with the Iran supreme leader, Ayatollah Ali Champing, who said Afghans must pull together and not allow the reconstruction efforts to become a pretext for outsiders to exercise political and cultural influence. The BBC Tehran correspondent said the Ayatollah is generally seen as responsive to Iranian conservatives some of whom are hostile to Hamed Karzai's government but he said the meeting seems to have gone well. Earlier addressing the Iranian Parliament Mr. Karzai said that Afghanistan would never forget Iranian support during its fight against the Soviet Union and against terrorists. He said no word of criticism of Iran harboring Al Qaida refugees and trying to destabilize Afghanistan; instead he spoke of Islamic solidarity.

The Pentagon had closed its strategic unit for information, which was casting favorable light on its war on terrorism. The Unit was established in the end of 2001 to reflect the events after the 11th September attacks. The Unit became known for spreading false stories among foreign journalist.

27 Feb 2002

The US defense Department said that the Al Qaida prisoners at Guantanamo are unlikely to be tried before military tribunals. Such tribunals are already ready to hear the cases but there are no cases yet. Interrogators at Guantanamo Bay have difficulties in building their cases. They are mostly interested in the whereabouts of Osama ben Laden and in preventing future attacks thus not past Al Qaida activities. US authorities arrested 20 employees of Boston international airport Logan in connection with the 11th September attacks. No charges and no reasons were given but there are speculations the arrested used false social security numbers that gave them access to the restricted areas of the airport. Security at Logan international airport has been heavily criticized following the attack on New York on the 11th September.

28 Feb 2002

A hunger strike broke out in the detention center Guantanamo Bay where 300 Al Qaida prisoners are held. The hunger strike broke out when prison guards removed forcibly the haircloth of an Al Qaida prisoner who was advised by prison staff and translators to remove his hair dress because it may contain weapons. He did not follow this "advice" and the hunger strike began. Later on it became clear the hunger strike broke out on 26 Feb 2002 when inmates refused their breakfast. The main reason for the hunger strike was the uncertainty for the future, which the Al Qaida prisoners face. US authorities said they are prepared to feed the prisoners forcibly. 4 days later the Al Qaida prisoners were still refusing to eat despite the "concessions" of the American authorities. US officials said they have refused at least 2 meals on Friday in a protest that began when guards removed a turban from one of the prisoners as he was praying.

112

02 Mar 2002

Heavy fighting has been taking place southeast of The-the Capital of Paktika province in Afghanistan-where the Americans say they think more than 500 Al Qaida fighters are hiding WITH THEIR FAMILIES. A spokesman for a senior local militia commander Kamal Wazir said American aircraft have been bombing the area since Friday night and Al Qaida fighters have been FIRING ROCKETS and heavy weapons. He said 600 Afghan ground forces were also involved in the fighting.

The next day the American intensified their bombing raids attacking Al Qaida positions at the mountains near the city of Gardez for a second day. B-52 bombers dropped 2 powerful bombs intended to destroy caves and underground bunkers, thought to have been used as hiding places. They also dropped other bombs designed to suck off Oxygen from the caves and to suffocate the inmates. Some Afghan officials said the number of the Al Qaida fighters is far higher than the initially thought 500. The American B-52 bombers were in action again over the mountains where is BELIEVED the Al Qaida fighters were hiding. But journalists were not allowed along the road to the remote snow-covered mountains where the operations were taking place. The Governor of Paktika province Tadge Mohamed Wardag said he believed the Al Qaida and THEIR SUPPORTERS would be defeated within the next few days. Other officials put that period as one week. The governor said he believes there are more than 450 Al Qaida fighters who were sheltering in caves. Local officials said there had been another ground offence. On Saturday 3 Americans have been killed by heavy artillery as they tried to advance on Al Qaida positions. Later next day a US helicopter was shot down by Al Qaida from their positions south of Gardez together with a number of soldiers. The US said it was the first helicopter shot down over Afghanistan. Other reports said the helicopters were 2. The BBC correspondent in Kabul Suzanne Price was not sure whether small firearms shot down the helicopters or it was an arm launched "STINGER" missile. The US defense Secretary Donald Rumsfeld warned in a broadcasted speech that the Al Qaida victims were over 200 and they will be more-killed and wounded. He did not say they were given a chance to surrender; nor he did elaborate what will happen with he THE WOUNDED AND THEIR FAMILIES. In its annual report on Human Rights the State Department condemned the Northern Alliance of killing, rape, robbery and looting among other human rights abuses such as persecution and displacement of ethnic Pashtun in northern Afghanistan. In radio broadcasts the Democratic Congressmen Vick Schneider and Denis Crusenic condemned the new raids on Afghanistan: "We must expect further casualties in the future" Vick Schneider said. In a broadcasted interview with the BBC correspondent in Kabul Suzanne Price the BBC moderator tried to blame the weather conditions for the helicopters' misfortune but Suzanne Price said the weather was fine, blue clear skies and the weather conditions were the same for both sides. General Tommy Franks and General Richard Myers by contrast blamed the weather conditions for the downing of the 2 American helicopters. They said 2,000 American, Afghan and Alliance force have surrounded the Al Qaida fighters and they expected them soon to be defeated. No word was spoken on their surrender by both generals; they spoke clearly of defeat. Only 2 days later the Pentagon confirmed that the number of the downed US helicopters was 2 and the US soldiers killed were 7.A US spokesman in Florida said the attack on the mountainous position will continue until the Al Qaida fighters there were killed: "We even expect further American casualties", he said "but this is part of the US strategy which

113

President Bush declared already at the begin of the Afghan war". However all US newspapers and all talk shows spoke clearly in support of the operation and of President Bush, said the BBC correspondent in Washington Michael Buchanan. Till now the American public opinion was in favor of the war because there were no American casualties. Now there is a little decline in the opinion polls but no one speaks of peaceful solution. Most of the Al Qaida fighters encircled are Chechens, Egyptians and South-East Asians who have no place to go if they escape so that they prefer to face the death on their positions. Finally it became clear the number of the deployed US troops 1,000 plus British, French, German and Australian units. The number of the surrounded Al Qaida fighters was already put at 450 fighters.

06 Mar 2002

The US has intensified its bombing raids in eastern Afghanistan attacking Al Qaida positions in the mountains near the city of Gardez for a second day. B-52 bombers dropped 2 powerful bombs intended to destroy caves and underground bunkers, thought to be used as hiding places. The American B-52 bombers were in action over the mountains where it's believed the Al Qaida fighters were hiding. But journalists were not allowed along the road to the remote snow-covered mountains where the operation took place. The Governor of Paktika province Tadge Mohamed Wardag said he believed the Al Qaida and THEIR SUPPORTERS would be defeated within the next few days. The Governor said he thought there were more than 450 Al Qaida fighters who were sheltering in caves. Local officials said there had not been another ground offensive during the day.

On Saturday 02 Mar 2002 3 Americans were killed by heavy artillery as they tried to advance on Al Qaida positions. The Americans were sending troop reinforcements and ground-attacking aircrafts to the mountains of eastern Afghanistan as their attacks on Al Qaida and Taleban positions intensified. A US spokesman said the guerrillas were still putting up stiff resistance despite heavy casualties in the fighting, which is concentrated around caves 3,000m up in the snow-covered mountains south of Gardez. Despite the heaviest bombing of the campaign overnight small groups of Al Qaida guerrillas are said to be darting from caves and bunkers raining heavy fire on American forces before withdrawing back into hideouts. 100 Al Qaida were said to be killed on Wednesday alone, 06 Mar 2002, and more than 400 since the fighting started. The Americans estimate the Al Qaida fighters killed at 450.

07 Mar 2002

2 German and 3 Danish soldiers were killed in Kabul when a rocket exploded in their hands when they tried to defuse it. The Americans did not comment on the incident. There were street protests in Germany against the war in which Germany was involved-they said-illegally; there was no information on what was going on in Afghanistan the protesters said, at least not in German language. There were only 100 German troops in Afghanistan from a 300,000 German Army but they were ill equipped and inexperienced. They took the leadership from the British recently. 34 German soldiers died recently in Kosovo, Bosnia and in Macedonia from shooting, landmines and illnesses, said the chief editor of The Zeit Constanze Stolzenmueller.

10 Mar 2002

Major Brian Hilferty -US military spokesman at Bagram airbase in Afghanistan-said the military operation near Gardes has come to an end after the US troops met no significant resistance in the past 3 days. No Al Qaida fire came from the caves and from the bunkers in the mountains south of Gardez and this allowed 400 American troops to retreat safely to their military base near Bagram. He mentioned with no word neither the Afghan and Al Qaida casualties in this conflict nor how many Al Qaida fighters were captured. The general assumption is that no Al Qaida prisoners were taken in this recent American blood bath. The Bulgarian Foreign Minister Isaac Solomon Pasi visited Washington and assured President Bush of the wholehearted Bulgarian support in the war against terrorism. This was sheer caricature of support because Bulgaria is small country with 7 million population, with huge foreign debts, high unemployment,high criminality, weak, shaky and controversial government: practically it cannot support the USA; for many years Bulgaria is been waiting in vain to be accepted as a NATO member but it has always failed because of its poor economy.

At the same time China, Russia and Iran demanded clarification from Washington for the latest American declaration on readiness to use nuclear weapons on these 3 countries among 4 other. Iraq was also enlisted as a possible target of nuclear war but did not join the declaration of China, Russia and Iran. The American Vice-President Dick Cheyne who was visiting London dismissed the media reports as exaggerated.

12 Mar 2002

The interim Afghan government concentrated massive troops in the mountains south of Gardez for a final push on the encircled Al Qaida fighters in Paktika province. The Afghan troops are backed by US-troops and US-tanks. A US spokesman at the Bagram airbase near Kabul did not spoke of a final push but he said that the Afghan allies are aggressive, highly motivated and determined to exterminate the Al Qaida fighters. American planes continued to bombard the Al Qaida positions; local residents spoke of a major ground offence as also the BBC correspondent Adam Brooks put it. The Afghan troops said they have captured key areas from the Al Qaida fighters. Many caves and bunkers were full of dead bodies of Al Qaida fighters, their wives and their children; some accused the US of Using chemical weapons in breach of Geneva conventions. At dawn the Afghan government troops, which served, as cannon fodder in the recent past days will start to clear up the caves, cave after cave; they have claimed already major victory.

An Al Qaida prisoner managed to contact the journalists outsides of the Guantanamo base in Cuba; he shouted that Al Qaida inmates were on hunger strike for 14 days already but they have received nothing; he claimed shouting in English they have received nothing. He claimed shouting at the journalists outside in English that the prisoners have sent 300 pieces of post according to the Geneva convention but they have received no answer: "We have no human rights and we are in full isolation", he said to the waiting journalist outside of Guantanamo bay in Cuba.

At the same time the interim Afghan leader Hamed Karzai flew to Moscow for two days talks with President Putin. This is the third visit of leading Afghan to Moscow; earlier the Interior Minister and the Defence Minister visit Moscow to reassure Russian support for Afghanistan and reconstruction of the Afghan army and the interior forces. Concretely Hamed Karzai wants the Russians to renovate the destroyed Afghan factories: there are some

170 plants built by the Soviets in the 1960s and 1970s. Hamed Karzai wants them renovated by the Russians. At the same time he is viewed as a pro-Western leader in the interim Afghan government not as a pro-Russian. Both sides signed altogether 17 contracts for rebuilding the country by the Russians. President Putin said his only aim is to see independent, prosperous and friendly Afghanistan.

13 Mar 2002

The US Vice President Dick Cheyne threatened again Iraq with the use of nuclear weapons during his visit to Jordan and Egypt. He said the US will retaliate with nuclear weapons if Iraq does use chemical or biological weapons.

Chapter 8

AL QAIDA

5 months after the start of the US war in Afghanistan Al Qaida showed it could still wreak havoc. US defense Secretary Donald Rumsfeld admitted on 06 Mar 2002 Al Qaida was still putting a strong fight: "As I've said repeatedly the task is FAR FROM OVER; not all Al Qaida and Taleban forces have been defeated. Substantial pockets of resistance remain, they are determined, they are dangerous, they would not give up without a fight, they are hiding in villages and in the mountains and just across the borders in a number of directions in Afghanistan and they are waiting for their opportunity." This will disappoint any American who will hope that six months after the 11th September the Al Qaida threat was eliminated. But Washington never promised a swift result. Speaking in October 2001 President Bush made it clear the war against terror may last a long time: "People often asked me how long this will last. This particular battle front will last as long as it takes to bring Al Qaida to justice; it may happen tomorrow, it may happen a month from now, it may take a year too but we will prevail and what the American people need to know as our allies know-I am determined to steer the curse." And despite the last week's set back the US does believe it will succeed in severely undermining Al Qaida ability to operate both inside Afghanistan and elsewhere. Edward Olden, a journalist with the "Financial Times" newspaper has been following the story from Washington: "What they have discovered from the documents, from the computer hard drives, from interrogations in Afghanistan is that there was a massive drive. What they say is a result of the invasion into Afghanistan, we have Al Qaida on the run. They don't have a place where they can assemble, coordinate their operations, communicate with each other and that has been very disruptive to the Al Qaida. "thousands of Al Qaida members are believed to have fled Afghanistan long before the Americans arrived expecting a response to the 11th September. And even before that many Al Qaida operatives were based outside of Afghanistan-in some 60 countries. Tackling such a scattered organization posed a huge challenge. But Dr. Magnus Ranstorp, an expert on terrorism at St.Andrew's University believes the counter terrorism efforts of the last 6 months have had considerable success:" There has been a tremendous number of arrests in the USA certainly foiled some planned further terrorist attacks in the US, so they have disturbed their activities. Of course in Europe there has been a tremendous law-enforcement success actually foiling a whole range of terrorist activities but the difficulty is that these organizations mutate and can be replenished". The roots of Al Qaida date back to the 1980s when guerrilla fighters went to Afghanistan to wage "a holly struggle against the Soviet occupation" They received religious and military education there; than often went elsewhere to fight other wars. It was around 1987 when intelligence sources said that Osama ben Laden formed the Al Qaida movement bringing Muslim warriors together with the mission to kill Americans and their allies. But the Al Qaida structure was deliberately kept non-hierarchical, said Magnus Ransdorp; 'There have been so many diverse groups and therefore they have such a loose

structure and it was obviously held by new means of communication - not only by satellite phones but also by Internet, which means that one could link up in order to maintain its capability to mutate should one pressure some parts of the organization." While Al Qaida diffused groups drew their inspiration and financial support from Osama ben Laden they often carried out their operations independently. So even with its radical Afghan heartland in tatters the different parts of the organization could still continue to operate. Abdul Barry Aquan is editor of the London based Palestinian newspaper, who wants to meet and interview Osama ben Laden. He said the Al Qaida leader always expected an early death and even this would happened his organization would not be weakened: "Al Qaida is not really a one-man show; definitely it is more than that because it is based on many strong bases and the strongest of them is the Islamic faith-radical interpretation of Islamic Jihad. Second thing is its hatred towards the US and its policies. So if Osama ben Laden is killed or captured Al Qaida will not finish". It is not known whether Al Qaida plans to regroup in a particular place though some recent reports suggest that Pakistan would be the favored new home. And although Pakistan had joined the US war against terror there are certainly areas in the country which are extremely difficult to police. The same goes for other places it is thought Al Qaida cells may try to operate from-Somalia, Kashmir, Chechnya. This explains in part why the US had chosen an ally-the Philippines-to make its second military stand against terrorism. Philippine journalist Marites Vito has written a book on the Muslim insurgency in the South of the Philippines:" I tend to believe what some of the Americans are saying that the US needs A QUICK VICTORY AFTER AFGHANISTAN. And where else to go but the Philippines which is an ally and one of the first in South-East Asia to support President Bush in his anti-terror campaign". American assistance has been provided in the Philippines to combat the small but fierce Abu Sayyaf guerrilla groups there. But Vito is skeptical whether it has anything to do with America's war against Al Qaida :" The evidence have been so far indirect; the main evidence is that the brother-in-law of Osama ben Laden, Sheikh Said, is to have international Islamic relief and research organization in the Philippines and he diverted part of the funds to the Abu-Sayyaf. However for the Abu-Sayyaf is very difficult to determine how many of them trained in Afghanistan and this was since the 1990s but there has been no report on it". Marites Vito pointed out that there were a handful of arrests recently of Muslim Philippines purporting to be members of two groups-a Philippine Radical Islamic Group and a South-East Asian Group known as Jemaah Islamiyah which some say has links with Al Qaida . This was the group said recently to be behind an alleged plot to blow up embassies in Singapore, Indonesia and Malaysia. But many of those who have studied the problem say it is immaterial whether any group claims links with Al Qaida or not; it's their conviction that counts. Jean-Louise Bougiere is a French judge who has been investigating Islamic radical activities for a decade: "Even if Al Qaida is not operative at all the threat does not decrease: Al Qaida is one part of the threat. But there are a lot of cells which are not connected to the Al Qaida ". And newspaper Editor Abdul Barriath agrees there will always be Islamic radical groups willing to sacrifice their lives attacking American and Western targets unless a preventative campaign of a different kind is launched: The campaign he envisions is one of hearts and minds rather than bombs and arrests: "The Americans actually refused to listen to many people who were trying to tell them to look at their unjustified foreign policies, they have to understand the grievances of the Muslim world, they have to look at the Arab-Israeli conflict which is the source of all terrorism in the whole world-not only in the Middle East; but the Americans are not listening to-they are Using B-52s and they believe by B-52, by Tomahawk missiles, by F-16 they can put an end to the terrorism". So far there has been little evidence the US is thinking of changing their strategy. Journalist Edward Olden says

118

Washington has not heard suggestions it should try reach Muslims who feel aggrieved by American policies: "I don't know weather it was ever taken seriously: the Vice-President Dick Cheney was giving a speech at Council for foreign relations in February and he was asked repeatedly about this: "Do you see any need to redress the economic-underline the economic-causes of this sort of hatred" but he deflected all these questions; he was asked for instance what is the crucial need in Afghanistan - a lot of people said Afghanistan needed a massive aid to reconstruct its infrastructure, its water system, its agriculture and Dick Cheney

Chapter 9

ANTHRAX

10 Oct 2001

US-Embassies round the world started to pile up antibiotics in case of anthrax-attack.

11 Oct 2001

Anthrax-letters in Germany.

14 Oct 2001

Many new anthrax cases.

15 Oct 2001

Democrat Senator Tom Daschle received an anthrax letter.

17 Oct 2001

Both Houses of Senate closed because of anthrax.

Anthrax found in the house of the Governor. of New York George Pataki.

USA and Britain closed their embassies in Sarajevo, Banja Luka and Mostar.

18 Oct 2001

Anthrax in Kenya from a letter posted in USA on 08 Sept 2001.

19 Oct 2001

Anthrax panic in India; Taleban denied any link to the anthrax.

20 Oct 2001

Canadian Government decided to by-pass Bayer pharmaceutical antibiotic "Cipro" designed to combat anthrax.

22 Oct 2001

New anthrax cases in USA: a postal worker in Washington-Brentwood contracted the disease after 2 further postal workers had already expired from anthrax; a special anthrax-website was established: www.uspost.gov

23 Oct 2001

Anti-anthrax measures taken in Washington including irradiation of the postal envelopes with low-level radiation machines. The purchase of the machines, which will bombard the mail with radiation, will cost $1,000,000,000.

26 Oct 2001

New anthrax cases were reported in the USA.

Anthrax was also found in the mailroom of the US Supreme Court in Washington, the CIA and the military medical research center in Maryland.

25 Oct 2001

3 new cases of anthrax were registered in the USA-between the contracted was a NBC journalist.

29 Oct 2001

Anthrax found in the Justice Department of the USA, which remained closed. In New Jersey a female post worker had been diagnosed with the most deadly form of inhalation anthrax. The specialists say that one person that had lived in the US for a while has written the last 3 letters. The specialists think it is a case of one local extremist. Till now anthrax was found in 3 buildings: the US Justice Department, the US Supreme Court and the Cohen building which houses several agencies.

30 Oct 2001

In New York a hospital worker is critically ill with inhalation anthrax; it is the 2nd time FBI is warning Americans that further terrorist attacks could be eminent, although there is no specific information on how or where they might happen.

The new alert came as new cases of anthrax were reported in New Jersey and New York. The latest came in Manhattan, where a 61 years old hospital worker tested positively for inhalation anthrax; it is the most serious form of the disease and the first case in New York.

31 Oct 2001

A 61 years old Vietnamese hospital worker Kathy Nguyen died from inhalatory anthrax-the most deadly form of the disease. She was checked in Manhattans Lennox Hill hospital.

No anthrax letter and no anthrax spores were found at her workplace so that her social life needs to be reconstructed.

01 Oct 2001

Anthrax found in the post room of the American Embassy in Lithuania. It is the first case anthrax is found Europe. The anthrax has been carried in by a diplomatic bag, the deputy director of Lithuanian Institute for Epidemic disease said. The mailroom of the Embassy had been sealed off for further investigation. Professor Rainhard Kurtz-Director of Robert Koch Institute in Berlin was called for assessment.

02 Nov 2001

New cases of possible anthrax spores sent in by post had been reported from Pakistan and Germany. A popular Pakistani newspaper said it received a letter last week (!) containing white powder, which tested positive for anthrax. The Pakistani government said there have also been other suspected cases and ordered full investigation. Meanwhile the German authorities said initial tests had found anthrax spores in a letter in the eastern state of Thueringia and more examinations had been carried out.

In Europe are 2 cases of suspected anthrax surface in Germany. Initial tests had shown positive signs of anthrax bacteria in a letter delivered to an unemployment office in the eastern state of Thuringia. The letter has been now flown to Berlin for further analyses. The 2nd case emerged in the Northern state of Schleswig-Holstein and is still under investigation, reported BBC Berlin correspondent Rob Brumby. The suspect package was received in the unemployment office of the East-German town of Rudolstadt. The letter had a German postmark but an Arabic name on the cover and Pakistani return address. The Health Ministry in the state of Thuringia said that 2 separate tests on the suspect package had proved positive for signs of the anthrax bacteria. The Health Ministry spokesman Thomas Schulz said on the base of their experts' advice there is now serious suspicion on anthrax.

He said there is no danger to the population or to other workers because the package had not been opened. It had been passed instantly to the laboratories of the city of Jena for tests. 3 people tested for anthrax in the office receiving the package were found to be clean. The letter was flown to Berlin for further analyses on the Robert Koch Institute and the final results are expected in the course of the evening. Chancellor Gerhard Schroeder was informed on the cases by on-board telephone during his flight back from China. If confirmed this will be the first case in Germany only the second in Europe as a whole. In the last few weeks a hundreds of suspicious letters had been tested for anthrax in the country all had proved to be hoaxes.

05 Nov 2001

The Pentagon said cases of anthrax have been found in the post office of the building-the first report of anthrax in the headquarters of the US military. A defense department spokesman said that area was decontaminating during the weekend (very fresh piece of news) and further cases all proved negative. He said the anthrax spores were found in 2 post-office boxes, one that was not in use and the other-rented by a Navy service member. In the past month 4 people had died of anthrax in the USA and 17 others have been infected.

06 Nov 2001

American official said that anthrax has been found in letters sent to US consulates in Pakistan and Russia. They said that white powder contained in the letter sent to the Pakistani city of Lahore has tested positive for anthrax. These are the latest of series of anthrax discoveries made in mail and buildings belonging to the US state department in Washington and oversees. All are described as negligible amounts of anthrax were found in a diplomatic bag and from Washington to the consulate in Yekaterinburg. Another envelope containing suspicious white powder has been found in Lahore.

Preliminary tests on the powder have proved positive and samples had been sent to the US for further investigations. If the Pakistani envelope does contain anthrax that will be a new development as the suspect package has been mailed within the country.

09 Nov 2001

4 further people contracted anthrax in New Jersey. The FBI issued a scientific profile of the suspect who is said to be a man. President. Bush increased spending by 25% for more protection on airports against anthrax.

22 Nov 2001

A 5th victim of inhalation anthrax died in the US.

05-12-2001

The man who was sending false anthrax letters to abortion clinics was arrested. His name is Clayton Lee Wagner. He escaped from prison in February and was wanted by the FBI for a series of bank robberies, car thefts, firearms and violence.

13-12-2001

A case of inhalation anthrax was confirmed in the US Embassy in the Austrian Capital Vienna.

Chapter 10

AFGHAN DATES

09 Sept 2001 Assassination of the Chief of the Northern Alliance Ahmed Shah Masood by 2 suicide fighters of Osama ben Laden posing as Arabic journalists

11 Sept 2001 suicide plane attacks on the World Trade Center in New York and on the Pentagon in Washington

18 Sept 2001 The head of the anti-Taleban Northern Alliance in Afghanistan offered to help the USA to trace down and arrest Osama ben Laden.

21 Sept 2001 Colin Powell said in BBC-interview that he does not know for sure where is Osama ben Laden but he assumes he is in Afghanistan.

23 Sept 2001 Arab countries' foreign ministers meeting in Jeddah to discuss how much to cooperate with the USA.

24 Sept 2001 President Bush froze all financial assets of Osama ben Laden. Mullah Omar urged Washington to withdraw all troops from the Middle East and stop its support for Israel in the combat against terrorism or to face all-out war

24 Sept 2001 Iranian President Khatami denounced sharply US-policy and demanded the closure of the Mudjahedeen-Office in Washington.

25 Sept 2001 Saudi Arabia broke diplomatic relations with the Taleban

26 Sept 2001 US Embassy in Kabul set afire. NATO Secretary General George Robertson gave false evidences against Osama ben Laden in Brussels. He could not say if they have intercepted a phone call with Osama ben Laden giving instructions to destroy the World Trade Center neither he was able to produce any voice record of recent conversations of Osama ben Laden with his Mother and his friends.

27 Sept 2001 The Taleban asked Osama ben Laden to leave Afghanistan; Italian Prime Minister Silvio Berlusconi spoke of the superiority of Western nations.

28 Sept 2001 Pakistani Delegation in Afghanistan tried to persuade the Taleban to hand over Osama ben Laden to the Americans

01 Oct 2001 Talks in Rome between the Northern Alliance, special US-Senate delegation and the former King of Afghanistan Zahir Shah.

03 Oct 2001 USA asked formally NATO for support logistical and military. Russian President Vladimir Putin in Rom for talks with Silvio Berlusconi

07 Oct 2001 Taleban said they might arrest Osama ben Laden and put him on trial; the same day USA started the war against Afghanistan by US air strikes

07 Oct 2001 Begin of the US-air strikes on Afghanistan to revenge the suicide plane attacks on the World Trade Center in New York and on the Pentagon in Washington

11 Oct 2001 Assassination of the 10 years old son of the supreme Taleban leader Mullah Mohamed Omar by American air raids at Kandahar

11 Oct 2001 The Northern Alliance took the northern town of Chah Charahn while Americans bombarded civilian objects and hit a mosque in Jalalabad. US used bunker-buster bombs that penetrate deep underground and destroy bunkers and facilities.

14 Oct 2001 Taleban senior leader Mullah Osama Kabir offered to surrender Osama ben Laden to a neutral country but President Bush refused any negotiations with Kabul.

18 Oct 2001 Tony Blair in Turkey for talks. Concretely he wants Turkish troops to occupy Afghanistan . Turkey rejected his proposal.

19 Oct 2001 US-ground troops entered South Afghanistan. Taleban denied this report

19 Oct 2001 first deployment of US ground troops in Afghanistan

23 Oct 2001 the Saudi Defence minister Prince Sultan spoke for piece in the Afghan conflict

25 Oct 2001 Donald Rumsfeld said USA may never succeed in capturing Osama ben Laden;

25 Oct 2001 Donald Rumsfeld said again USA might never succeed in catching or killing Osama ben Laden. Even if they succeed the activities of Al Qaida will continue, said Donald Rumsfeld in a newspaper interview with "USA-Today". Repeated the question, if they can capture Osama ben Laden, Donald Rumsfeld answered: "Well, you are trying to get me again ".

26 Oct 2001 deployment of British ground troops in Afghanistan

26 Oct 2001 assassination of Abdul Hak Senior Mujahedeen Commander, opposed to the US strikes on Afghanistan; he was arrested and executed by the Taleban on 26 Oct 2001

30 Oct 2001 speech of UN High Commissioner for refugees Ruud Lubbers in Islamabad

31 Oct 2001 Tony Blair in Syria and in Saudi Arabia for talks with regional leaders

03 Nov 2001 Osama ben Laden criticized the UNO for its support of Israel and international terrorism

6-8 Nov 2001 General Pervez Musharraf in Iran, Turkey, France and Britain

09 Nov 2001 American ally the Saudi foreign minister Prince Saud al Feysal told the New York Times that President Bush can "make a sane man go mad".

10 Nov 2001 the city Mazar-e Sharif in Northern Afghanistan was captured by the Northern Alliance

11 Nov 2001 British ground forces started to operate in Afghanistan In Fox-TV interview Donald Rumsfeld said Kabul was destroyed by the Soviet Union.

12 Nov 2001 Plane crash in New York

13 Nov 2001 the fall of Afghanistan Capital Kabul and the town of Bamian to the Northern Alliance. Controversial anti-terrorist measures in Britain

14 Nov 2001 begin of the OPEC-conference in Vienna

15 Nov 2001 Donald Rumsfeld said Osama ben Laden may try to slip out of Afghanistan

16 Nov 2001 at 12:37 GMT BBC moderator Alex Prody said in BBC-newshour: "I cannot understand is there crisis in Afghanista or there is no crisis?" Well,it was a war raging.

125

17 Nov 2001 begin of the Muslim holy month of Ramadan but no stop of American war on Islam

25 Nov 2001 revolt of imprisoned Taleban fighters in the prison complex Qala-e-Janghi near Mazar-e-Sharif. All rioters were said to have been killed. Northern Alliance spokesman Abdul Wahid Yasa said 300 Taleban soldiers were killed in cold blood.

27 Nov-05 Dec 2001 Conference in Germany of all Afghan tribes including a representative of the former King Zahir Shah.

30 Nov 2001 George Harrison died in Los Angeles aged 58. The former Afghan President Burhanuddin Rabbani questioned the legitimacy of the Bonn talks. Haji Kadir walked out of the conference saying the Pashtun were underrepresented. 1,000 US marines were flown into the desert airfield outside of Kandahar. The Northern Alliance captured Al Qaida leader Ahmed Abdul Rahman who was responsible for training and recruitment. He will be handed over to the Americans.

03 Dec 2001 Autobiography of one of Osama ben Laden's lieutenants was published in London.

05 Dec 2001 The conference in Bonn-Koenigswinter in Germany ended after 8 days intense negotiations with the appointment of Hamed Karzai for a head of the interim administration and Hedayat Amin Arsala for new finance minister; the Northern Alliance got 17 seats out of 29 including the interior, defense and foreign ministries.

13 Dec 2001 President Bush cancelled the ABM treaty with Russia after he assured logistic Russian support in the Afghan war. The Pentagon released controversial videotape proving the involvement of Osama ben Laden in the 11th September attacks on New York and Washington; many Arabs said the videotape was faked.

14 Dec 2001 British Parliament approved new anti-terrorists laws including the right of the authorities to detain non-British suspects without charge or trial. Civil liberties groups have said they intend to challenge the new powers.

16 Dec 2001 the last Al Qaida stronghold Tora Bora fell to the Eastern Alliance; Osama ben Laden was not there. Donald Rumsfeld visited Afghanistan for talks with the interim leader Hamed Karzai.

18 Dec 2001 Hamed Karzai visited Rome via London for talks with the former King Mohamed Zahir Shah. Nothing was reported on his London talks.

22 Dec 2001 Inauguration of the new interim Afghan government under the leadership of Hamed Karzai.

24 Dec 2001 Pakistani President General Pervez Musharraf visited China for talks

26 Dec 2001 Osama ben Laden released a new videotape in which bitterly criticized the West for the bombing of Afghanistan during the Islamic holy month of Ramadan. The videotape was broadcast by the Qatari based Al Jazzera satellite TV station. Al Jazzera did not say how it obtained the tape but said it will broadcast the full 30-minute length the next day.

27 Dec 2001 Donald Rumsfeld dismissed the videotape saying he had not watch it and said in a press conference: "Osama ben Laden may be in Afghanistan, in some other country or may be dead."

28 Dec 2001 President Bush admitted they have lost the tracks of Osama ben Laden.

02 Jan 2002 Alleged terrorist Zacarias Moussaoui appeared in a court in Virginia where he said: "In the name of Allah I have nothing to plead".

04 Jan 2002 The first US soldier shot dead in Afghanistan in Khost-Khost area

05 Jan 2002 The Taleban Ambassador to Pakistan Abdul Salam Zaif arrested by the Americans in breach of international asylum law; he had asked earlier asylum in Pakistan but was refused. The Americans have N O jurisdiction in Pakistan. The new US envoy to Afghanistan Zalmay Khalilzaid arrived in Kabul to take the reigns.

06 Jan 2002 American anti-war activist Charles Bishop aged 14 flew his plane into the Bank of America block in the center of Tampa in Florida in a suicide mission.

07 Jan 2002 The British Prime Minister Tony Blair visited the Bagram airbase in Afghanistan amid tight security and almost secretly.

18 Jan 2002 Pakistani President Pervez Musharraf said Osama ben Laden may be dead as he suffers kidney problems and needs kidney dialysis machine; Islam bin Laden registered his trademark "bin Laden"

21 Jan 2002 Conference on Afghanistan in Tokyo with US Secretary of state Colin Powell

22 Jan 2002 A US human right organization has brought to an L.A. court the conditions in which Al Qaida prisoners were held at Guantanamo base in Cuba. It said the conditions under which the prisoners were held are in breach with the Geneva conventions. An US helicopter shot down 60km from Bagram air base North-West of Kabul.

26 Jan 2002 General Tommy Francs said the US is still keen to track down the head of the Al Qaida network Osama ben Laden and the Taleban leader Mullah Mohamed Omar.

28 Jan 2002 Meeting between Hamed Karzai and President Bush in Washington; Bush promised additional help of $50,000,000

29 Jan 2002 the niece of President Bush Noelle Bush was arrested when she tried to obtain the banned drug Xanax using false prescription. Xanax is similar to Valium and treats anxiety problems. In 2001 aged 19 she was arrested again for underage alcohol drinking.

30 Jan 2002 Clashes in the Afghan town of Gardez. Rival factions fired mortars and rockets at each other while the Northern Alliance watched but did not intervene.

01 Feb 2002   NATO Secretary General Lord Robertson said in the World Economic Forum in New York that USA must prove evidence against each nation, which may be subject to American aggression.

07 Feb 2002   President Bush said the Geneva conventions will be applied to Taleban but not to Al Qaida fighters hold prisoners at Guantanamo base but both categories will N O T be treated as prisoners of war.

09 Feb 2002 the former Taleban foreign minister Wakil Ahmad Mutawakel surrendered to the Americans, which began interrogating him in breach with the Geneva conventions and their own decisions not to interrogate Taleban. Meanwhile the interim government in Afghanistan released 300 rank and file soldiers to return home paying them small amount of money. Mutawakel by contrast will be tried by American court. The International Red Cross continues to disagree about the faith of the Taleban prisoners arguing that only an international court not the glorious power may trial them.

10 Feb 2002   the head of the new Afghan Army General Mohamed Fahim arrived in Moscow for 5-day talks with the Russian leadership and to buy Russian military hardware for the new Afghan Army. The Iranian authorities have closed down the offices of the Afghan faction Hezb-e-Islami that is headed by the

former Mujahedeen Gulbuddin Hekmatyar. It became clear that American Army beat villagers in Uruz-Gan that were mistaken for Al Qaida fighters. The 27 civilians were beaten, punched, kicked and dragged until they lost conscience. 21 other civilians and were killed in the raid and 1 US soldier wounded.

16 Feb 2002 The funeral of the assassinated civil aviation minister Abdul Rahman; In Britain Government minister Joe Moe forced to resign after her remark that unpopular decisions could be passed on 11th September.

08 Mar 2002 The UNCHR Commissioner Mary Robinson came to Kabul for a 4-day visit. No further reports came about her talks.

09 Mar 2002 President Bush got the permission of the Congress to use atomic weapons against 7 named countries in the crusade against terrorism: China, Russia, Iran, Iraq, Syria, Libya and North Korea. The media paid very little attention to this very important peace of news. The Pentagon report leaked to the media already in January 2002

10 Mar 2002 BBC Defence correspondent Jonathan Marcus predicted the US will start the war on IRAQ in August or in September 2002. US Vice-President Dick Cheney started several days visit to Britain and to the Golf states.

10 Mar 2002 a powerful bomb exploded outside the American Embassy in Kabul. The Iranian media reported widely on the event while Western media were silent.

12 Mar 2002 the interim Afghan leader Hamed Karzai visited Moscow for two days talks with President Putin. He wants the Russians to reconstruct 17O Soviet-built plants and factories destroyed by the war.

13 Mar 2002 The US Vice President Dick Cheney threatened again Iraq with the use of nuclear weapons during his visit to Jordan and Egypt. He said the US will retaliate with nuclear weapons if Iraq does use chemical or biological weapons.

14 Oct 2002 The next court trial of alleged terrorist Zacarias Moussaoui in the USA; his judge is Nyoki M Brinkema

AFGAN CITIES

Alah Kuzi
Alimardah
Anar Darreh
Andkhvoy
Aqcheh
Aybak
Baghlan
Bahram Chah
Bala Morghab
Balkh
Bamian *
Barakht-e
Baraki Barak
Belcheragh
Busham
Chaghcharan
Chahar
Chahar Borjak
Chalas
Charikar *
Dahane
Dalaram
Darakht-e Yahya
Dashti Qala
Deh
Dowlatabad
Eshkashem
Eslam
Eslam Qaleh

Farah *
Feyzabad
Gardez
Gereshk
Gozar-e Shah
Gusgy
Hazrat-e Soltan
Herat *
Jalalabad *
Jaldak
Jan
Kamdesh
Kariz-e Flyas
Karizak
Karize Elyas
Karokh
Khanabad
Khane Baqat
Kheyrabad
Kholm
Khowst
Kojabahuddin
Kowte Ashrow
Landay
Lash-e Joveyn
Lashar Gah
Mahmude Eraqi
Malenj
Mandel

Mashuray
Mehtar
Mir Bachcheh
Moqor
Mushaki
Nalenj
Nawah
Now *
Orgun
Oruzgan
Panjab
Pir
Qalat
Qaleh
Qeysar
Qonduz *
Qowmghi
Qurugh
Robat
Rostaq
Rowzanapak
Rudbar
Sange Masheh
Sarafsar
Seyyedabad
Shahr-e Safa
Sheberghan
Shindand
Sukhten Qaleh

Taloqan
Torzi
Uzhdah Mandah
Vashir
Zadeh
Zaranj
Zarghun Shahr
Zenden
Ziba

Appendix 2

WWW LINKS & EMAIL ADDRESSES

www.BBC.co.uk/worldservice/whatstheproblem-practical advice
www.globalsecurity.com-independent defense organization run by John Pyke
www.jihad.com-webside on the wholly war jihad
www.opensourcessociety.com-Webside on espionage
www.tradingweapon.com-weapon information website.
www.transparency-international organisation on corruption worldwide
www.uspost.gov-special anthrax-website
newshour @ BBC.co.uk-for comments and views
talkingpoint @ BBC.co.uk-for comments and views

LIST OF NAMES USED IN THIS BOOK

Abdul Hak-Highest Mujahedeen Commander, arrested and executed by the Taleban on 26 Oct 2001

Abdul Hak-Senior Mujahedeen Commander, opposed to the US strikes on Afghanistan, killed by the Taleban on 26 Oct 2001

Abdul Mashud-Hamaz activist killed by car bomb on 15 Oct 2001

Abdul Nasser Mastri-Senior Taleban official

Abdul Rahid Yassir-Spokesman of the Northern Alliance, Doctor

Abdul Raid-Senior Northern Alliance commander at Mazar-e Sharif where riots broke out among the captured Taleban fighters at the Qala-e-Janghi prison complex

Abdul Rushed Dostum-Northern Alliance general, tragically known from the blood bath of Qala-e-Janghi prison complex

Abdul Satar-Pakistani foreign minister

Abdul Zatar Zirat-Professor, probably the chief of the future Afghan interim administration; from the King's party

Abdullah Shatah-BBC Pashtun service

Abdullah Sinusi - Libyan Intelligence Chief

Abdulaghan-area in North Afghanistan where the starvation is very strong

Achtar Lakhdar Brahimi-UN special envoy to Afghanistan; met Pervez Musharraf on 30 Oct 2001 but was forbidden to meet Taleban officials

Adam Brooks-BBC correspondent in Quetta

Adam Ingram-British armed forces Minister

Adnan Imram-Syrian information minister

Adolfo Rodriguez Sar-new interim Argentine President

Afghan Islamic Press Agency-the Taleban Press Agency

Ahmed Abdul Rahman-one of the Al Qaida leaders, son of the blinded Egyptian cleric Omar Abdul Rahman

Ahmed Fawzi-speaks good English

Ahmed Forsey-spokesman of the UN special envoy to Afghanistan

Ahmed Maha-Egyptian foreign minister

Ahmed Pakistani-Pakistani writer with splendid English

Ahmed Waley Masood-London based spokesman of the Northern Alliance

Al Calipha bin Laden-Mother of Osama ben Laden

Al Jihad-Ottoman castle in Mecca torn down by the Saudi authorities in 2001

Al Barakath-financial sponsor of Al Qaida

Al Gore-former US Vice President from the previous Clinton administration

Al Hayed-Arabic newspaper in London

Al Jazzera-Arabic TV station active in the Middle East, based in Qatar

Al Lakhud-London based Arab newspaper

Al Mahajirune-British Muslim organizations member of which joined the Taleban

Al Mohajirune-Islamic organization in Pakistan, which recruited fighters in Britain

Al Qaida -the militant organization of Osama ben Laden

Al Shakh al Swakh-Arab newspaper in London

Al Taqua-Arabic financial organization, Al Qaida 's sponsor

Alain Richard-French defense minister against the war in Iraq

Alan Johnston-BBC correspondent in Kabul

Ali Abdullah Sale-Yemeni President

Ali Abdullah Saleh-Yemen's President

Ali Abuzakub-American Muslim Council

Alim-Afghan title for Mullah

Amanaula Gozar-Northern Alliance commander

Amr Secretary-Secretary General of the Arab League

Amir Khan Mutaki-Taleban education minister

Amir Khan Mutaki-Taleban Education Minister

Andre Sprostrana-Columbian President

Andrew Marr-BBC political editor, joined Tony Blair during his Middle East tour

Anwar Ohidi-Pashtun tribal representative; Doctor

Ariel Sharon-Israeli Prime Minister

Armina Azali-the head of Afghanistan's official women's movement

Attaf Abdul Gawa-Arab journalist in Washington: " The videotape was faked! "

Atal Behari Vaajpee-Indian prime minister

Ayatollah Hameini-Iranian Supreme religious leader

Ayman al Zawahari-Osama ben Laden's Egyptian deputy, author of a book

Azis Abdul Khan-Pakistani foreign ministry spokesman

Badawi-activist of the Organization of Islamic Conference in London; Doctor of Law

Badris-East Afghan provinces

Baka Moan-Chief of BBC Pashtun and Persian service

Bagram-Afghan town North-West of Kandahar

Bagram-airport near Kabul

Bakez-northwest province in Afghanistan

Baka Moan-head of BBC Persian & Pashtun Service

Balkh-province around the northern Afghan city of Mazar-e Sharif

Bamako-Capital of Mali in Africa

Barbara Hatch-Rosenberg-American Federation of scientists working group on biological weapons

Barnet Rubin-US Afghan expert, scholar at New York University

Basher el Asad-Syrian President, son of the late President Hafez el Asad

Basher Riaz-Press officer of the former Pakistani President Benazir Bhutto in London

Belmarsh-prison in London (see Pentonville)

Ben Bradshaw-British foreign office minister, whom anti-war protesters sprinkled with blood

Bernard Russell-British anti-nuclear protester

Beruz Afak-BBC Central Asia editor

Beruz Afrak-BBC Afghanistan analyst

Blunt-former BBC director; became chairman of British Telecom

Breadwinner-children book on Afghanistan

Brian Baron-BBC correspondent in Kandahar

Brian May- Queen guitarist, awarded by Queen Elizabeth with Knighthood; against the Afghan war

Brian Wilson-British energy minister

Brian Taylor-Scottish political editor

Burhanuddin Rabbani-former President of Afghanistan, Northern Alliance Commander, leader of the opposition, lives in exile in Tajikistan

Bahrain Rabbani-the ousted President of Afghanistan

Caliph Daud-Egyptian journalist, speaks fluently English: "The tape was faked by the Yankees"

Carl Rove-senior advisor of President Bush

Caroline Hawley-BBC correspondent in Jerusalem

Caroline Stuart-Member of the EU Parliament (MEP) who demonstrated in Laaken on 14-12-2001

Chamani-border crossing point between Afghanistan and Pakistan where many refugees were stranded Oct 2001

Charles Bishop-a 15 years old pilot who flew a plane into the Bank of America office in Tampa in Florida on 07-01-2002

Chokokarez-Afghan village flattened by American air attacks on 01 Nov 2001

Chris Davis-new Labor Director of the BBC together with BBC Chairman Greg Dyke

Chris Yanovski-UNHCR activist

Christine Gayak-spokeswoman of Xavier Solana

Christine Lamb-British journalist of Daily Telegraph, reserved a ticket under the name O. B. Laden

Christopher Stock-from the American aid agency MSF

Cynthia Schneider-US Ambassador to the Netherlands

Clair Boldowson-BBC correspondent in Washington

Clark-spokeswoman of the Pentagon (also Victoria Clark)

Colin Powell-US Secretary of State

Condoleezza Rice-American National Security Advisor to President Bush

Damian Grammaticas-BBC correspondent in Taipei

Damian Grammaticas-BBC correspondent in Tora Bora

Dan Isaac-BBC correspondent in Lagos, Nigeria

Daniel Lack-BBC correspondent in Peshawar

Daniel Marx-Argentinean deputy economy minister

Darra Yusuf-area south of Mazar-e Sharif

Daud Khan-senior Northern Alliance commander

David Bamford-BBC correspondent in Libya

David Hicks-young Australian aged 26, who fought for the Taleban and for the Kosovo Liberation Army

David Loin-BBC correspondent in Bamian

David Willis-BBC correspondent in Rom

Defodi Bunger-from UN food program

Dick Cheney-US Vice president

Donald Leader-leader of the team British troops, which arrived in Kabul on 16-12-2001

Donald Rumsfeld-US defense minister whom on 25 Oct 2001 denied the chance to capture Osama ben Laden

Dr. Badawi-activist of the Organization of Islamic Conference in London

Ede al Fitah-festival at the end of the Muslim holy month of Ramadan

Edward Sturton-BBC correspondent in Malaysia

Electra Naysmith-BBC correspondent in Peshawar

Elephant's mountain-volcanic outcrop near Kandahar where the Taleban situated their anti aircraft defenses

Emamudin-Taleban General who changed fronts shortly before the Northern Alliance offensive

Emin Zahwari-Egyptian Jihad leader, right hand of Osama ben Laden, killed in Afghanistan together with his 5 children by American raids

Eminal Amin-former Taleban security chief in Spin Boldak in the southern border area

Emma-Jane Kirby-BBC correspondent in Pakistan

Esqay Lamba-special Indian envoy to Pakistan

Evanal Sheikh Alibi-Senior Taleban leader arrested on 05-01-2002; had run Al Qaida training camps

Eunice Khanuni-Leader of the Northern Alliance delegation in Koenigswinter in Germany; Northern Alliance interior minister; interior minister also in the interim body

Fahim-Commander of the Northern Alliance; general

Faysabad-town in north Afghanistan where President Rabbani has his palace

Fergal Parkinson-BBC correspondent in Washington

Fernando dela Rua - Argentinean President forced to resign

Fort Brag-US military base in North Carolina

Frahatulla Babar-Press officer of the ousted Pakistani president Benazir Bhutto in Islamabad

Franc Gardner-BBC correspondent in Damascus

Francesc Vendrell-UN deputy special envoy to Afghanistan; urged USA to bring Afghanistan in its coalition

Francis Kennedy-BBC correspondent in Rome

Fred Scot-BBC cameraman in Kabul

Frederick Forsyth-author of the book "The day of the jackal"

Gaaz Tadin Sadiki-Leader of the Islamic Parliament in Britain

Gaidar-Pakistani interior minister

Gazi-Jemaah Islamiya

General Fahim-defense minister of the Northern Alliance

George Joffi-expert on Islamic politics

George Fernandes-Indian defense minister

George Kerry-Arch-bishop of Canterbury

George Robertson-Secretary General of NATO; Lord

Global Exchange-American human rights organization

Gor Heshad-the most beautiful mosque in Herat built; by a woman

Gordon Brice-UNICEF representative in Islamabad

Gore Vidal-US publicist: "We have in America one-party-system with 2 right wings": BBC interview on 12-11-2001 at 21:55 GMT

Gore-northwest province in Afghanistan

Gorkan Ayokhan-former Pakistani foreign minister

Graham Richard-President of EU Commission of Human rights, civil liberties and home affairs

Grant Ferret-BBC correspondent

Green Humor-American giant bomb

Greg Quake-Rear admiral; Pentagon spokesman; in BBC interview on 03-01-2002 at 21:33 GMT

Gregorio Fuentes (104 years old)-Cuban who inspired Hemmingway to write his book "The old man and the sea"; 2001 awarded by the World Game fish Association

Guantanamo-US military base in Cuba where many Al Qaida fighters were imprisoned

Gul Bedin-Pashtun tribal leader; warned he will raise his weapons against the new Afghan administration

Gula Aga-former Mujahedeen Pashtun governor of Kandahar

Gula Mohamed-the commander of Midensharh 30km from Kabul were Taleban forces were encircled by the Northern Alliance

Gula Shah Mazy-governor of Kandahar

Gulbudin Hekmatiar-former Afghan Prime minister now living in exile in Iran

Guram Farukhazam-former minister of Burhanuddin Rabbani, now living in exile in London, chairman of the Afghan Forum: "The Western media does not cover this war sufficiently"

Burka-cloth that covers the head and the shoulders

Guy Goodwin-Professor of Law at Oxford University

Guzny-central Afghan province

Hajji Abdul Kadir-Afghan delegate in Bonn who walked out to protest against the under representation of the Pashtun; governor of Nangahar province with Capital Jalalabad, Brother of Abdul Hak;

Hajji Basher-opposition commander who took Kandahar from the Taleban; his reign was looting and robbing after the fall of Kandahar

Hajji Imam-local commander in the Tora Bora battle

Hajji Mustafa Bakik-Afghan planning minister in the new interim government

Hajji Zahir-local militia commander in Tora Bora

Haha-Afghani town in the Hindukush Mountains where commander Mohamed Daud from the Northern Alliance was active

Hakati Jihadi Islamia-Kashmiri militant organization, which fought together with the Taleban

Haled el Naim-English speaking Arab journalist

Halid Pashtun-spokesman of Gul Aga, the former ruler of Kandahar

Hamed Galoni-representative of the Peshawar group on the talks in Germany

Hamed Gool-Northern Alliance General

Hamed Gul-the man who ran the Pakistani Intelligence Service ISI as the Taleban rose to power

Hamed Karzai - prominent Afghan leader, comes from the same Pashtun Clan as the former King; diplomat of the pre-Communist era

Hamed Mir-biographer of Osama ben Laden; in a BBC interview with Judy Swallow said: "A superpower against single man"; Urdu newspaper editor

Hanabad-town 20km north of Kunduz, which fell without a gun, shot to the Northern Alliance

Hanabad-town about 20km from Kunduz

Haraton-Afghan port at the river Amu-Daria just across the Uzbek town Termez

Harvey Harris-Metropolitan police London Chairman

Hasan Bin Tellal-Jordanian Prince

Hasrat Ali-local militia commander round Tora Bora

Hawala-Arabic method of money transfer

Hazard Ali-Local anti-Taleban commander who captured Tora Bora on 16-12-2001

Hazrat Ali-leader of the ground assault in Tora Bora

Hazward Ali-anti-Taleban leader in Tora Bora area

Hedayat Amin Afsala-the new finance minister of Afghanistan in the interim body; he is from the King's party named also Rome Party

Helen Sheban-The Times journalist

Helene Bamboo-from the US medical foundation "Victims of cruelty"

Helmut Sturisch-editor of Die Standard-newspaper in Vienna

Hilary Anderson-BBC correspondent in Kabul

Hindu-Islamic insult; call someone Hindu is a great insult among the Muslims

Hodgan-town in south Tajikistan close to the Afghani border

Hodgebaldin-modern Afghan town in the north close to the Tajik border near the place where Alexander the Great built fortification 2,500 years ago.

Holumn-village in Afghanistan almost fully obliterated by US-bombing on 14 Oct 2001

Hosni Mubarag-Egyptian President

Khost-town in eastern Afghanistan where Americans massacred 65 civilians and injured 40 others on 22-12-2001.Donald Rumsfeld admitted the massacre.

Hu Jin Thao-Vice President of China

Hussein Anwari-Northern Alliance Commander

Hussein Emez-Leader of Jemaah Islamiya in Pakistan

Hussein Khanuni-Northern Alliance Commander

Ibrahim Halal-al Jazzera editor in chief; speaks good English

Ibrahim Moodnier-Hezbollah head, accused by the Israeli intelligence service Musad of organizing the September attacks

Igor Ivanov-Russian foreign minister

IMU-Islamic Movement for Uzbekistan; Uzbek Taleban militia who seeks to topple the Uzbek President Islam Karimov

Iod as Abu Chusk Rasini-journalist of the Ash Shakr al Ashwad, Arabic daily published in London

Ian Gun-BBC correspondent in Vancouver

Ian Mc William-BBC correspondent in Kabul

Ian McWilliam-BBC correspondent in Afghanistan

Ian Pummel-BBC correspondent in Kabul

Irene Khan-Secretary General of Amnesty International

ISI-Pakistani Intelligence service

Islam bin Laden-Brother of Osama ben Laden, lives in Geneva

Islam Karimov-Uzbek President

Islam Mashadov-Chechen separatist

Islamic Relief-refugee organization based in Birmingham

Ismail Khan-Mujahedeen governor of the western Afghan city of Herat

Ismail Khan-Pakistani analyst

Ismail Khan-spokesman of the Northern Alliance, former Mujahedeen Governor of the Western city of Herat

Ismail Sadath-BBC Pashtun service

Ismail Sadath-BBC team helper in Kabul

Jack Straw-British foreign minister

Jalala Khali-cave complex in the Khost area bombarded by the Americans on 10-01-2002

Jalalaldin Harkani-Taleban commander in the Sawara area in eastern Afghanistan who opposed the Americans even in January 2002

Jamah Ath-tribal force opposed to the Northern Alliance, which took Kabul on 13 Nov 2001

Jamaah Islamiya-one of the leading factions in the Northern Alliance

Jamaah Tablia-Islamic missionary group

James Aitkin-former US Ambassador to Saudi Arabia

James Dobbin-US special envoy to Afghanistan

James Hill-New York Times photojournalist who saw many charred bodies in Qala-e-Janghi; Pulitzer Price winner

James Lindsey-from the Brooklyn institution in Washington

James Reynolds-BBC correspondent in Jerusalem

James Richey-American businessman who spent his childhood in Afghanistan

James Wolfonson-World Bank President

Jane Peel-BBC correspondent in New York

Jaswan Singh-Indian foreign minister

Jeff Barrack-editor in chief of JerusalemPost

Jeff Hoon-British defense minister

Jeffrey Tempa-former advisor of President Reagan

Jeremy Cook-BBC correspondent in Jerusalem

Jeremy McDermott-BBC correspondent in Bogotá

JIA-Algerian terrorist organization

Jill McGivery-BBC correspondent in Islamabad

Jim Muir-BBC correspondent in Herat

Jim Welsh-Chief medical official of Amnesty International

Johannes Sutton-French journalist from Radio France International killed in Afghanistan

John Ashcroft-US Attorney General

John Bolton-US Undersecretary of State for arms control

John Gallagher-Labor MP

John Gilligan-BBC correspondent in Pakistan

John Line-BBC correspondent in Washington

John McClain-charity "War Child" in Iran

John Pike-security analyst from www.globalsecurity.org

John Spenser-from the Heritage Foundation

John Stufflebeem-Rear Admiral spokesman of the Pentagon

John Walker-Nickname Abdul Hamed; at 16 converted to Islam after he read the Autobiography of Malcolm X; later on went to Yemen to learn Arabic; is under way to become US national martyred.

John Walker-young American Taleban who fought for the Taleban in Mazar-e Sharif. His Father was an Irish catholic; his Mother-Buddhist. Donald Rumsfeld said he is likely to be tried for treason by a secret anti-terror military court.

Jonathan Stevenson-International Institute for Strategic Studies

Johnnie Diamonds-BBC correspondent in Washington

Jonathan Marcus-BBC defense analyst

Jordan Day-World Food Program spokesman

Joseph Pique-Spanish foreign minister

Joseph Bidon-head of the US Senate Foreign Relations Committee; visited Afghanistan on 13-01-2002

Jun Jix-Chinese foreign minister

Justin Pierce-BBC correspondent in Angola

Justin Webb-BBC EU correspondent

Kasha Gari-refugee camp near the Pakistani city of Peshawar, visited by the Dutch Prime Minister Kok on 28 Oct 2001

Qala-e-Janghi prison complex 10km from Mazar-e Sharif where riots broke out among the captured Taleban fighters

Kamal Ahib-Islamic terrorist arrested in Britain extradited to France on 04 Oct 2001

Kamal Kharazy-Iranian foreign minister

Kamram Khan-Pakistani defense analyst

Karabas-town north of Kabul

Karnebad-US military base in Uzbekistan

Karri Ama Dula-head of intelligence for the Taleban killed in December 2001 in American air raid

Katakala-area near the Tajik border where the Americans bombarded the Taleban positions on 28 Oct 2001

Kate Clark-BBC correspondent in Kabul

Katherine Davis-BBC correspondent in Uzbekistan

Kenton Keats-American coalition spokesman

Kenton Keats-US spokesman in Pakistan

Khaled Mansur-World Food Program spokesman in Islamabad

Khust/ Khowst -town in southeast Afghanistan where some 30 civilians were killed in a bomb raid on 04-01-2002

Khamati Islamiya-jihadi group in Upper Egypt

Kharun Amin-Northern Alliance representative in Washington, speaks excellent English

Khor-north Afghan province

Kilifayso-border transit camp in Pakistan

King Fahad-King of Saudi Arabia

Kofi Annan-Secretary General of the UN, awarded with the Nobel Peace Price

Koja-Bahoudin - town in northeast Afghanistan

Korol Koram-the main road from Northern Pakistan to China blocked by angry anti-war protesters on 27 Oct 2001

Kunduz-Taleban stronghold in northern Afghanistan east from Mazar-e Sharif where heavy battles took place

Kvazhnin - Alexander, Russian Commander, general

Lashka Itoyba-Pakistani militant organization blamed for the assault on the Indian Parliament on 13 Dec 2001

Lashkagor-Afghan town near Kandahar

Lies Doucet - BBC correspondent in Kabul

Lindsey Davis-World Food Program in Islamabad

Lord Ahmed-British Labor MP who is critical on the Afghan war; his phone was bugged

Loren Fabeus - French finance minister

Lotsi Raisi-Algerian pilot detained on 26 Oct 2001 on suspicion for participating in the plane attack on New York

Louis Hidalgo-BBC correspondent in Afghanistan

Loya Jerga-a grand council of all the tribes' representatives in Afghanistan

LUS Harding-The Guardian journalist in Afghanistan who witnessed the blood bath of Qala-e-Janghi

Lucy Frears-BBC reporter in Berlin

Madeleine Albright-former US foreign minister

Mahajan-Indian minister for parliamentary issues

Mahmud Zahir-Hamas spokesman

Mahreb-remote province in North-East of Yemen

Major Joe Blair-instrutor from the (terrorist) School of Americas: "It is organized uniformed Mafia" BBC interview on 08-11-2001 in 18:11 GMT; it is renamed now into Western Hemisphere Institute of Security

Malcolm Chesan-British deputy Health minister

Malcolm Hicks-Canadian journalist kidnapped for ransom near the South Afghan town of Spin Boldak

Maled Otman-al Fahid newspaper in London English speaking Arab journalist

Malyam Baba-The News newspaper in Islamabad

Maragon-town in western India where protesters clashed with police on 27 Oct 2001: 7 people were killed

Marc Southerner-South African Internet tycoon who will became the 2nd space tourist in April 2001

Maria Lordi-Pakistani lady Ambassador to Washington; Doctor

Marianne Barber-diplomatic correspondent for the Pakistani newspaper "The News"

Marianne Barber-diplomatic editor of the Pakistani newspaper "The News"

Marianne Blakey-National Transportation Safety Board Chairwoman

Mark Fisher-former Labor minister

May Stijf-from the organization "Lawyers for peace" in The Netherlands

Meshad Shejara-Islamic Human Rights Commission

Metwedin Sheikh-Pakistani foreign Secretary

Michael Adin-American Enterprise Institute in Washington

Michael Boyce-Admiral, Chief of the British Defence Staff

Michael Connelly-Center of terrorists studies in London

Michael Griffin-author of the book "Taleban"

Michael Klein-from the ICRC International Committee of the Red Cross in Kabul

Michael Williams-BBC correspondent in Afghanistan

Michel Perar-French journalist detained by the Taleban

Midensharh-location 30km southwest of Kabul where the Taleban forces are said to be regrouping

Mike Fox-BBC correspondent in New York

Mike Huggins-World Food Program spokesman

Mike More-Director General of WTO

Military Studies in the Jihad Against the Tyrants-terrorist handbook used by Al Qaida

Mir Vise-son of the former Afghan King Mohamed Zahir Shah

Mohamed Abil-spokesman of the new Afghan Defence Ministry

Mohamed Adar-UNHCR spokesman

Mohamed Afroze-Indian terrorist trying to hijack a plane in London on 11th September

Mohamed Afsal-leader of the terrorist Jashi Mohamed group who organized the killing in the Indian Parliament on 13-12-2001

Mohamed Ali-American boxer born on 17-01-1942, heavy weight champion; refused to fight in Vietnam under US flag

Mohamed Chalabi-Algerian terrorist deported to Algiers after serving 8 years in France; JIA member

Mohamed el Baraday - Director of the international Atomic Energy Agency

Mohamed Fahim- Afghan defense minister; General

Mohamed Fahim-defense minister in the new interim Afghan government

Mohamed Hak-Egyptian writer

Mohamed Hayb Aga-spokesman of the Taleban government

Mohamed Ishlamawi-Algerian extremist deported from France to Algiers on 09-11-2001

Mohamed Kaplan-Turkish extremist serving time in Germany

Mohamed Khatami-Iranian President

Mohamed Mohatir-Prime minister of Malaysia, in 2003 stepped down voluntarily

Mohamed Riaz Khan-Pakistani Government spokesman

Mohamed Zeman-Anti-Taleban Afghan commander

Molano Fazlo Reman-radical Pakistani Islamic group leader

Monica Wittlock-BBC correspondent in Tashkent

Moultan-city in central Pakistan where anti-war protests took place

Mowan Kanavany-spokesman of Yasser Arafat

Muhammad Junaid-young American Taleban who fought for the Taleban in Afghanistan; charged with treason by the US authorities

Muhammad Mohakekh-Northern Alliance commander in charge of Kabul

Muhsin Amin Zadey-Iranian deputy foreign minister

Mullah Abidula-Taleban defense minister

Mullah Dardula-Taleban commander of the town of Kunduz

Mullah Gaddulah-Taleban Commander

Mullah Mohamed Omar-Taleban supreme leader, born 1959

Mullah Nagibulla-Pashtun tribal leader rival of Mullah Aga

Mullah Sadun Ean-Taleban industry minister

Mullah Soupi Mohamed-Local leader of Tanzia Niphat Isheriat Mohamedi

Mullah Turabi-Taleban Justice minister

Mulkaleyba Haidar-Pakistani defense minister

Mussa Amin Rhade-deputy foreign minister of Iran

Mustafa Zahir-grand son of the former Afghan King Zahir Shah

Nabil Shat-Palestinian minister, extremely clever man

Nageb Sabri-Iraqi foreign minister

Najiba Kashre-from BBC Pashtun service

Naim Beg-Islamic Circle of North America

Nairobi-Kenyan capital where mighty anti-American protest demonstration took place on 26 Oct 2001

Najib Sabri-Iraqi foreign minister

Naour-district south of Kabul

Benjamin Britain-British musician

Niazi Kaleh-Afghan village in Paktika province near the town of Gardez bombed by the Americans on 30-12-2001; 100 villagers died in the raid.

Nicholas Somas-shadow British defense minister

Nick Brian-BBC correspondent in Washington

Nick Childs-BBC correspondent in Kabul

Nicole Fountain-President of the EU Parliament, speaks no English

Niem-German chief prosecutor

Nisram Islam Beg-former Pakistani General

Norman Minetta-US transportation agency spokesman

Nyoki Brinkemi-the judge of Zacarias Moussaoui

Obidula Akhund-Taleban military minister

Omar Abdul Rahman-blinded Egyptian cleric Omar Abdul Rahman; in US jail for bombing of the World Trade Center in 1993

Organization of Islamic Conference-moderate Islamic organization

Osama ben Laden-Saudi born dissident; Al Qaida network leader;

Otto Schilly-German interior minister

Owen Bennett Jones-BBC correspondent in Jalalabad

Oxfam-international aid agency

Paktika-Afghan province east from Kabul

Patricia McKelly-BBC correspondent in Dublin

Patrick Butler-BBC correspondent in Frankfurt

Paul Nielsen-EU Commissioner for food for Afghanistan

Paul Reynolds-BBC correspondent in Washington

Paul Wulfowitz-deputy US defense secretary

Pentonville prison-prison in the center of London

Pervez Musharraf-Pakistani President, Army General who seized power in 1999

Peter French-Audio forensic expert, Doctor

Peter Greste-BBC correspondent in Kabul

Peter Haynes-British European Minister

Peter Masden-author of the book "The Taleban"

Pierre Moskovich-French European Minister

Pilnesh-US general, member of the Council for foreign relations

Prince Hasan Bin Tellal-Jordanian Prince

Prof. Rainhard Director-Director of Robert Koch Institute in Berlin

Pulicharki-river near Kabul

Pulikumri-town in North Afghanistan taken by the Northern Alliance on 11-11-2001

Quetta-town in northwestern Pakistan, capital of the province Balujistan

Rachel Harvey-BBC analyst

Ragae Omar-BBC correspondent in Kabul

Rahamori Yusuf Zaif-BBC correspondent in Peshawar

Rahim Makdun-the new Afghan minister of information and culture

Rahmasivi Inkriminayka- Sri Lankan President

Rahu Bedhi-Indian journalist from the Daily Telegraph in India

Rushed Daud-Pakistani commerce minister

Rushed Kareshi-Pakistani Presidential spokesman, Army General

Rushed Kurashi-spokesman for the Pakistani President Pervez Musharraf

Richard Goldstone-S. African judge, former Chief Prosecutor at the War crime Tribunal in The Hague

Richard Hollander-Chairman of Metropolitan West Financial

Richard Loy-director of Landmine Group UK

Richard Lloyd Parry-British journalist from the Independent newspaper

Richard Masirb-US Regulatory Commission

Richard Murphy-US Ambassador to Syria

Richard Pearl-Chairman of the defense board of the Pentagon

Richard Reed-British terrorist who tried to blow up a plane with an explosive hidden in his shoe

Richard Shelby-senior member of the US Congress; Senator

Rick Wakeman-British musician

Rob Ruiter-Dutch KLM airlines official

Rob Watson-BBC correspondent in Washington

Robert Fisk-British journalist whom Osama ben Laden wanted to establish contact to

Robert Fox-Evening Standard journalist

Robert Muller-FBI director

Rogani-refugee camp near the Pakistan town of Quetta set up on 11-11-2001

Rodger Harvey-BBC Middle East analyst

Romano Prody-President of the European Commission

Rory Stewart-author of a book on Afghanistan, former British diplomat aged 29

Roy Bourgeois-School of Americas Watch activist

Rudolph Scharping-German Defence minister ,dismissed for his lavish and exuberant life style

Ruggiero-Italian Foreign Minister

Rupert Winfield Haze-BBC correspondent in Taloqan

Ruud Lubbers-UN High Commissioner for refugees; visited the stranded refugees near the border crossing Chamani on 28 Oct 2001

Sacram Prince Abdulah - Crownprince of Saudi Arabia

Sadaka Ogato - Japanese special envoy to Afghanistan, former UNHCR High-Commissioner

Sadik Saba-BBC Persian service

Sahad al Faagy-Islamic movement for reforms in (Saudi) Arabia

Said Hamed Albar (al Bah)-Malaysian foreign minister

Sala al Khala-Jordanian information minister

Saud al Feysal-Saudi foreign minister; Prince

Sawara-area near Khost in eastern Afghanistan

Sergey Ivanov-Russian defense minister

Sergey Lawrow-Russian Ambassador to the UN

Sergey Yastrazhenski-security advisor to President Vladimir Putin

Shah Yassin-Leader of Hamas who is blind and bearded

Shalkud Aziz-Pakistani finance minister

Shamir ben Caliph Amini-the Emir of Qatar

Shamsi-American air base in the West of the Pakistan where a US plane crashed on 09-01-2002

Sharigan-prison in Mazar-e Sharif where most Taleban prisoners were held

Sheba Der Derba-Nepalese Prime minister

Shikan-a village in the eastern Afghan province of Paktika raided by US planes after the end of the war on 29 Dec 2001; 15 people were killed

Shipigan-northern Afghan town where a number of Al Qaida fighters are kept in prison, many of them wounded

Shipigan-northern Afghan town, hometown of the ethnic Uzbek war lord Abdul Rushed Dostum, who is now Afghanistan's deputy defense minister

Shura - religious council in Afghanistan

Sidney Paterson-Director of the Swedish Committee for Afghanistan

Simon Ingram-BBC journalist who was allowed to visit Kandahar on 31 Oct 2001

Simon Reef-author of the book "The new jackals" on Osama ben Laden and the future

Sir John Stevens-Metropolitan police London official

Spin Boldag-town in Afghanistan near Kandahar where Taleban looted UN property on 31 Oct 2001

Stanley Hoe-Macao casinos' owner with 17 children

Stephanie Bunkerk-UNO spokeswoman

Steve Rosenberg-BBC correspondent in Moscow

Steven Eek-BBC Eurasia analyst who was not in Afghanistan

Steven Hess-professor at the Brooklyn Institution in Washington

Steven Schwarz-British anti-nuclear protestor, publisher of the nuclear disarmament bulletin in London

Steven Youngman-US lawyer brought in a petition to a L.A. court against the unlawful detention of Al Qaida prisoners in the US military base at Guantanamo

Stipe Masic-Croatian President

Sual Rahman-Pakistani journalist, speaks fluently English

Suzanne Price-BBC correspondent in Islamabad

Taleban-book by Michael Griffin

Town-town in Northern Afghanistan near the Tajik border

Tamrin Falial-from Pakistani based Revolutionary Association of Afghan women against the bombing of Afghanistan: "We don't want to see the Mujahedeen back in power because we cannot forget what they inflicted to the Afghan people 1992-96!"

Tamyes-Uzbek border town where an US bridgehead was established to attack Taleban from the North

Tanzia Niphat Isheriat Mohamedi-radical Pakistani Islamic organization

Tarrin Kowt- Afghani village 80km north from Kandahar entirely destroyed by US-strikes on 25 Oct 2001

Tayab Agar-Taleban spokesman in the city of Kandahar

Taylor Hicks-"The News"-photographer in Kabul

Termez-Uzbek town on the border with Afghanistan

Terry Stiastny-BBC correspondent in London, former Europe-Today moderator with a very strong and pleasant voice

Thomas Reek-military correspondent of the Washington Post

Thomas Willington-Institute of defense studies at the King's college in London

Tim Francs-BBC correspondent in Washington

Tom Carver-BBC correspondent in Washington

Tom Francs-BBC correspondent in Texas

Tom McKinley-BBC correspondent in Nairobi, Kenya

Tom Rich-US Director of Homeland Security

Tommy Franks-US senior general, chief commander in the region who held talks on 29 Oct 2001 with the Uzbek president Islam Karimov

Tony Blair-British Prime Minister criticized to be acting as American foreign secretary after the September 11th attacks on New York

Tora Bora -area in Afghanistan were US planes killed over 100 civilians on

Tora Bora -mountain base in eastern Afghanistan where Osama ben Laden was believed to be hiding

Ulu Zagal-province in Afghanistan

Uruz-Ghan - province in Afghanistan

Usatah-Northern Alliance General who ventured to contradict against general Dostum

Valid Madud-advisor of the Northern Alliance on the conference in Koenigswinter

Vertum Eisenhower-German journalist from the English version of the Frankfurter Allgemeine Zeitung

Verwighen-Belgian Justice minister

Wesley Clark-former NATO Supreme Commander for Europe; on BBC on 30 Oct 2001 he denied the chance of NATO ground troops to enter Afghanistan. Presidential candidate in the 2004 US elections

William – British prince,second to the Throne,son of the legendary Princess Diana,student at St. Andrew University in Scottland. At 7 was hit with a golf club into his head, suffered depressive
Scull fracture and has 24 stitches into his skull. Took actually no position to the wars in Afghanistan and Iraq in which British troops were sent to fight along with the Americans: (BBC_World , 16 DEC 2003, 00:14)

William Hirsh-US journalist; described in the New Yorker magazine the raid on Mullah Omar compound from 20 Oct 2001

William Nash-retired US general

William Reef-BBC Correspondent in Afghanistan, former Kabul correspondent

Williams-a candidate for the post Archbishop of Canterbury; Doctor, author of a book on Afghanistan in which criticized Western leaders and the morality of the Afghan war

Wim Duisenberg-President of the European Bank

Wulf Strongberg-Swedish journalist killed in Afghanistan by armed robbers in the northern town of Taloqan

Xavier Solana-EU commissioner for external relations; criticized the US for the condition under which it kept Al Qaida prisoners in Guantanamo military base in Cuba

Yasser Arafat- senior Palestinian leader

Yasser Assiri-Egyptian dissident charged with conspiracy to kill the leader of the Northern Alliance Ahmed Shah Masood

Yvonne Riggley - journalist of Sunday Telegraph arrested by the Taleban authorities but later releases

Zacaria Moussaoui - French terrorist arrested in the USA; he enjoyed French consular protection not to face the dead penalty

Zacarias Moussaoui -French "terrorist" accused of involvement in the September attack on New York; but he was jailed already on 16 Aug 2001!

Zafar Abaz-BBC correspondent in Islamabad

Zaher Shahin-Taleban deputy representative in Islamabad

Zahir Shah-the former King of Afghanistan who was living in exile in Rome, Italy aged 86

Zahir Tanin-from BBC Pashtun service

Zambwanga-town in the Philippines where a bomb went off on 28 Oct 2001 against American soldiers

Zawa-Killi - area of Eastern Afghanistan bombed by the Americans on 15-01-2002

Zermay Harrizad-the new US envoy to Afghanistan

Ziad Mustafa Kazimi-Agriculture minister in the new interim Afghan government.

Printed in the United States
By Bookmasters